Wakefield Press

Out of the Silence

The History and Memory of
South Australia's Frontier Wars

Robert Foster is Associate Professor in the School of History & Politics at the University of Adelaide. Amanda Nettelbeck is Professor in the School of Humanities at the University of Adelaide. Their previous co-authored books, also published by Wakefield Press, are *Fatal Collisions: The South Australian Frontier and the Violence of Memory* (with Rick Hosking, 2001) and *In the Name of the Law: William Willshire and the Policing of the Australian Frontier* (2007).

Out of the Silence

The History and Memory of
South Australia's Frontier Wars

Robert Foster and Amanda Nettelbeck

Wakefield
Press

Wakefield Press
16 Rose Street
Mile End
South Australia 5031
www.wakefieldpress.com.au

First published 2012
This edition published 2018

Copyright © Robert Foster and Amanda Nettelbeck 2012

All rights reserved. This book is copyright. Apart from any fair dealing for the purposes of private study, research, criticism or review, as permitted under the Copyright Act, no part may be reproduced without written permission. Enquiries should be addressed to the publisher.

Cover design by Stacey Zass, Page 12
Typeset by Wakefield Press

ISBN 978 1 74305 582 3

 A catalogue record for this book is available from the National Library of Australia

 Wakefield Press thanks Coriole Vineyards for continued support

CONTENTS

Introduction		1
Part 1	'The war between the races'	
Chapter 1	Foundations	13
Chapter 2	British subjects or enemy aliens?	21
Chapter 3	'Our declared enemies'	40
Chapter 4	The trials of the criminal justice system	55
Chapter 5	'The secrecy with which these transactions have been cloaked': The culture of the settler frontier	78
Chapter 6	'The natural working of an unsound system': Administrative responses to frontier violence	87
Chapter 7	'These war-like preparations': The Mounted Police and the tyranny of distance	100
Part 2	Negotiating the past	
Chapter 8	Paving the way back	131
Chapter 9	The great Australian whispering	142
Chapter 10	Placing the past in the present	167
Conclusion		181
Notes		187
Bibliography		211
Index		227

ACKNOWLEDGEMENTS

Some sections of this work have previously been published in different versions: 'The Rule of Law on the Australian Frontier', *Legal History*, vol 13, no 2 (2009); 'Colonial Judiciaries, Aboriginal Protection and South Australia's Policy of Punishing with "Exemplary Severity"', *Australian Historical Studies,* vol 41, no 3 (2010); 'Commemorating the Past: Foundation in Regional Memory', *History Australia,* vol 7, no 3 (2010); 'The Australian Frontier in the Museum', *Journal of Social History* (Summer 2011). We would like to thank the editors of those journals and the anonymous readers who provided us with valuable feedback.

In this book we revisit some of the events we first addressed in *Fatal Collisions: the South Australian Frontier and the Violence and Memory*; it has been necessary to do so because these events form an integral part of the more comprehensive analysis of the trajectory of the South Australian frontier which is undertaken here.

The authors would like to acknowledge the support of the Australian Research Council in supporting this project through an ARC Linkage Grant, and our industry partners, the South Australian Museum and the State Records of South Australia. We would especially like to thank Skye Krichauff and Jude van Konklenberg for their patient and methodical research, and Bain Attwood for his astute comments and corrections. Many thanks also to Michael Bollen and the staff at Wakefield Press for their continued support.

INTRODUCTION

In 1835 Britain's House of Commons established a Select Committee to inquire into the conditions of Aboriginal people in British settlements. Chaired by the evangelical politician Sir Thomas Fowell Buxton, famed for his role in the abolitionist movement, the Select Committee was symptomatic of a building reformist politics over the past decade as Britain sought to reconcile the economic strength of its empire with an increasing sense of humanitarian duty towards Aboriginal peoples across its colonies.[1] The Committee's report of 1837 was forthright in its condemnation of past British policy toward 'the uncivilized nations of the earth'. This had been a policy that had not only sacrificed many thousands of lives, it stated, but continued to have disastrous consequences for Aboriginal peoples:

> Too often, their territory has been usurped; their property seized; their numbers diminished; their character debased; the spread of civilization impeded. European vices and diseases have been introduced amongst them, and they have been familiarized with the use of our most potent instruments for the subtle if violent destruction of human life, viz. brandy and gunpowder.[2]

The Select Committee's report spoke strongly of rights. Aboriginal peoples had a 'plain and sacred right' to their soil, and Europeans had not only intruded upon that soil, but had then punished the original inhabitants for presuming to 'live in their own country'.[3] But although it issued a compelling reminder of the wilful neglect of Aboriginal rights across Britain's colonies, the Select Committee's report refrained from acknowledging the sovereignty of the Aboriginal peoples of Australia, whose political and social systems it regarded as being too 'destitute' to warrant that status. Instead, it argued, these peoples must be secured 'the due observance of Justice' through the extension of 'civilisation' and 'Christianity'.[4] The 1837 report illuminated a paradox at the heart of colonial endeavour in Australia from this time onwards, for although its language of humanitarian liberalism challenged a history of British settlement in which Aboriginal rights had been usurped, it did not fundamentally challenge Britain's continuing possession of new territories.[5]

At the same time as the Select Committee was conducting its inquiries into the effects of colonisation on Aboriginal peoples across Britain's empire, plans were evolving to establish the new colony of South Australia, which was formally proclaimed on 28 December 1836. South Australians now know this day as Proclamation Day, and celebrate it every year with a ceremony at the 'Old Gum Tree' near the beach-side suburb of Glenelg. This is the place where the colony's inaugural governor Captain John Hindmarsh read 'The Proclamation of South Australia' and formally announced British possession.

The Proclamation was a remarkable document for the fact that, despite being one of the legal instruments by which Aboriginal sovereignty was overturned, well over half of it was devoted to the question of the rights and welfare of Aboriginal people and, in particular, their status as British subjects. In insisting upon this principle, the Colonial Office was mindful of the violence that had marked earlier Australian colonies, and was determined that the unequivocal extension of British legal rights to Aboriginal people would not only be a humane intervention but also a means of deterring the kind of settler excesses that had occurred elsewhere. In this respect the importance of South Australia's Proclamation lay not only in what it claimed to offer Aboriginal subjects of the Crown, but in the caution it offered to its European ones. As British subjects, Aboriginal people were unambiguously 'under the Safeguard of the law', and any 'acts of violence or injustice' toward them would be punished 'with exemplary severity'.[6]

The nature and extent of frontier violence after 1836, and the degree to which the law operated to provide Aboriginal protection as British settlement unfolded, are therefore significant questions not only in understanding the character of South Australian settlement but also in analysing more broadly the terms on which British settlement in Australia took place after the 1830s. Having established authority over previously sovereign peoples, could colonial governments fulfil the promise of providing them with legal protection as British subjects, a promise which formed the moral underpinning of the assertion of British sovereignty?

The Australian frontier and the rule of law
Until this time in the Australian colonies, the treatment of Aboriginal people under British law had been marked by ambiguity and vacillation.[7] Although

the principle that Australia was settled rather than conquered implicitly suggested that Aboriginal people were British subjects from the moment of British occupation, their relation to British law was 'largely a matter of chance'.[8] The early instructions to governors in Van Diemen's Land and New South Wales to attempt 'conciliation' with Aboriginal people were framed as a matter of intention rather than as a legal imperative.[9] As a result, occasional efforts to afford Aboriginal people protection under the law were, for at least the first fifty years of British settlement in Australia, 'certainly not the general rule'.[10] Given that Aboriginal people could neither give evidence in a court of law nor be expected to understand its proceedings, the only course, according to New South Wales' early Judge Advocate Richard Atkins, was 'to pursue and inflict such punishment [on them] as they merit'.[11] Atkins' blunt assessment describes the broad shape of early Australian settlement. After an outbreak in the Bathurst region of New South Wales in 1824, in which the Wiradjuri had killed seven stockmen, Governor Brisbane declared martial law west of the Blue Mountains.[12] Governor Arthur also employed this strategy on several occasions, most famously in August of 1830 when authorising the 'Black Line', his attempt to drive all the Aborigines from the settled districts.[13] Though perhaps desirous of conciliating where possible, there is little sign that the Governors of Australia's earliest colonies felt obliged to treat Aboriginal people as subjects of the Crown.

Interestingly, Tim Castle has shown that of the 363 executions that took place in New South Wales in the decade before 1836, only four of the executed were Aboriginal men; the vast majority were male convicts, not only indicating that convict crime rather than frontier violence was regarded as the most significant threat to social order, but also demonstrating the legal uncertainty that pertained well into the 1830s about the amenability of Aboriginal people to British criminal law.[14] A case that seemed to clarify the status of Aboriginal people took place in New South Wales in 1836, the same year that saw the foundation of South Australia. This was the murder trial of *R. Vs Murrell*, in which the New South Wales court decided that an *inter se* case where one Aboriginal man had killed another was within its legal jurisdiction to try under British criminal law. However, the court's reluctance to find Murrell guilty indicated continuing uncertainty about the treatment of Aboriginal people as British subjects, and despite the precedent set in taking this case to trial, judges elsewhere across Australia's colonies continued for at least the next decade to express doubt that their courts held jurisdiction over Aboriginal peoples – peoples who not only shared no understanding of British law, but had shown no sign of submitting to it.[15]

Perhaps the most telling marker of continuing ambiguity about Aboriginal people's status in the eyes of the law is that across Australia's colonies, very few Europeans were brought to legal account over the course of the nineteenth century for the murder of Aboriginal people. The execution in 1838 of seven white men for the Myall Creek massacre in New South Wales – in defiance of considerable public pressure to acquit them – was an exception to the more enduring rule that the law 'nearly always failed … to protect Aboriginal subjects'.[16] Indeed, shortly after this event, Governor Gipps declined to prosecute New South Wales police who had shot dead a dozen or so Aboriginal people in a frontier clash in order to avoid offending the volunteer police force.[17]

In the Port Phillip district (later Victoria), Aboriginal protection under the law proved equally elusive. Susanne Davies has shown that between 1841 (when the district had its first resident judge) and 1847, five Aborigines were hanged for the killing of Europeans, despite doubts about their capacity to understand the proceedings and the inadmissibility of their testimony in court.[18] In the same period, the death sentence of an Aboriginal man tried for murdering another Aboriginal was commuted, indicating the judiciary's discomfort at invoking British law in *inter se* cases and continuing legal doubt about the status of Aboriginal people as British subjects. In contrast, only two cases in colonial Victoria saw Europeans tried for the murder of Aboriginal people, and in both cases the defendants were acquitted.[19] To put this in perspective, Richard Broome has argued that Aboriginal fatalities on Victoria's pre-1850 frontier can be calculated at 700 or more.[20]

In colonial Queensland, too, judicial punishment was directed more concertedly against Aboriginal and other non-European people, and even after capital punishment reform which prohibited executions as public spectacle, Aboriginal people continued to be gathered together to witness the hanging of their countrymen as an educational example and deterrent against 'committing outrages upon settlers'.[21] The 'lawful violence' practiced against Aboriginal people in colonial Queensland from the time of its separation from New South Wales in 1859 is perhaps best exemplified by the notoriously violent operations of the Native Police. In working to secure European settlement through the second half of the nineteenth century on Queensland's northern and western frontiers, the corps of the Native Police worked through an implicit legal contradiction: on the one hand, Aboriginal people were in theory British subjects due the protection of the law; on the other hand (as Queensland's Aboriginal Commission noted in 1875), 'without an armed force the frontier settlement could not be maintained'.[22]

Western Australia might suggest a different pattern in so far as, like South Australia, it promised Aboriginal protection under the law not just as a vacillating 'afterthought'[23] but as a foundational principle. When Lieutenant-Governor Stirling proclaimed Western Australia as a British colony in June 1829, he stated (though without quite the definite force of intention expressed by Governor Hindmarsh in proclaiming South Australia in 1836) that anyone behaving in a 'fraudulent, cruel or felonious manner' towards Aboriginal people would 'be liable to be prosecuted and tried for the offence as if the same had been committed against any other of His Majesty's subjects'.[24] Again, however, the historical record suggests that in Western Australia 'both courts and the colonial government [realised] that Aborigines could not really be treated as British subjects', and exercised a mixture of 'legal and illegal remedies' in responding to Aboriginal 'crime' well into the 1840s.[25] And though technically British subjects, Aboriginal people would be policed on Western Australia's remote northern frontiers with deadly force until the early twentieth century, while in contrast it proved virtually 'impossible' to investigate settlers for crimes against Aboriginal people.[26]

Bruce Kercher has noted that South Australia would seem most likely amongst Australia's colonies to have an effective rule of law because, unlike other Australian colonies, a clear judicial system was established there 'almost from the beginning'.[27] As he puts it, legal 'amateurism' defined the first decades of New South Wales justice, as well as justice in the early Moreton Bay settlement under New South Wales' jurisdiction before Queensland's separation in 1859; Port Phillip had no resident judge until 1841 or Supreme Court until its separation from New South Wales in 1851; and although Western Australia had a civil court from 1832, its judges were 'flexible about the application of English law' until a Supreme Court was established in 1861.[28] However, although South Australia's judicial structure may have been clearly established from the outset, implementing a rule of law on the frontiers of settlement proved to be altogether another matter.

Given that South Australia was distinctive in its explicit promise to protect Aboriginal people under the law, the history of how its settlement took place, and of Aboriginal resistance to it, has remained surprisingly under-researched in the historical scholarship of Australia's frontiers.[29] Likewise, although there is some excellent scholarship addressing the relationship between Aboriginal people, police and the law in colonial Australia, there has been surprisingly little sustained analysis of the practical processes by which Aboriginal people were brought under the authority of the colonial state.[30] This book considers the ways in which these processes unfolded across the evolving frontiers of South Australia, and examines how governments and settlers dealt, in policy and in practice over the course of decades, with Aboriginal resistance to incursions upon their land. While these reveal a set of specific policing strategies and administrative mechanisms (with varying levels of effectiveness), they also demonstrate a process of wheels repeatedly being re-invented, most particularly because there was no global Aboriginal resistance but rather the singular response of dozens of Aboriginal nations faced with invasion of their lands.

Despite the foundational principle that Aboriginal people were to be considered British subjects under the law – a principle intended to set South Australia apart from the violence that had marked other Australian colonies – through the second half of the nineteenth century a unifying theme concerning the colony's governors and administrators was whether and how Aboriginal people were in fact amenable to the rule of law. In 1863 South Australia's Police Commissioner Major P.E. Warburton responded to Aboriginal attacks against settlers in the colony's north by dispatching more mounted troopers and ammunition to the district. When the Protector of Aborigines protested against these 'war-like preparations', the Commissioner responded angrily that the police were 'directed to endeavour to secure the *legal* punishment of these offenders, but this is next to impossible – These savages cannot be made to understand our Laws whatever pains we may take to teach them … they will not yield to the covenants of the Law whilst they have the least power of resistance'.[31] On the one hand, the Police Commissioner was duty-bound to uphold the principle of the rule of law, which required the protection of Aboriginal peoples as British subjects; on the other, he knew his primary task in managing the frontiers of European settlement was to suppress Aboriginal resistance.

In this study we use the term 'frontier' to refer to that phase of European settlement from the time when settlers first intruded into Aboriginal country to the point when colonial authority over Aboriginal people was effectively established. In this respect South Australia's were pastoral frontiers, driven further and further inland by settlers in search of fresh grazing land for their sheep and cattle. South Australia's frontiers incorporated not only the largest territory amongst Australia's colonies but also the longest-lived and most protracted struggles for British settlement because until 1911 it included within its jurisdiction the Northern Territory, which only earnestly began to fill with settlers from the 1870s after the establishment of the Overland Telegraph Line. In a detailed sense, however, our history of how these frontiers were managed concludes in the 1870s when the limits of good grazing land within South Australia's current northern borders were reached; from that time to the end of the nineteenth century, the patterns by which the Central Australian frontier evolved would prove to be relentlessly repetitive of those that had emerged between the 1840s and the 1870s further south.[32]

The frontier phase in most regions was typically characterised by Aboriginal resistance to the invasion of their lands, which took the form of attacks on settlers, their stock and their property. Aboriginal resistance was met in turn by an assertion of European force designed to suppress that resistance. As Henry Reynolds has argued in regard to Aboriginal sovereignty, a key characteristic of the Australian frontier – one that proved to be as true of South Australia as of Australia's earlier colonies – was the uncertainty of Britain's effective occupation: if a rule of government 'extends as far as ... its administrative machinery is in efficient exercise', then in Australia, British sovereignty was only of 'a qualified and limited order'.[33] In this respect the frontier phase, as Julie Evans has argued, highlights the 'unsuitability' of the rule of law, which remained insecure until such a time as the Aboriginal peoples it purported to protect had been dispossessed.[34] Tom Griffiths has made a similar point somewhat more bluntly: it was in the very nature of the frontier 'to undermine the rule of law and the legal method'.[35]

Remembering the frontier

The question of whether and how a rule of law operated on Australia's frontiers has been central to recent critiques of frontier historiography. In his controversial book *The Fabrication of Aboriginal History*, Keith Windschuttle argued that, with some notable exceptions, most of the violence of Australia's frontiers occurred in the context of legitimate police actions; colonial authorities were dealing with Aboriginal criminality, not warfare. The ideal of the rule of law, which assumed that Aboriginal peoples would be protected and if need be punished as British subjects, was certainly central in the thoughts of British policy-makers at the same time the colony of South Australia was being planned, but how did it translate into practice? A close examination of how the settler frontier evolved 'on the ground' and how it was policed suggests that not only was the rule of law an ideal impossible to implement but that, perversely, the often genuine attempts to impose it undermined its effectiveness by diminishing settlers' faith in its capacity to protect their interests, and encouraging their own forms of 'frontier justice'.[36]

This question is critical to the issue of how frontier conflict between Aboriginal people and Europeans has been recorded and remembered. In 1968 W.E.H. Stanner famously observed the remarkable absence of

Aboriginal people from twentieth century histories of Australia.[37] Although his insight is largely true of the national histories produced at that time, the very prominence of the idea risks obscuring a much more complex, ever-evolving, and often contradictory story of remembrance. As Tom Griffiths has astutely observed, Australia's was a 'strange frontier' of 'fear and distain', not easily conceivable in terms of 'a romance of campaigns and heroes'.[38] In large measure, this can be traced back to the foundational fiction that Aboriginal people were protected as British subjects and that, by association, Australia was settled rather than conquered. In reality the colonial state, as well as settlers, were required to use force to secure the lands they claimed and affect the subjugation of Aboriginal people to state authority. Wars were fought, but these were wars that could not generally be openly acknowledged. The inherent tension between Aboriginal people's nominal status as subjects of the Crown and the lived experience of violent dispossession shaped the way frontier conflict was reported and remembered.

The records of European settlement leave little doubt that war was being levied against Aboriginal people to dispossess them of their lands and ensure their subjugation to state authority. Governors and Police Commissioners, Mounted Police and settlers understood this fact full well, and they also understood the tension between this reality and the ideal that a rule of law prevailed. A good deal of the violence that occurred on Australia's frontiers happened beyond the reach of metropolitan surveillance and before the arrival of police and colonial officials whose task it was to uphold the law. Privately recorded accounts of conflict suggest that frontier clashes often went officially unreported, and if news of them did come to the notice of attentive officials, time, distance, and settler solidarity made them difficult to prove. Settlers were often caught between a desire to record their experiences and a reluctance to incriminate themselves. This tension can be seen in the written records of settlers, especially in a euphemistic language that recorded, while at the same time masked, the violence of the frontier: the 'Natives were dispersed', for instance, or perhaps they were 'taught a lesson'.[39] These forms of language, writes Tom Griffiths, 'reveal that many colonists accepted murder in their midst; but they reveal, too, an awareness that it could not be openly discussed'.[40]

South Australia presents a particularly useful case for examining at closer range the historical memory of Australian settlement and its counterpart of Aboriginal dispossession because, from amongst all of Australia's former colonies, it has always cherished a reputation for the humanitarian treatment of Aboriginal people. South Australia prides itself on its 'sense of difference'.[41]

Perhaps the most comprehensive examination of this idea remains Douglas Pike's 1957 work *Paradise of Dissent,* a history of the colony's first thirty years which focuses on its social, political and economic foundations. Pike explores the qualities that set the Province apart: foremost among them was that it was a colony free of the 'convict stain'; it was a planned colony, built on Wakefield's theory of systematic colonisation; and it was a colony predicated on liberal ideals of religious and political freedom.[42] The idea that it was a colony more liberal in its approach to the treatment of Aboriginal people came to adhere to this overarching idea of 'difference'. The origins of this claim can be traced to the colony's founding documents: the Letters Patent, which acknowledged prior Aboriginal title to the land, and the Proclamation, which undertook to place Aboriginal people under the protection of the rule of law as British subjects. These were innovations of the British Colonial Office rather than ones welcomed by South Australia's founders, yet even by the late nineteenth century they became seen as emblematic of the colony's 'benevolent intentions' toward its Aboriginal subjects.

Yet despite its often covert face, and despite the fact that it has more recently emerged as an apparently 'hidden' history, the story of frontier conflict has never disappeared – at least entirely disappeared – from public view. In contrast to W.E.H. Stanner's famous conception of the 'great Australian silence', which expresses the exclusion of the story of Aboriginal dispossession from Australia's 'textbook' history throughout most of the twentieth century, local historical narratives have always kept the story of Aboriginal and European conflict in view. In the memoirs of settlers, in published local histories, and in memorials and commemorative tributes to the past, the history of a violent frontier is something that may be remembered with partiality, but is never quite forgotten. The events of the past, and the questions of how they were recorded and remembered, are not separable ones but are inexorably linked, and those links maintained in memory. Aboriginal peoples have always remembered the violence of their dispossession; but South Australia's settler-descended communities have also always engaged with this aspect of their history, although its forms have shifted and changed through time.

Our society, writes philosopher Janna Thompson, is an 'intergenerational community' of institutions and moral relationships that 'persist over time and through a succession of generations', and its 'moral and political integrity' relies upon 'its members accepting transgenerational obligations and honouring historical entitlements'.[43] This conception of society as an intergenerational community informs our approach to this history and underpins our concern with the nexus between history and memory. What do we find when we compare the recoverable history of the frontier with the patterns of how it is both remembered and forgotten? What, in turn, might this suggest about the status of our nation's history, as well as its legacies in the present? These questions are the subject of this book.

Part 1

'THE WAR BETWEEN THE RACES'

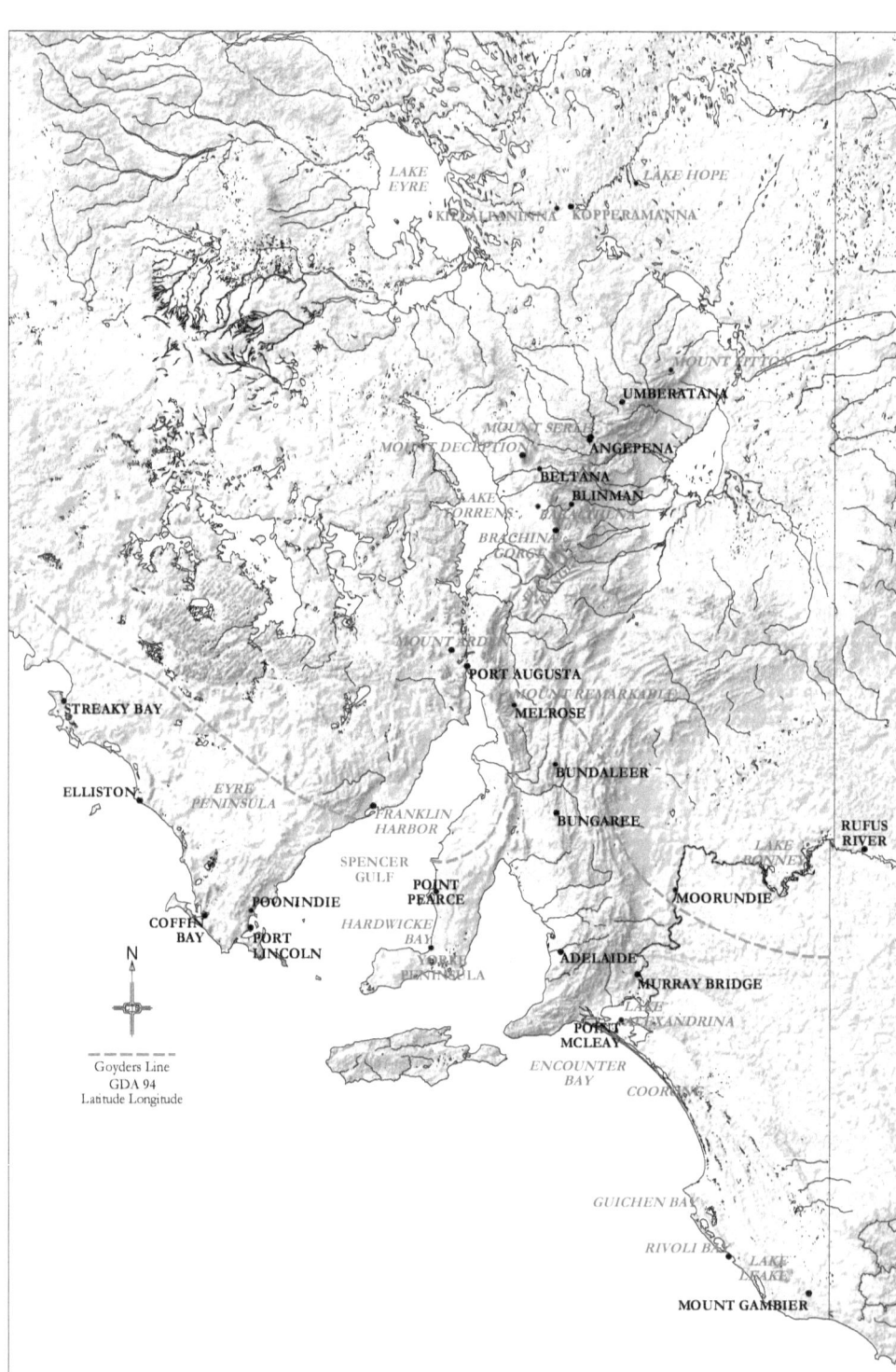

Chapter 1

FOUNDATIONS

In January 1830 Charles Sturt was exploring the inland river systems of eastern Australia when he came upon a new river, which he would name the Murray, and decided to follow it to its outlet.[1] During this journey Sturt constantly encountered Aboriginal groups and actively sought their knowledge of the country and their assistance as guides. To smooth his passage through their lands he conscientiously observed Aboriginal diplomatic protocol by approaching each group cautiously and openly, distributing presents and requesting assistance. In his journal of the expedition Sturt commented on the nature of the protocol and the importance of Aboriginal aid:

> They sent ambassadors forward regularly from one tribe to another, in order to prepare for our approach, a custom that not only saved us an infinity of time, but also great personal risk. Indeed, I doubt very much whether we should ever have pushed so far down the river, had we not had the assistance of the natives themselves.[2]

Sturt's conciliatory approach proved invaluable on one of the few occasions when he feared that violence was imminent: as a group of Aborigines was threatening his party an Aboriginal man he had encountered earlier came to his assistance and persuaded the aggressors to retreat.[3] Having been guided down the river, the expedition finally arrived at its terminus, a body of water that Sturt named Lake Alexandrina. Intent on finding where it flowed into the sea Sturt's party rowed across the Lake, and observed a chain of smoke signals rising from the surrounding hills; their approach was being watched.[4] When they attempted to land a large body of Aborigines came toward them, 'fully equipped for battle' and intent on opposing them, but they retreated when Sturt levelled his musket at them.[5] He was surprised at this response. How did they know about muskets, when other groups further up the river certainly had no knowledge of the weapon? What he may not have realised is that whalers and sealers had worked the region for the past 30 years from their base on Kangaroo Island, often raiding the coast in search of Aboriginal women. As Sturt's party set up camp that night, conscious that all around them were Aboriginal camps, the explorer looked out upon the scene and imagined the future landscape of European settlement on rolling hills 'that seemed to invite civilised man to erect his dwellings upon them'.[6]

In the course of his expedition, Sturt regularly commented on the numbers of Aboriginal people he encountered: 'We found the interior more populous than we had any reason to expect; yet as we advanced into it, the population appeared to increase'.[7] On another occasion he wrote, 'we seldom communicated with fewer than 200 daily'.[8] Yet despite the extensive Aboriginal population, and the hospitality of his hosts, Sturt never saw them or wrote about them as the owners of the country through which he travelled. What he saw, in his mind's eye, was a patchwork of neatly cultivated fields, wisps of smoke rising from scattered farm-houses, vessels plying their trade along the river, and church spires in the distance. Towards the end of his journal Sturt speculated on the prospects of the region. This was, he suggested, a spot 'to which the colonist might venture with every prospect of success, and in whose valleys the exile might hope to build for himself and for his family a peaceful and prosperous home'.[9]

Planning a colony

Meanwhile in London a small group of men interested in both the practice and principles of colonisation was beginning to coalesce. Robert Gouger, who planned to emigrate, and Edward Wakefield, who studied emigration while in debtor's prison, met and began developing the notion of systematic colonisation. One of the problems of colonisation elsewhere, Wakefield argued, was that land could be acquired too cheaply and too quickly, leading to an inefficient dispersion of settlement and a shortage of labour. His proposal was that land be sold at a price low enough to attract middle-class capitalists, but not so low as to encourage working men as land investors. Instead, he proposed, a percentage of the moneys derived from land sales should be used to fund the emigration of labour, and in this way a rational balance between capital and labour might be maintained. By July 1829 a 'Sketch for a proposal for colonising Australia' had been forwarded to the Colonial Office.[10]

Here was a plan for a colony, but as yet no place to locate it. News of Sturt's explorations reached London during 1830 and by January of 1831 Gouger's promotional pamphlets were now referring to 'the new colony of South Australia'.[11] By the end of 1833 the South Australian Association had been formed to garner support and promote the proposal of this new colony to the Colonial Office.[12] As a charter for the proposed colony was being drawn up, some in the colonial office expressed the reservations that it was too 'republican', and that it might not be genuinely self-supporting.[13] The view of James Stephen, legal counsel to the Colonial Office and soon to be its Under Secretary, was blunt:

> There is no joint-stock – no proprietary body – no Chartered Company. It is simply a Plan for selling the Lands of the Crown and applying the Proceeds to the foundation of a Colony to which at the expense of the Crown, Poor Persons are to be conveyed as emigrants.[14]

Negotiations and compromise continued until in July and August 1834 the Act establishing the Province of South Australia passed both Houses of the British Parliament. The preamble to the Act declared all the lands of the colony 'waste and unoccupied'. There was not a single reference to the significant Aboriginal population Sturt had observed just a few years before. Indeed, the planners of the colony had given almost no thought to how they would deal with that population once they set foot on the ground. Not long after the Act was passed, a new Whig government came to power under Lord Melbourne. Evangelical reformers were now in the ascendency, and men who had campaigned against slavery now turned their attention to the question of Aboriginal people's rights in British colonies. They also, for the first time, questioned the South Australian Colonisation Commissioners charged with supervising the establishment of the colony about their plans regarding Aboriginal people.[15]

In 1835 Governor George Arthur, hearing that measures were being proposed to secure justice for the Aborigines of Australia and that a new colony was to be established on Australia's southern shores, wrote to the Secretary of State with his thoughts on the matter. Noting that the Aboriginal population of Van Diemen's Land had been reduced to no more than 130 souls due, in part, to 'the warfare so long waged' between the Aborigines and settlers, he offered cautionary advice drawn from his own experience:

> On the First occupation of the colony – It was a great oversight that a treaty was not, at that time, made with the natives, and such compensation given to the Chiefs, as they would have a fair equivalent for what they surrendered – a mere trifle would have satisfied them; and that feeling of injustice which I am persuaded they have always entertained would have had no existence.[16]

Arthur was in a good position to offer this advice, having witnessed in his long term as Lieutenant Governor the escalation of violence between Aboriginal people and settlers in Van Diemen's Land. 'Every effort', he suggested, should be made to come 'to an understanding with the natives of Southern Australia' on the cession of lands before settlement commenced. The failure to secure the goodwill of the Aborigines would make it 'impossible to prevent a long continued warfare, in which the whites as well as the Aborigines becoming more and more inflamed as their mutual injuries accumulate will destroy each other in detail'.[17]

Responding to Arthur's concerns, Sir George Grey wrote to the South Australian Colonisation Commissioners, quoting Arthur's letter, and asking what provisions were being made for the welfare and protection of the Aborigines? The Commissioners, who had a considerable investment in the new colony and were anxious to make a start, initially responded with soothing but essentially platitudinous noises.[18] Grey would not be assuaged by platitudes, and again demanded to know what consideration was being given to the rights and interests of the Aboriginal people. The territory covered by the new colony extended far into the interior of New Holland, he observed, and would 'embrace in its range numerous Tribes of People whose proprietary Title to the Soil, we have not the slightest ground for disputing'. Before His Majesty could approve anything, he added,

> He must have at least, some reasonable assurance that He is not about to sanction any act of injustice towards the Aboriginal natives of that part of the Globe. In drawing the Lines of demarcation for the new province or provinces, the Commissioners therefore, must not proceed any further than those limits within which they can shew, by some sufficient evidence, that the land is unoccupied, and that no earlier and preferable Title exists.[19]

For men who had never set eyes upon the lands, and who had used Sturt's account of his Murray River explorations as their real estate guide, these were most difficult things to do. In their efforts to appease the Colonial Office, the Colonisation Commissioners gave a variety of undertakings: they agreed to the appointment of a Protector devoted solely to the welfare of Aboriginal people; they would negotiate land cession treaties where this was required; they would provide any necessary medical and material aid; and they would promote the spread of 'Christianity' and 'civilisation'. As the negotiations continued, the Colonial Office indicated that it wanted the 1834 Foundation Act amended to take their concerns into account, especially those relating to Aboriginal rights to land. It was suggested that perhaps settlement be postponed until these matters were addressed.[20] The Chairman of the Colonisation Commission was devastated; he is reported to have said that if the objections of the Colonial Office were not withdrawn 'the colony was pretty well ended'.[21] The Commissioners took the offensive. Chairman Torrens met with Sir George Grey and outlined his view that the requirement to meet all these measures would be 'fatal' to the prospects of the colony. Grey softened, agreeing that the colony would go ahead without changes to the Act, which could be amended at a later date. The delays, he argued, had been occasioned by his desire to avert 'from the Aborigines of that part of New Holland the calamities under which that race of men' had been 'overwhelmed' in the other Australian colonies.[22]

Grey's concern about the need to clarify Aboriginal rights within the Foundation Act was well grounded. The 1837 report that emerged from the Select Committee inquiry into the condition of Aboriginal peoples in British settlements considered that the legal status of Aboriginal peoples up until this time had been uncertain and inconsistent.[23] This was an apt appraisal. For the first fifty years of Australian settlement, colonial policy toward Aborigines was encapsulated in the instructions issued to Captain Arthur Phillip.[24] Governor Phillip was directed:

> To endeavour by every means in his power to open an intercourse with the natives, and to conciliate their good-will, requiring all to live in amity and kindness with them; and if any of our subjects should wantonly destroy them or give any unnecessary interruption in the exercise of their several occupations, it will be our will and pleasure to cause such offenders to be brought to punishment, according to the degree of the offence.[25]

These were sentiments rather than injunctions. Phillip was to 'endeavour' to 'conciliate' Aboriginal good-will and to protect them from 'unnecessary' interference, but nowhere was the precise relationship between Aboriginal people and the State defined in a legal sense. Right of discovery justified British possession of Australia, and the Aborigines were not regarded as a conquered nation with their own rights and laws. As an almost accidental consequence of British occupation, Aborigines were taken to be British subjects. Yet for the first fifty years of Australian settlement, as David Neal puts it, 'the colonial legal system had trouble deciding whether the Aborigines should be treated as subjects of the Crown or foreign enemies who could be hunted down in reprisal raids and shot'.[26]

In April 1801, when Aborigines gathered in large numbers near Parramatta, Governor George King ordered that they be driven back from the settlers' habitations by firing at them. Later that year similar orders were issued to protect wheat crops on the Georges River from Aboriginal incursions.[27] Circumstances such as these led Lord Hobart in 1805 to raise the question of the Aborigines' legal status. The Judge-Advocate of New South Wales, Richard Atkins, pointed out that although Aborigines were technically under the protection of His Majesty's government, they could hardly be expected to plead in a court of law when they did not understand the proceedings. He considered that to bring Aboriginal people before the criminal courts, whether as criminals or witnesses, 'would be a mocking of Judicial Proceedings, and a Solecism in Law'.[28] Certainly, prior to the 1830s, colonial governors acted on this view that Aboriginal people could not readily be treated as subjects of the Crown. In New South Wales and Van Diemen's Land, martial law was declared against Aboriginal people on occasions where a strong assertion of state power seemed expedient.[29] The periodic declaration of martial law underlined the ambiguity of Aboriginal people's status as British subjects across Australia's colonies: this was a status of which they could be conditionally deprived when it was deemed necessary to authorise the use of punitive violence.

On occasions in the course of Australian settlement, even the formality of martial law was dispensed with. Following the deaths of settlers in the Hunter River District of New South Wales, Governor Darling advised landholders that they should take 'vigorous measures for their own defense' and indeed the government assisted them in doing so by supplying settlers with muskets from the government store. In 1825 Lord Bathurst wrote approvingly of this approach:

> In reference to discussions, which have recently taken place in the colony respecting the manner in which Native Inhabitants are to be treated when making hostile incursions for the purpose of plunder, you will understand it to be your duty, when such disturbances cannot be allayed by less vigorous measures, to oppose force by force, and to repel such Aggressions in the same manner as if they proceeded from subjects of any accredited State.[30]

In this instance, Aboriginal people committing aggressions against settlers were to be regarded as enemy aliens – subjects of a potentially separate nation state – against whom war could be levied. From the arrival of the First Fleet until the late 1830s, the relationship between Aboriginal people and the State was loosely defined and readily reinterpreted. In essence, Aboriginal people were subjects of the Crown when they acquiesced to its dictates. When they did not, they might be considered as being beyond the ordinary reach of the law.

The Ideal of Protection

The recommendations that emerged from the 1837 report of the Select Committee were an attempt to clarify the legal status of Aboriginal peoples across Britain's colonies and set a line of policy around the principle of 'protection'. This had a number of tiers. The idea that Aboriginal people needed to be 'civilised' and 'Christianised' was central to a plan which imagined that their only future lay in their eventual assimilation into the new colonial order. With this aim in mind, the Select Committee report recommended that Protectors of Aborigines be appointed to supervise the interests and welfare of Aboriginal people. This would include a duty to look to Aboriginal people's education and provide for their employment. There was also some scope for a limited recognition of Aboriginal customary lifestyle, for so 'long as agriculture is anathema to them, they should be provided with the means of pursuing the chase without molestation'.[31] While it was acknowledged that expecting 'ignorant hordes of savages' to observe laws they had no knowledge of 'would be palpably unjust', it was nonetheless seen as crucial that Aboriginal people not be placed 'beyond the pale of the law'. To this end it was conceded that 'a temporary and provisional code for the regulation of the Aborigines' might be put in place 'until advancing knowledge and civilization shall have superseded the necessity of any such special laws'.[32]

Despite the best intentions of the Select Committee's recommendations, the task of Protectors would prove to be embedded with the same kind of ambiguities that remained intractable for colonial governments in determining Aboriginal people's status as British subjects. On the one hand, Protectors were to serve as advocates for Aboriginal peoples, charged with protecting their welfare where that was threatened by the spread of colonial settlement. On the other hand, Protectors would serve as agents of the colonial state, charged with mediating between Aboriginal peoples and settlers in ensuring the secure and peaceable passage of the colonial project. In the absence of any clear policies on Aboriginal rights, this mediating role between competing agendas would often place the Protector in an incongruous and invidious position.

In hindsight, the entire logic of the policy of protection seems perverse: Protectors would serve both to protect Aboriginal people from the effects of colonial settlement, and ensure its progress; imperial authorities who were sanctioning the dispossession of Aboriginal people were simultaneously endeavouring to protect them from its consequences. What was being conceived was a kind of schizophrenic paternalism in which the

Crown – through its proxies, the Governor and the Protectors, and its trust in the majesty of the law – held two worlds apart while imagining their assimilation. The Colonial Office's Under Secretary James Stephen eloquently captured the dilemma when he noted that perhaps the only way of saving the Aborigines from the settlers 'would consist in teaching them the art of war and supplying them with weapons and ammunitions – an act of suicidal generosity which of course can never be practiced'.[33] However flawed the conception of Aboriginal protection might seem in hindsight, the rationale was clear enough at the time: if the rule of law was applied vigorously and impartially, and if 'mediators' such as Protectors of Aborigines could be put in place, then the excesses of violence that had characterised earlier Australian settlements might be avoided.

The founders of South Australia understood the mood of the Colonial Office, and attempted to demonstrate that they too had its goals in mind. The First Report of the Colonisation Commissioners in July 1836 concluded with a passage that portrayed their enterprise as one in which the benefits of colonisation to Aboriginal people would flow automatically from benevolent intent. Without the instruction of 'civilisation', the Aborigines were depicted as lacking even 'the instinctive apprehensions of some of the inferior animals'. But by virtue of the settlers coming among them, they

> will be lifted up from this degradation; they will be gradually reconciled to labour for the sake of its certain reward; they will be instructed in the several branches of industry, and they will possess in their reserves property increasing in value as the colony expands. Colonization thus extended to South Australia, though it should do nothing for the colonists, and nothing for the mother country, would yet deserve, in its influence upon the Aborigines, Lord Bacon's character of a 'blessed work'.[34]

By the time the first colonists were sailing for South Australia aboard the *Buffalo* in the middle of 1836, the Colonisation Commissioners had provided the Colonial Office with a set of understandings regarding the treatment of Aboriginal people. They had agreed that a Protector of Aborigines would be appointed. They had agreed to recognise Aboriginal proprietary right to land, where such a right was found to exist, and to negotiate for the sale of that land if necessary. They had undertaken to promote the spread of 'civilisation and Christianity'. Most importantly, they undertook to extend the protection of the law to Aboriginal people. This last principle was the centrepiece of Governor Hindmarsh's first Proclamation in the Colony.

Chapter 2

BRITISH SUBJECTS OR ENEMY ALIENS?

On the ground

On 28 December 1836 settlers gathered around a gum tree near the coast to witness a ceremony in which the colony's first Governor John Hindmarsh formally read the Proclamation establishing His Majesty's Province of South Australia. The Governor called upon the settlers to conduct themselves with 'order and quietness', to 'respect the laws,' and through 'industry and sobriety' to 'prove themselves worthy to be the founders of a great and free colony'.[1] This brief preamble was followed by a much lengthier directive on their dealings with the Aboriginal population. This was a document that distilled precisely the ideal of protection articulated by the Colonial Office:

> It is ... my especial duty to apprise the Colonists of my resolution to take every lawful means for extending the same protection to the Native population as to the rest of His Majesty's subjects, and of my firm determination to punish with exemplary severity all acts of violence or injustice which may in any manner be practised or attempted against the Natives, who are to be considered as much under the safeguard of the law as the Colonists themselves, and equally entitled to the privileges of British subjects. I trust therefore, with confidence, to the exercise of moderation and forbearance by all classes, in their intercourse with the Native Inhabitants, and they will omit no opportunity of assisting me to fulfil His Majesty's most gracious and benevolent intentions toward them, by promoting their advancement in civilization, and ultimately, under the blessing of Divine Providence their conversion to the Christian faith.[2]

In subsequent years, 28 December would become an annual holiday celebrating South Australia's foundation, an event marked and remembered with each passing year for its particular injunction to protect Aboriginal people from violence and injustice through the extension of rights as British subjects.

At the first sitting of South Australia's new Supreme Court in May 1837, Chief Judge Sir John Jeffcott reiterated the Proclamation's sentiments. He quoted at length from the first report of the Colonization Commissioners, drawing particular attention to the bloody history of previous colonial enterprises. Stressing the colonists' obligations toward the Aborigines he stated unequivocally:

> They have been declared British Subjects – As such they are entitled to the full protection of British law, and that protection, while I have the honour of filling the situation which His Majesty has been pleased to confer on me, shall be fully and effectually afforded to them. I will go further and say, that any aggression upon the Natives, or any infringement on their rights, shall be visited by greater severity of punishment than would be in similar offences committed upon white men.[3]

The assumed consequence of Aboriginal people's declared status as British subjects, of course, was the negation of Aboriginal sovereignty in relation both to land and to law. Aboriginal customary law was rendered null and void on the presumption that whatever laws governed Aboriginal society would be swept away by the 'superior' civilisation. Legal pluralism – in which traditional law could continue to function under the umbrella of British law – was a feature of some dominions within Britain's empire, but was not considered in South Australia. In the past, it had offered Britain an approach to the governance of subject peoples that was considered not only morally just but also politically astute, for to make newly colonised peoples immediately subject to laws of which they had no knowledge would be to risk alienating the people whose sovereignty was being overturned, and invite resistance to the imposition of British rule. Yet South Australia's establishment coincided with a time when the British government was losing faith in a system of legal pluralism within its colonial possessions.[4] Rather, the political mood of liberalism in the aftermath of Britain's abolition of slavery favoured the principle that for Aboriginal peoples to become assimilated into the empire's 'imagined Christian community', they must be regarded as subjects of (and therefore subject to) the Crown.[5] While it has been suggested that an implicit form of legal pluralism pertained in the Australian colonies after the 1830s,[6] in South Australia the imposition of British law was conceived in terms of the 'gift' of British subjecthood, and a necessary part of the 'civilising process'.

How was this to be reconciled with the undertaking by South Australia's Colonisation Commissioners to recognise Aboriginal proprietary title to land and, where necessary, to negotiate for the purchase of that land? The Letters Patent which defined the extent of the new Province contained the rider that nothing

> Shall affect or be construed to affect the rights of any Aboriginal Natives of the said Province to the actual occupation or enjoyment in their own Persons or in the Persons of their Descendants of any Lands therein actually occupied or enjoyed by the Natives.[7]

The Colonisation Commissioners had distinct instructions to the effect that no land was to be disposed of which had not first been voluntarily ceded by its original owners and due compensation paid.[8] But when the first settlers arrived in South Australia there was no attempt to establish the nature and extent of Aboriginal proprietary rights, and nor was there a crown-appointed Protector of Aborigines to press the issue. This promised appointment was frustratingly delayed. It had been first offered to George Augustus Robinson, the 'Conciliator' who had worked under Governor Arthur in Van Diemen's Land, and who declined the offer in preference to a similar post in Port Phillip. The office of Protector was then held by a succession of interim officers, appointed locally and compromised in their degree of independence. It was initially held, for only a few months, by George Stevenson, the Governor's Private Secretary. It was then filled in April 1837 by Captain Walter Bromley, an elderly man with failing health who within three months was invited to resign for reasons of 'physical and mental imbecility'.[9] Next it was taken up by William Wyatt, a colonist who had emigrated as ship surgeon, and who held the post until Dr Matthew Moorhouse, the Crown appointed Protector, arrived in July 1839.[10] Moorhouse would serve in that role until 1856, the year self-government was granted to the province.

In his brief time as Protector, Wyatt at least endeavoured to have some reservations of land set aside 'to the benefit of the aborigines'.[11] Yet as he was aware, the very limited terms of his instructions – to protect Aboriginal proprietary rights, but only where that land was employed for cultivation, identified with a fixed residence, or used for funeral purposes – excluded the meaningful possibility of any such protection. He took this problem to Governor Hindmarsh, who advised him to address it to the Resident Commissioner, James Fisher. Oddly, although the position of the Governor incurred specific instructions to honour Aboriginal people's 'enjoyment' of their own lands, the Governor himself did not have the power to pursue this in law. Under the peculiar structure set up under the Foundation Act, the Governor had political authority as the representative of the Crown, while the Resident Commissioner had authority over the sale of land. Wyatt duly appealed to the Resident Commissioner for the reservation of Aboriginal land, only to be told that 'as the Act of Parliament admitted of no reservation of the kind, my application was useless'.[12] Eventually, these obstacles were resolved by an amendment to the Foundation Act in 1838, which included the passage from the Letters Patent recognising Aboriginal proprietary rights, and which moreover vested the powers of the Resident Commissioner in the Governor.[13] This meant that Governor Gawler, who replaced Hindmarsh in 1838, did not have the problems of divided authority that had hampered his predecessor. He was furnished with instructions that 'no land which the natives may possess' should be offered for sale 'until previously ceded by the natives to the Commissioners'. The Protector was to provide evidence to substantiate the sale.[14]

When a new set of surveys was completed in July 1840, Governor Gawler instructed Protector Moorhouse to reserve sections of land on behalf of Aboriginal people before they were opened to selection by colonists. Moorhouse set aside several parcels of land in districts that seemed to correspond to areas associated with particular Aboriginal clans. Despite the modest size of these reserved lands, representatives of the South Australia Company, including the former Resident Commissioner Fisher, were furious. The preliminary land orders they had purchased in England, they complained, gave them the right to have first choice. Governor Gawler responded with what must be one of the most passionate defences of Aboriginal rights to land ever heard in the Australian colonies. Aboriginal people, he said, 'have exercised distinct, defined, and absolute rights of proprietary and hereditary possession ... from time immemorial'.[15] He reminded prospective land owners of his instructions, which commanded him to protect Aboriginal people in 'the free enjoyment of their possessions ... and of which they are not disposed to make a voluntary transfer'.[16]

Yet despite this unequivocal statement on Aboriginal proprietary rights, Gawler ultimately implemented a much more compromised policy, based on the view that Aboriginal people would, given their 'limited knowledge', be put at disadvantage if they were to enter into treaties and bargains. Gawler's instructions as both Governor and Resident Commissioner certainly gave him authority to enter into land cession treaties of the sort that were regularly being negotiated in British north America, but he did not pursue his authority in this way. Instead he directed the Protector to select such land for the natives, in moderation, as he may deem likely to be necessary for their future use, support, and advancement in civilisation: such land being afterwards secured in the Governor, and Council, and the Protector of Aborigines, as trustees.[17]

Before long, the passage of the Imperial Waste Lands Act of 1842, which gave Governors the discretionary power to set aside lands for Aboriginal use, would settle the question. Henceforth, parcels of land would be set aside for Aboriginal people, but only to the extent that this would serve their eventual 'civilisation' and 'Christianisation': that is, they could have land if they farmed it. Although Gawler's compromised approach seemed to signal a contradiction between rhetoric and policy on Aboriginal propriety rights, it actually echoed the paradoxical logic of the 1837 Select Committee report: on the one hand, Aboriginal people, in Buxton's words, had a 'plain and sacred right' to their soil, a right at least acknowledged in some other British territories where land cession treaties were negotiated; on the other hand, Australia's Aboriginal people were regarded as being insufficiently advanced in 'civilisation' to have this 'plain and sacred right' recognised in law.

In South Australia, as across Australia's other colonies, the failure to adequately deal with Aboriginal rights to land was fundamental to the violence that followed in the path of the pastoral frontier wherever it spread. This failure rendered Aboriginal people both state-less and property-less, the consequences of which were anticipated by Governor Arthur when he wrote to the Colonial Office in 1835 pressing the necessity of land treaties. Aboriginal people may have been made British subjects, but by virtue of that nominal status they were instantly made the unsovereign trespassers on their own land. District by district and year by year, as the frontiers of European settlement spread into the interior, dispossessed Aboriginal peoples responded to European aggression with aggression.

The *Maria* Massacre

On 25 July 1840 the police at Encounter Bay, about 100 kilometres south of Adelaide, received news that a ship had been wrecked on the south coast and that the survivors had been murdered while attempting to return overland to Adelaide.[18] The ship was the brig *Maria* which had departed Adelaide for Hobart on 7 June 1840 with a crew of ten, and sixteen passengers.[19] A party under the Marine Surveyor, Captain Pullen, set out from Adelaide to search for survivors, but no one had been spared. They recovered a number of bodies buried in the sand, and the victims' scattered belongings.[20] The murder of the twenty six survivors of the *Maria* was the largest massacre of Europeans by Aboriginal people in Australian history.

In Adelaide, the murder of a large group of European settlers in a remote district of the colony caused consternation, fear and outrage. Governor Gawler, relatively new in his role as Hindmarsh's successor, faced a crisis that neither his predecessor nor the colony's founders had anticipated, and it was the first significant occasion on which the legal status of Aboriginal people beyond the settled districts could be put to the test. The demand for 'exemplary' action jostled with the requirements of the law. Yet in the face of the massacre of twenty six Europeans, Gawler had few precedents in determining how to respond. With colonists calling for immediate action, Gawler called a special meeting of the Executive Council to advise him. Judge Cooper and Advocate-General Hanson argued that the crime had been committed 'beyond the reach of ordinary British Law'.[21] Being unable to take an oath, Aboriginal evidence would be inadmissible in any case that might go to trial; and in the absence of survivors, there was no European evidence. Given the legal advice he had received, and 'considering the district in question as in a disturbed state', Gawler decided to proceed 'on the principles of martial law'.[22]

No formal proclamation of martial law was made, since the Council feared that making public the adoption of the 'principles of martial law' might injure the reputation of the colony.[23] This, however, was effectively what it was. A police party was sent to the district to secure summary justice against the offending tribe. This was to be the first significant occasion in South Australia, though by no means the last, on which the police force would be enlisted against an entire Aboriginal group in the cause of punitive action.

Until this point, there had been little reason to consider the role of the police as one that would involve serious action against the newly identified Aboriginal subjects of the Crown. When Aboriginal people murdered shepherds William Duffield and James Thompson in the Adelaide area in 1839, acting Governor James Stephen, in Gawler's absence, cancelled all government rations to Aboriginal people in Adelaide and lectured as many Aboriginal people as could be mustered to a public meeting on the principle that the government would 'always protect white men and punish wicked black men'.[24] The editor of the *Register* protested that the acting Governor's actions risked placing Aboriginal people beyond British law, a violation of the principle of the Proclamation, and indeed when Governor Gawler returned, he immediately restored the rations that had been withheld, and to further prove his friendly intentions, invited Aboriginal people from the Adelaide area to a dinner in the grounds of Government House to celebrate Queen Victoria's birthday.[25]

In 1840, in fact, the colony's police force, still in its fledging state, was neither intended nor organised to fight a war on any significant scale against any Aboriginal aggressions that might arise. Its manpower was limited, and its primarily metropolitan peace-keeping role thus far had been committed to duties such as apprehending drunk and disorderly persons on the streets of Adelaide, preventing the disorderly from discharging firearms or fireworks, fining culprits who let their livestock stray into the streets, and ensuring the registering of dogs.[26] In the absence of a large body of enlisted men, Governor Gawler had early in that year encouraged the formation of a voluntary militia, furnished with arms provided by the Colonisation Commissioners, which would supplement the police force and be called out in 'exceptional circumstances'.[27]

The police force quickly took form, however, under Gawler's commitment to it as an essential public service. When the *Maria* tragedy occurred, the new office of the Commissioner of Police had just a month previously been established. This office was held by Major Thomas O'Halloran, a former military man who had served as an officer in the British army in India. Another former military man, Alexander Tolmer, was appointed his second in command as Sub-Inspector of police. According to Robert Clyne, the new Commissioner of Police was a 'frustrated soldier' who 'frequently displayed an inability to appreciate the civil function of the police department'.[28] Trained within a military environment, both he and Alexander Tolmer would be influential in organising the fledging South Australian police into a para-military force. Both would have a significant impact on the consolidation of the police as a security force in the coming years.[29]

Before his party left for the site of the murders on the south coast, O'Halloran's instructions were 'to apprehend, and bring to summary justice, the ringleaders in the murder, or any of the murderers (in all not to exceed three).' Although further bloodshed was to be avoided if possible, O'Halloran had the Governor's assurance that if he had to 'resort to extreme force against the whole tribe', he would not be held accountable. If deemed to be guilty, the Aboriginal suspects were to be hanged or shot on the spot.[30] As Robert Clyne has pointed out, Commissioner O'Halloran's instructions in this case took the police's civil role as a putative peace-keeping force to a martial role of administering 'belligerent rights against a declared enemy'; and as commander of this expedition, O'Halloran would serve as 'judge, jury and executioner'.[31]

O'Halloran's party left Adelaide on 15 August. Upon reaching their destination they found ample evidence of violence: blood-stained clothing, the scattered leaves of a bible, the ship's mail, and part of the ship's log. On 23 August they rounded up 13 men, 2 youths, and 50 women and children, although they later let the women and children go. Two Aboriginal men seen fleeing the area by swimming across the Coorong were shot. On interrogation the captive group implicated two men, Moorcangua and Mongarawata, as those involved in the murder of the *Maria* survivors. On 24 August the two men were unanimously found guilty by a tribunal formed from members of the expeditionary force, and on the following day they were hanged over the graves of the *Maria* victims.[32]

Over the following month, the government sought to justify the decision to invoke martial law. At a meeting of the Executive Council on 15 September, 1840, the most unequivocal defence was offered by Advocate-General Hanson who began by asking: in what position do the Aborigines of the Province stand in relation to the Government? He argued that the doctrine which declared the Aborigines as British subjects should hold only under certain conditions. To those who were in constant intercourse with colonial society, exhibited friendly dispositions, and were advancing in civilisation, 'the ordinary forms of our constitution and laws may be beneficially and effectually applied'.[33] But British law could extend no further than this:

> it would be assuming too much to hold that the same maxims and principles must be applied without modification to distant tribes, inhabiting a territory beyond the limits of our settlement, with whom we have never communicated under friendly circumstances, whose language is equally unknown to us as ours is to them, and who betray, in all their intercourse with Europeans, the most savage and brutal hostility – who have never acknowledged subjugation to any power, and who, indeed, seem incapable of being subjected to authority, or deterred from atrocious crimes, except by military force.[34]

If further bloodshed and plunder were to be prevented, he argued, it was necessary that tribes such as the Milmenrura, the people accused of the crime, be considered a 'separate state or nation'. He cited Vattel's influential *Law of Nations* to argue that those who 'disdain to cultivate their lands, and choose rather to live by plunder, are wanting to themselves – are injurious to their neighbours – and deserve to be extirpated as savage and pernicious beasts'. Hanson also argued that the Milmenrura had a history of hostility, and it was therefore necessary that measures 'summary and severe were adopted to terrify the whole tribe by a sense of our power and determination'.

Their crime should be regarded 'not as that of individual British Subjects, but of a whole hostile tribe, that is *a nation at enmity with Her Majesty's subjects*'. His defence of the government's decision was completed with an assertion that Hindmarsh's Proclamation was directed more towards ordering the conduct of the settlers, than in extending the benefits of the British constitution to all Aborigines.[35]

On 30 September a bill was introduced in Council to allow Aborigines to be received as competent witnesses in criminal cases. With the question again raised of the Aborigines' constitutional position, Gawler had another opportunity to defend his actions in the *Maria* case. He characterised the Aborigines' 'proper position in the eye of the law' as a 'question of the greatest difficulty throughout the whole continent of Australia'.[36] While he admired the British constitution, its extension to the Aborigines of South Australia posed difficulties. The constitution, he stated, had gone through a thousand years of development, and

> it cannot be fully received or properly appreciated even by civilized nations of an inferior class, much less by the savages of Australia, who stand in the lowest degree in all the earth in religion, government, arts and civilization. In all these respects they are morally, as in material things they are physically, the antipodes of Britain – and it is not an easy thing to make antipodes meet.[37]

Gawler argued that even in Britain there were people under the same incapacity as the Aborigines. 'Atheists, idiots, and very young children' were under the protection of the law, but they were also 'deprived of great liberties and privileges'. If such people, he argued, were gathered together in an isolated mass, occupying great tracts of country and speaking an unknown language, 'our present laws would be in reference to them ... powerless, and that to have law at all a very great change would be required in the principles and practice of the parent state'. If the murderers had been given the protection of British subjects, he concluded, 'crime would have followed crime, the blacks intermixed among us would have caught the example, other persons of another description might have become emboldened by the impunity enjoyed by the blacks, and even the settled portion of our territory would have witnessed scenes of blood, robbery, and desperate contention'. His interpretation of the extension of rights as British subjects was that they were conferred 'as a boon and not as a right, in the rate and degree at which they would be beneficial to the natives, and safe for natural born subjects, and not all at once'.[38]

Shortly afterwards Justice Cooper, who had advised Gawler that the case lay beyond the reach of British law, also felt compelled to justify his views in a statement to the Court sessions. He appealed to the idea that summary justice represented a kind of commensurate law in the Aboriginal world; he could see no reason why the Milmenrura people should feel that they owed any allegiance to the British law, but their crime was a crime against nature, and one for which they themselves would have inflicted death.[39]

Outside of the Executive Council, Gawler's view enjoyed considerable support. The *Southern Australian* newspaper steadfastly defended his actions, suggesting that his 'energetic system' of administering punishment to the Aborigines was efficient, and approving of his assertion that the extension of the rights of British subjects to the Aborigines was a boon rather than a right.[40] Plenty of correspondents from among South Australia's colonists agreed. One respondent argued that just because Aboriginal people might 'reside' in a British province, it did not follow that they deserved British rights.[41] Another considered that Aboriginal people were amply compensated for the loss of their lands by colonists' goodwill, and the extension to them of British subjecthood was too much to expect.[42] Another argued that the executions of the Milmenrura men fulfilled divine justice, a higher law than man's, and therefore Gawler could be defended by the most unimpeachable authority of all.[43] A letter of address to His Excellency expressing 'public approval and appreciation' of his actions was circulated and made available to be signed at various offices, and *The Southern Australian* urged all to 'come forward with promptness and decision' to add their name to the list of supporters.[44] The deaths of twenty six Europeans had caused fear as well as outrage, and legal debate about the status of Aboriginal people was of less import to many colonists than their future security. In September, *The Southern Australian* spread alarm with a report that 'the Milmenrura nation, after having massacred the unfortunate people of the *Maria*, had invaded the neighbourhood of Lyndoch Valley in a most formidable number'. The *Register* immediately responded with a counter-report in an attempt to diminish unnecessary anxiety, with a correction that 'only about half a dozen blacks' were seen on a hunting excursion, were not of the Big Murray tribe, and had 'heard nothing of any attack or any disturbance'.[45]

In his report of the punitive expedition, published in the *Register* in September 1840, Commissioner of Police Major O'Halloran showed no doubt about the primary function of punitive action, which had little to do with the legal technicalities being debated in other quarters: 'The impression ... left on the natives' minds of our activity in thus sweeping their entire country, will, I am persuaded, give them a high notion of our power, and teach them to dread it for the future'.[46] Even in to the following year, newspapers expressed support for a 'white man's law' that bypassed the niceties of the court. In July 1841, the *Courier* complained:

> we hear of nothing but British law and trail by jury – as if, in the first place, the utter extermination of such a tribe would have been a matter of the slightest regret; and as if, in the next place, the enactment of a formal trial before a civil Court were not a complete farce. In all such instances summary justice is the best preventative against the repetition of crime, and is more likely – by striking terror at once – to get at the truth of events than a tedious process of law.[47]

But the execution of Aboriginal subjects without trial caused doubt and consternation in other quarters, most particularly in numerous editorials by George Stevenson, the editor of the *Register*, who challenged the government's justifications of its action. Stevenson characterised the Advocate General's description of the Milmenrura as a people beyond British law as the artful side-stepping of a barrister. He pointed out that the clear intention of the Proclamation, which he himself had worded, was to extend the protection of British law to all the Aborigines of the Province. Rather than 'framing the law,' the Proclamation merely stated what was already law – something approved of by the Home Government and already tested in the colony's courts. Stevenson scoffed at Hanson's description of the Milmenrura as a separate nation, pointing out: 'If we treat the Murray tribe as a nation, we must concede to them the right to make their own laws, and what is more, we must deny the right of the South Australian nation to object to these laws, whatever they may be'.[48]

Through the mouthpiece of the *Register*, George Stevenson also emphatically rejected the authority of O'Halloran's police party to employ summary justice. Although the police acted according to 'moral conviction' and were sanctioned by their instructions, it was impossible to reconcile their proceedings 'either with the acknowledged rights of all natives within the province of South Australia, or with the inviolable principles of the British Constitution'.[49] In essence, the hanging of the Milmenrura men was undertaken 'by an unrecognised and unconstitutional tribunal'.[50] He also rejected the logic of the view that ordinary law must be deferred because the case could not be legally tried; if it could not be legally tried, he argued, there was no other option than to consider the Milmenrura men legally innocent.[51] In all, he rejected the 'vigorous efforts' being made 'to justify an act which, legally and constitutionally, is unjustifiable'. At issue was the power of the

Governor to order 'the summary execution of any human being within the Province'.[52]

Stevenson made a steadfast point of distinguishing between the 'moral' grounds of punitive action and the requirements of the government's own law. 'Whether the natives themselves can be bound by the proclamation in question, or whether they recognise or value the title of English subjects, may admit of argument; but the Government, at least, is bound by its own act'.[53] In contrast to those who justified the hangings as divine justice, there were many from among the colonists who agreed with the *Register*'s editor. 'No man's life', argued one correspondent, whether that 'of a British subject, or a savage native — can be taken away on the moral belief of his guilt, and in the proclaimed absence of "all legal evidence of crime"'.[54] When the *Register*, despite its views, acknowledged that there was 'a long and respectable list' of people who expressed support of Gawler's action,[55] a correspondent wondered why no such list of names had appeared in print: 'Is it that the absence of names of old and influential colonists would show too plainly how far it was from obtaining general approval'?[56] Mary Thomas, in a letter to her brother George Harris, wrote that Gawler's decision entailed 'a most flagrant breach of the laws and constitution of England' as well as an assumption of governmental power 'which even the Sovereign does not possess'.[57]

The reaction in Britain was unambiguous: when details of the summary trial and execution were received by the Colonial Office the opinion of Crown Law officers was that the Governor had acted illegally and that he and O'Halloran were liable to be tried for murder.[58] The Aborigines Protection Society in England met and roundly condemned Gawler's actions.[59] Within the year, the over-expenditures of this government would lead the Colonial Office to recall George Gawler and replace him with George Grey. Gawler had begun his governorship of South Australia with the determination to maintain peaceful relations between the colonists and the Aborigines of the province, yet with the *Maria* affair, his term ended in controversy and some degree of shame. Grey began his term with a similar determination to faithfully implement the principle of the rule of law set out in the Proclamation, yet within a year this determination was compromised, as Gawler's had been, by events unfolding on the ever-expanding frontier.

Overlanders and the Rufus River Massacre

By 1839, as new surveys were completed, settlers began to move into country further distant from Adelaide. Enterprising pastoralists and adventurers saw an opportunity for profit, and provided the capital for overland expeditions to bring sheep and cattle from New South Wales. Two principal routes emerged: one through the Port Phillip district via the Lower South East of South Australia, and the other following Sturt's path along the Murray/Darling River system. It was the second that would be preferred in the years between 1838 and 1842: it was direct and there was a sure supply of water for the stock. The first to bring cattle overland along this route was the explorer Edward John Eyre. In late December 1837 Eyre assembled a party of 8 men, three teams of bullocks and 300 head of cattle on the Limestone Plains of New South Wales. Although Charles Sturt had given him advice about the route, it would nonetheless prove to be a long and difficult journey. By June of 1838 his party reached the junction of the Darling and he knew there were just 250 miles to go before he reached Adelaide. Eyre was cautious about his dealings with Aboriginal people and completed the journey in July with nothing more serious to report than a hostile but harmless confrontation near the Rufus River.[60] But in the following months and years, the traffic on the Murray/Darling route would grow exponentially. At its height there was an almost continuous train of sheep, cattle, bullock drays and horses, snaking their way along the river system from Sydney to Adelaide. Many of these entrepreneurs were much less reticent than Eyre to use violence to ease their passage.

Certainly there was good money to be made. James Crawford, who travelled the route in 1838, made a profit of £3000 from about 700 head of cattle.[61] To put this in perspective, the annual salary of the Protector of Aborigines, Matthew Moorhouse, was about £100. The prospect of huge profits also entailed the risk of great losses. What was less clear at this time was the human cost of the passage. In October 1840 a correspondent to the *Register* suggested that the cost in Aboriginal lives was high:

> There has seldom been an arrival by land from Port Phillip or Sydney, which on its reaching Adelaide, did not bring some tale of boasting and butchering the natives on the way. There are few in Adelaide who have communicated with the degraded ruffians employed in driving stock to this country, who have not heard them vaunt their exploits in shooting or 'peppering' the natives in their route. And there are well authenticated instances where both the stockkeepers and their masters have related tales of their shooting or hunting down the natives, which they have promptly recanted when it was ascertained that they were affording grounds for a dangerous enquiry into their own conduct. That firearms have been unhesitatingly and unscrupulously used by overland parties there is no doubt ...'[62]

These, of course, were just rumours, but the journal of Alexander Buchanan's overland expedition in the second half of 1839 appears to bear out the claims. Buchanan set out from Sydney in July 1839 and arrived in Adelaide in December of that year. His arrival went virtually unnoticed in the press, but his own journal suggests that it was far from an uneventful passage. On 1 October he recorded: 'We gave the men the muskets and ammunition to-day as we may expect to fall in with the blacks'. On 15 November, when Buchanan's party encountered an Aboriginal party at the junction of the Murray and Darling Rivers, he recorded:

> the men fired upon them and we from the opposite bank fired upon them also and killed the old chief, when they all took to the Murray and we kept firing as long as they were within shot. There were five or six killed and a good many wounded.[63]

On November 22, 'a black was seen in some reeds and the carter fired upon him and killed him. He had come with no other intention but to spear sheep, so his plant was fixed.' Buchanan's journal records that he fired upon Aboriginal people on half a dozen occasions, killing at least eight and wounding 'many others'. The last of these clashes occurred on 7 December when Buchanan coolly noted that they saw 'a good many blacks on the opposite bank of the river, fired upon them and killed one, the rest made off immediately'.[64] There seems little doubt that Buchanan's actions were pre-emptive. Just two days later Buchanan fell in with a settler party that included Governor Gawler, which had sailed up from Lake Alexandrina on a tour of the river. Asked whether 'the blacks had been troublesome', Buchanan records: 'We told them they had been pretty quiet except at the Darling they annoyed us a little. Did not say we shot any'.[65]

As Aboriginal attacks on overlanding parties became more concerted and widespread, the need for secrecy about the use of guns diminished. In October 1839, when an overlanding supply party was attacked, the expedition leader McLeod reported that 'after about half an hour's sharp firing, which the natives stood admirably,' the attackers were driven off.[66] Shortly afterwards this party came across another overlanding party which had also been attacked nearby, and one of their number killed. Governor Gawler issued a public statement about the escalating violence. He had no doubt that Aboriginal hostility existed, in part, because of the 'injudicious treatment' they had received from Europeans; 'it is certain that the natives have been frequently fired upon and many of them killed and wounded'.[67]

In April 1841 an overland party led by Henry Field and Henry Inman was attacked by a Maraura group near Lake Bonney: the overlanders shot dead at least one Maraura man in fending off the attack, but five thousand sheep and eight hundred head of cattle had been dispersed.[68] The death of an Aboriginal man registered little mention; the loss of the stock, which represented a valuable import into the colony, caused wide consternation. Gawler, now in the last month of his governorship, immediately despatched a police party to the Murray River to retrieve the lost property. Members of the police force, which was still limited in manpower, were supplemented with volunteer militia. Major Thomas O'Halloran was in command of this expedition, as he had been of the punitive expedition following the *Maria* massacre the previous year. In his journal the Major noted that although the police 'shall be careful not to be the aggressor in any way', he anticipated that 'the punishment ought to be severe to prove to them our power … I think that a severe lesson to this fierce tribe would greatly conduce to the preservation of life hereafter.'[69]

The police party did not reach its destination, for news of Gawler's recall by the Colonial Office obliged them to turn back. Frustrated by the loss of the awaited sheep and cattle, settlers organised a volunteer party, led by Henry Field, to set out to recover the missing stock. Amongst the party was James Hawker, who in coming years would become an influential and successful pastoralist. His diary reveals that the settlers shot six to eight Aboriginal men on this expedition, but failed to recover the stock.[70]

Meanwhile in Adelaide, Gawler had been replaced with the new Governor George Grey. When news reached Adelaide in May that another overlanding party led by stockholder Charles Langhorne was on its way down the river, colonists petitioned Grey to send a strong party of volunteers and police to the Murray to protect the overlanders on the route.[71] Holding to an unambiguous understanding of Aborigines' legal status as British subjects, Grey rejected the petition. For a start, he argued, the police should not be considered as a private security force to protect the enterprises of overlanders. He was equally reluctant to sanction an expedition in which volunteer colonists, unaccountable to the police force, might take part in acts of retribution against the Aboriginal population. He also doubted that the recent attacks on overlanders were unprovoked. Above all, he emphasised that all Aboriginal peoples held the same rights of British subjects as did all settlers, and that 'to regard them as aliens, with whom a war can exist, and against whom Her Majesty's troops may exercise belligerent rights, is to deny that protection to which they derive the highest possible claim from the sovereignty which has been assumed over the whole of their ancient possessions.'[72] He did finally sanction an expedition, which would be led again by Major O'Halloran, but on conditional terms. Its primary function was to escort the overlanders to Adelaide, it would be accompanied by the Protector of Aborigines whose role was to 'act as protector and counsel of the natives', and weapons were only to be used when 'absolutely necessary' in self-defence.[73]

Before this third party reached the overlanders, Langhorne's party and the Maraura had already clashed, and four of Langhorne's stockmen had been killed. The Protector of Aborigines, Matthew Moorhouse, later reported to Grey that Langhorne's party had shot and killed at least five Maraura men, though no Aboriginal deaths were mentioned in Langhorne's report.[74] With the Governor's clear instructions against the use of firearms, the police party was obliged to return to Adelaide without having retrieved the stock. 'I much fear', O'Halloran wrote in his journal, 'that allowing these fellows to escape without injury will do much future Mischief & make them more bold & daring than ever.'[75]

In August, petitioners again pressed Grey to send armed protection to the Murray with the news that another overland party under the leadership of William Robinson was passing through the same contested territory.[76] Again Grey hesitated, reluctant to commit government resources to a cause which not only might 'involve alike the innocent and guilty, men, women, and children in its consequences' but also was 'a matter of private adventure, not of public utility'.[77] But again he agreed to endorse an expedition to the Murray, this time a smaller party commanded by the Protector of Aborigines Matthew Moorhouse. The Sub-Inspector of Police Barnard Shaw would be second in command. The 'main object', Grey instructed Moorhouse, was to prevent a collision between the overlanders and the Maraura; Moorhouse should take every opportunity to establish good relations between the two groups.[78] Yet when the Moorhouse/Shaw party met Robinson's party on August 27, it was to learn that the overlanders had been attacked the previous day and in defending the stock had killed five and wounded another ten Aboriginal men.

Within an hour of this meeting, Moorhouse's and Langhorne's parties were confronted with a large group of Maraura men, women and children on the banks of the Rufus river. Fearing imminent attack, Moorhouse gave over command to Shaw. Without waiting for Shaw's orders, Langhorne's party opened fire, followed by the police party from the opposite bank of the river. Moorhouse's report suggests that perhaps thirty Aboriginal people were killed and many wounded,[79] though other records suggest this figure to be higher. In his memoir published in 1899, James Hawker wrote: 'in after years, when I was residing on the Murray and had learnt the language of the natives, I ascertained that a much larger number had been killed, for Mr. Robinson's men were all picked marksmen'.[80]

When the party returned to Adelaide in September, Grey called an inquiry into the massacre. The resolution of the Bench of Magistrates was that the party's conduct was 'justifiable, indeed unavoidable in the circumstances'.[81] In this case, unlike the case of the *Maria* massacre the previous year, all the principles of the rule of law had been observed. Nonetheless, the final result was that when faced with strong Aboriginal resistance to European incursions, the government again sanctioned and justified the use of deadly force against a people deemed to be British subjects. The outcome on the Rufus River was the largest recorded massacre of Aboriginal people in the colony's history.

Grey's immediate response in the aftermath of the clash at Rufus River was to appoint the explorer Edward Eyre as Resident Magistrate and Protector of Aborigines on the River Murray. Eyre established his outpost at Moorundie, mid-way between Adelaide and the site of the clashes on the Rufus. He was directed to devote 'his attention to the suppression of outrages on the part of overland parties, and to the civilisation and improvement of the natives'.[82] These objectives were to be achieved in the following way:

> I have directed Mr Eyre to bring into operation a system of periodical distributions of flour to the natives; – this distribution being made dependent on their good conduct. They are to assemble on every other full moon, for the purpose of receiving these presents. Opportunities will thus be afforded them of bring under Mr Eyre's notice any grievances, under which they may be suffering; and he, at the same time, can impart to them any regulations or directions for their guidance. I confidently anticipate that the measures thus adopted will, for the future, prevent a recurrence of scenes similar to those which I have lately had to bring to your Lordship's attention.[83]

On the eve of quitting England to take up his post as Governor of South Australia, George Grey had written to the colonial office expressing his surprise at the 'total absence of any armed forces in South Australia', forces that might be necessary to repel an attack by foreign enemies, be brought to the aid of the Civil Power, or in the event of other emergencies. To this end, he asked if 'one of two companies of Infantry' might be granted the colony.[84] Just days after assuming the governorship of South Australia he addressed the issue again, this time in a letter to Governor Gipps in New South Wales requesting 'two or three companies of infantry'. Governor Gipps sent him a terse response declining his request and advising him that he was only authorised to send troops 'in a case of emergency'.[85] The violence on the overland route was just such an emergency. On 12 June 1841, as the rescue expedition under the command of Moorhouse and Shaw was heading up the river to give assistance to overlanders, Grey again requested Gipps to provide him with a detachment of troops:

> Your Excellency will also learn from other Despatches, which, if they can be prepared in time, shall be forwarded by this opportunity, that the natives of the river Murray near its junction with the Darling have assumed a more hostile attitude than the natives of this Continent have ever previously done, so that full occupation would be found in this quarter alone for a larger Police Force than this province is able to maintain. The Town and the other districts have been left for the last five weeks in a totally unprotected state.[86]

Governor Gipps directed a company of 80 men from the 96th Regiment based in Van Diemen's Land to be despatched to South Australia. Twelve men and a non-commissioned officer arrived at Moorundie in October, soon after the arrival of new Resident Magistrate and Protector Edward Eyre.[87]

During his three years at Moorundie, Eyre undertook three expeditions to the area of the Rufus River, and on each occasion travelled only with a few Mounted Police and Aboriginal guides rather than with the infantry company that had been sent to support him. The report of the first expedition, undertaken in January 1842, provides a fairly clear insight as to why the district was quiet. He estimated that there were approximately 700 Aboriginal people between his post at Moorundie and the Rufus and of that number he believed that no more than 200 were 'grown up men':

> Whilst in the neighbourhood of the Rufus, I observed many women in deep mourning for their husbands, who had been shot in some of the conflicts with the Europeans. Many children were pointed out to me as being fatherless from the same cause; and I have no doubt the loss of lives in these districts has been considerable from such affrays.[88]

The violence inflicted upon the Maraura by the overlanding parties, and by the police expedition sent to assist them, had devastated the population and had evidently had the desired punitive effect. Although Eyre proposed that a military post might be established at the Rufus, Grey declined to act on the suggestion, evidently satisfied that the crisis had passed. Writing of the event years later, colonist Henry Melville no doubt expressed the view of many of his contemporaries when he wrote: 'I am satisfied that the terror that the whites inspired amongst the tribes east of the Murray and the terrible lesson given them on the upper Murray was the means and I believe the only means of making the overland routes safe to travel'.[89]

The events over 1840 and 1841 indicated the degree to which Aborigines' status as British subjects had been exposed as a legal fiction in the minds of many colonists, if indeed it had ever been digested at all. For colonial officials, the principle that Aboriginal people were to be protected as British subjects had been tested and had failed in practice, readily suspended when the loss of European lives and property were at stake. Although Governors Gawler and Grey may well have hoped that these cases could be considered as exceptions to the rule, the years to come would demonstrate that they were far from exceptional.

Chapter 3

'OUR DECLARED ENEMIES'

Imagining invasion

In early October 1840, a year before his posting to Moorundie, Edward Eyre was camped at Port Lincoln preparing for his expedition to King George's Sound in Western Australia. The small harbour town had been established in March of the previous year when Captain Frank Hawson landed the first official settlers there.[1] The settlement grew slowly, and by the beginning of 1840 it had a population of 220 souls and about '30 houses, either finished or in the course of completion'.[2] The town was located at the bottom of what would eventually be named Eyre Peninsula, after the explorer himself. On the afternoon of 6 October, Eyre learnt that a 12 year-old boy, Frank Hawson, had been fatally speared by Aborigines about a mile and a half from the hut on his family's property, where he had been tending their flocks. Frank had been alone when a group of Aborigines approached requesting food. He gave them bread and rice, but when they wanted more provisions, he blocked them with a gun and sword. One of the Aboriginal children, Eyre was told, had given Frank a spear to throw, and in throwing it he had received two spears to the chest. Despite his injuries Frank fired his gun, hitting one person, and the party retreated. Hours later, Frank's older brother found the injured boy and took him into Port Lincoln, where he died not long afterwards. His death marked the beginning of what was to become a fearful and protracted conflict between Aborigines and settlers on the colony's western pastoral frontier.

Noting this event in his journal, Eyre asked himself what had motivated the attack on the young boy. He knew that Aborigines had been fired upon at various stations in the district; Frank Hawson's elder brother had fired upon a group at the station not long before, to 'frighten them'. Without more definite information Eyre suspended judgement, but the events gave him pause to reflect on 'the conduct of the Aborigines of Australia … towards the invaders and usurpers of their rights'. Aboriginal people, he felt, 'have seldom been guilty of wanton or unprovoked outrages' without 'some strongly exciting cause'.[3] What, he asked, were those causes?

Firstly, writes Eyre, 'our being in their country at all' is 'altogether an act of intrusion and aggression' which Aboriginal people could justly imagine is for the 'purpose of dispossessing them'. Although the Aboriginal people of a district that has been 'unceremoniously taken possession of' may choose to remain aloof at first, eventually they are compelled to return, 'cautiously and fearfully approaching what is their own'. When they do, 'often they are met by repulsion and sometimes violence'.[4] In a powerful passage Eyre ponders the extremes of settler behaviour on the Australian frontier:

> Passing over the fearful scenes of horror and bloodshed, that have but too frequently been perpetrated in all the Australian colonies upon the natives of the remoter districts, by the most desperate and abandoned of our countrymen; and overlooking, also, the recklessness that too generally pervades the shepherds and stock-keepers of the interior, with regard to the coloured races, a recklessness that leads them to think as little of firing at a black, as at a bird, and which makes the number they have killed, or the atrocities that have attended the deeds, a matter for a tale, a jest or boast at pothouse revelries ...[5]

But what of those settlers 'actuated by no bad intentions' and anxious to avoid violence? Such settlers find themselves 'alone in the wilds.' With few men to support them and cut off from ready assistance, and schooled in accounts of the 'ferocity' or the 'treachery of the savages,' they conclude that there is less trouble and risk in keeping the Aborigines away from the station. Should Aborigines appear, threats are made and weapons produced, even if 'no stronger measures are resorted to'. It would hardly be surprising, Eyre continues, that such displays should produce feelings of 'a hostile and vindictive kind' among the Aboriginal owners of the land. Is it any wonder that Aboriginal people, thus dispossessed and watching the intruders 'revelling in plenty near them,' choose to 'rob those who first robbed them?' The responses of Aboriginal people faced with such acts of 'intrusion and aggression', he concludes, are no different to 'what men in a more civilized state would do under the same circumstances':

> What they daily do under the sanction of the law of nations – a law that provides not for the safety, privileges, and protection of the Aborigines, and owners of the soil, but which merely lays down rules for the direction of the privileged robber in the distribution of the booty of any newly discovered country.[6]

Eyre's characterisation of the Australian frontier is a remarkably perceptive one. He leaves his readers in no doubt that the settlement of Australia was an invasion and that violence was a routine necessity in the process of Aboriginal dispossession. Perhaps the most unusual aspect of Eyre's account is his attempt to imagine the invasion of Aboriginal lands through the eyes, hearts and minds of the people confronting it. Such empathy is rare in the accounts of settlers; it was an emotion antithetical to the task of dispossession and the violence that inevitably accompanied it.

Port Lincoln under siege

By early 1842, more than a year after the fatal spearing of the boy Frank Hawson, Port Lincoln was a developing but still sparsely settled coastal port, more easily accessible from Adelaide by boat than by a long overland journey. Its scattered pastoral stations fanned out from the township and clustered around the coastal tip of a large, as yet unexplored inland peninsula. This was the country of the Battara people and Nauo people to the north, who vastly outnumbered the settler population. Given its distance from the administrative centre in Adelaide, colonial government at Port Lincoln was represented in the figure of the Government Resident, an occasional position assigned to outlying districts.

Occupied by a respectable pastoralist, the role of Government Resident combined the roles of Protector of Aborigines, distributor of rations and Magistrate. Yet although the position represented the presence of colonial government, the scope of its authority was deliberately vague. When the Government Resident appointed to the south east in the early 1850s requested clarification of his instructions, the Colonial Secretary responded that 'the duties of the Governt. Resident at that station are not permanently defined, – they are only such as may be directed – from time to time – by the Governor.'[7] The instructions issued in 1841 to the new Government Resident at Port Lincoln called for a similar degree of flexibility. In particular, in the absence of a nearby court of law, discretionary decisions were acceptable with regard to 'punishment of the Natives'. These, Grey wrote, might include the withholding of rations for minor offences such as 'pilfering', and corporal punishment, or whipping, which he recommended be carried out by the Aboriginal relatives of the offender, and affected 'in the sight of the assembled Natives'. For other light crimes, the Government Resident was effectively authorised to determine any 'such other punishment as you may see fit to award'.[8]

Yet the discretionary powers of the Government Resident at Port Lincoln were inadequate to the crisis to come. In the late summer of 1842 Aboriginal hostility to settlement in the district began to increase. The Government Resident Dr Harvey described the escalating violence in his report dated 8 March 1842. On Monday 14 February there was an attempt to plunder Samuel White's hut. On 20 February about 30 Aborigines endeavoured to steal sheep from the station and threw spears at his shepherd; two constables were sent to his station but despite their presence Aboriginal people still 'shewed every disposition to be hostile'. On 25 February an attempt was made to rob Charles Dutton's station and one of his fences was set alight.[9] According to the Lutheran missionary Reverend Clamor Schurmann, who knew the local people and language, the aggressors were men of the Battara tribe who occupied the inland hills and valleys.

The first settler deaths since Frank Hawson died happened in March, when pastoralist John Brown and his hutkeeper Lovelock were killed on Brown's station. Lovelock was speared by Morldalta in the course of robbing his hut, and Brown was speared because he had earlier beaten Ngarbi with the butt end of his rifle.[10] Charles Dutton wrote to the *Register* at the end of March detailing the spiralling violence and noting that, within days of the murders of Brown and Lovelock, his own station had been attacked again.[11] Writing in his journal on 5 March, the Government Resident reported the sense of agitation in the district:

> In consequence of these depredations, Messrs White had abandoned his second station. The parties in the bush – with the exception of Mr Dutton, who is least protected of any, and 30 miles off – are very much alarmed and are sending into town, repeatedly, for men to come out on hire at high wages, merely to protect them; but no one can be found to go.[12]

Shortly afterwards, the station of police sergeant McEllister was attacked by a party of 80 Aboriginal men, forcing his workers to flee.[13] The attacks were not only in quick succession but were also reasonably widespread. The Aboriginal people inland of Port Lincoln, the Government Resident worried, were showing 'altogether a strong unfriendly feeling'.[14]

The townspeople petitioned the Governor for immediate aid. 'The depredations and outrages', they wrote, were now of 'such magnitude' as to make them fear 'for the general safety of life and property'. They were afraid that the township itself might be attacked and 'each dwelling might be destroyed in detail'. Their petition included a list of all the men resident in the district, and all they had by way of arms and ammunition. Feeling insufficiently armed for the threat facing them, they requested that a detachment of the military be sent to their aid, and that additional arms and ammunition be dispatched to them from the government store.[15] Governor Grey replied that because of the serious constraints on government spending he was unable to assist them; besides which, the military detachment was so small as to be barely adequate for the region around Adelaide.

The sense of crisis soon worsened. On 29 March, James Rolles Biddle's Long Pond station not far from the Port Lincoln settlement was attacked. Under a barrage of spears the four people resident at the station retreated into their hut. They fired upon their attackers, killing two, but were eventually overpowered. James Biddle, Elizabeth Stubbs and James Fastings were all killed, while Elizabeth's husband, James, who was left for dead, regained conscious after the attackers had left and was able to drag the body of his wife and companions from the hut that had been set alight.[16] According to Schurmann, who spoke with Stubbs after the attack, a number of their weapons had jammed, eventually rendering them defenceless. Biddle had nearly a dozen spear wounds, Fastings twenty three, while Elizabeth Stubbs was killed with a pitchfork by Ngarbi while she tried to hide under the bed. 'Little Jemmy', as she knew him, was a young man already implicated in the murder of Brown.[17]

To a settlement already alarmed, the attack on the Long Pond station produced an atmosphere of panic. The new Government Resident, Charles Driver, immediately raised a party of seven armed and mounted men to pursue the attackers.[18] They were accompanied by Reverend Schurmann and half a dozen 'friendly blacks' as guides. They set out on 2 April, riding northwest until they came upon an Aboriginal camp that Schurmann believed to contain the party that attacked Biddle's station. As they approached the Aborigines 'fled in all directions,' leaving only four men and a woman behind. In his account of what happened next, Schurmann writes:

> Driver ordered Stewart to shoot the native nearest to us. He repeatedly called: 'Knock him over'. I asked Driver why he ordered the man shot when he was unarmed and could have been taken prisoner. He said that he didn't want prisoners, since they were useless. Shots were fired at three of the fleeing natives, but none fell. However, our trackers told us that Nulta and Mulya were wounded. On the top of the hill we found a woman who was in advanced stages of pregnancy, trying to hide in the hollow of a tree, and I asked the Sergeant if he was going to shoot her.[19]

Driver's party collected up the stolen property found in the camp and, after burning all the Aboriginal belongings, they returned to town.

Charles Driver perceived a systematic plan in the Aboriginal attacks. In less than a month, five settlers had been killed and attempts made on the lives of others. These murders, he reported to the Governor, 'originate in no particular feeling of ill will towards the parties but are a natural termination of the game that has been playing the last year and a half'. So secure were the attackers that even after the attack on Biddle's station, 'they were forming a sort of winter's encampment within 3 miles of the scene of violence'. Port Lincoln had descended into a state of 'general panic'. The settlers, wrote Driver, 'are excessively alarmed and have all flocked into Town with their families; agricultural operations 'are suspended'; it was becoming difficult to retain employees at stations, even with wages 'more than quadrupled to make or persuade them to remain at all'; 'All the cattle stations are deserted and the Cattle running wild in the bush'. He requested that an 'efficient force be speedily placed at my disposal for a short period to enable us to make an example of the murderers and leave a wholesome impression on the minds of the natives generally'.[20]

The 96th Regiment

This time, Governor Grey bowed to his petitioners' request and ordered Lieutenant Hugonin and fifteen men of the 96th Regiment to proceed without delay to Port Lincoln 'with a view of affording protection to the settlers, and aiding the civil power'.[21] Hugonin was made a Commissioner of the Peace and magistrate, to underline the civil role his force would play and to allow him control of the police force in the district. In recognition of his rank he was also assigned a police officer to act as his orderly. His instructions were to capture the Aborigines 'concerned in the late outrages', if necessary to 'apprehend all natives against whom fair ground of suspicion may lie', and to detain them until sufficient evidence 'can be procured against them'. The Governor suggested that he base himself at Biddle's station, endeavour to secure horses from the local settlers 'to mount the force under your command', and to patrol the neighbourhood. It was again stressed that his task 'consists solely in apprehending the natives ... not in punishing them'; nonetheless they were to be 'captured at all risks' and if challenged 'you must use force to oppose force'.[22] Reverend Clamour Schurmann later recalled a somewhat blunter version of those instructions. Hugonin told him that he had been ordered to 'take the whole of the Port Lincoln natives either dead or alive without discrimination'.[23]

Lieutenant Hugonin's detachment arrived in Port Lincoln on 17 April 1842. The following day he and the Government Resident planned their expedition. Reverend Schurmann was invited to join the party as an interpreter.[24] Wary after his experience with Driver's expedition, Schurmann agreed to go in the hope of preventing the loss of 'innocent blood'.[25] The expedition established their initial base at Pallanna, 15 miles west of Port Lincoln. A party of 17 men departed Pallanna on 25 April, travelling northward along the peninsula's coast in the direction of Coffin Bay. Later that day they saw a group of Aboriginal people on the shore who, the tracker assured them, were not connected to the guilty parties. Yet despite being called upon not to fire, one of the soldiers shot a man standing in the water spearing fish, a man who had acted as a guide for Schurmann on previous occasions.[26] In his report, Lieutenant Hugonin defended his soldier's action, saying that a spear had been raised ready to throw.[27] As they left the camp, and the dying man in the company of his relatives, lamentations and shouts could be heard; the tracker said they were scolding Schurmann for bringing the soldiers to them and that 'bye and bye they would spear him'.[28] Upset with what had transpired, Schurmann left the party and returned to town.

A week after Hugonin's party returned to their base, news was received that about a hundred Aborigines were gathering on the coast not far from Port Lincoln. On 7 May, Lieutenant Hugonin and his men, together with some volunteers from amongst the settler community, set off with a plan to encircle the Aboriginal encampment and take prisoners. As they neared they found that most people had fled, with the exception of some old men, women and children. As he sent his men to surround the remainder of the encampment, Hugonin reported, he 'heard two shots fired on the shore':

> Running up I found that two of my men had come upon a party of Natives, who had endeavoured to take their flintlocks from them. They shot two, several shots were fired at the rest. I am inclined to think two more were wounded.[29]

Schurmann was appalled by the actions of Hugonin's men, which so far had taken the form of random reprisals rather than a structured effort to capture the guilty. 'So heinous are the whites!', he wrote in his journal. 'Mr Driver said the butchery will continue until they hand over the guilty ones. But it hasn't been proved that the guilty ones are among them'.[30] Information gathered from his Aboriginal friends led Schurmann to believe that those responsible for the attacks on Brown's and Biddle's stations were a division of the Parnkalla, known as the 'Battara Yurarri, or gum tree people', who inhabited the interior country. The camps that the 96th regiment were attacking were bands of Nauo, a coastal tribe that had no part in the attacks.[31]

After their camp had been raided by Driver's party on 2 April, the Battara had kept their distance from Port Lincoln. But after Hugonin's raids, they recommenced their aggressions. On 19 May, shortly after midnight, an Aboriginal party of about 200 men attacked Charles Driver's station, Pillaworta, which had been used as the base for Lieutenant Hugonin's operations. Lieutenant Hugonin, Driver, and the remainder of the detachment had only departed the station a few hours before, leaving it under the guard of several soldiers of the 96th Regiment. The soldiers fired nine rounds at their assailants and saw 'two natives fall', but in danger of being surrounded, they were forced to retreat while the attackers plundered the huts. Given the systematic nature of the attacks in March, and Driver's leading role in the retaliatory actions that followed, it is difficult not to think that his station was deliberately targeted. Lieutenant Hugonin promised to 'lose no time in the pursuit of these fellows who appear to be bolder than ever in their outrages'.[32]

This time Hugonin and Driver assembled a larger party of foot soldiers, Mounted Police, and volunteer mounted settlers. On 21 May, a day after leaving Pillaworta, they captured an Aboriginal boy whom they induced to guide them to an Aboriginal camp on the sea-coast. They raided the camp, and as 40 or 50 people fled, they captured one person and shot dead another who had thrown a spear at Sergeant McEllister.[33] On the party's return to Pillaworta, Schurmann was summoned to interpret for the prisoner. He was Ngarka, Schurmann reported, 'a native of the Eastern Coast tribe', who were not implicated in the recent attacks. At Pillaworta Schurmann was confronted by a gruesome spectacle. It was the head of Ngulga, whom the soldiers had shot. His head had been stuck on a pole, with a clay pipe forced between the teeth. Schurmann protested to the lieutenant about this behaviour, but 'could not prevail upon him to put a stop to it'. Neither Ngarka nor Ngulga, he wrote, was implicated in the murders. In outlining these events in a letter to the Protector, Schurmann observed that 'the destruction and removal of the innocent, or at least less guilty natives, while those who have taken lives escape with impunity, besides some other circumstances are gradually convincing me that my presence will not much longer be wanted in this part of the province.'[34]

In his own report of events that had transpired since Pillaworta had been so brazenly attacked, Charles Driver was depressed about the state of the district. 'For some time to come', he wrote, 'no friendly intercourse will result between the Europeans and Aborigines at Port Lincoln'. Aboriginal aggressions had been 'allowed too long without a sufficient check', and their mastery of the hinterland affords them so many advantages that the settlers must for the present at least, confine their operations to the immediate vicinity of the Town, unless a protective force is placed in the settlement to a much larger extent to what I imagine the local government has in its power to afford.

The recent events, he continued, had 'completely paralysed the industry of both the town and surrounding country'. All the flocks had been brought into town, resulting in a scarcity of feed; outlying stations had either faltered or been abandoned, the labour bestowed upon them 'thrown away'.[35]

Despite the lives they had taken, the activities of the 96th Regiment at Port Lincoln under the command of Lieutenant Hugonin could hardly be described as successful. In three expeditions over the course of three months, they had managed to capture only one man, Ngarka, on suspicion of being involved in the attacks in March, despite all suggestions that he had no involvement. During their raids they had shot and killed or wounded a number of Aboriginal people, but none of the camps they raided belonged to the tribe believed to have committed the murders. The only time the soldiers encountered the Battara people was when the Battara attacked Lieutenant Hugonin's own encampment at Pillaworta, forcing the soldiers to flee. The activities of the military in the Port Lincoln district – in hindsight at least – were regarded with some amusement. James Hawker, who was in the district in October 1842, commented on the absurdity of 'soldiers on foot, in heavy marching orders', trying to catch 'natives who knew every inch of the country and who could evade any attempt to make them prisoners!' With their old Brown Bess muskets, which would not carry a long distance, and their inability to cross swampy country, their presence was a 'miserable fiasco'.[36]

To be fair, Lieutenant Hugonin understood this point almost from the moment he arrived. In his first report, detailing the expedition to Coffin Bay, Hugonin praised the work of Schurmann and the settlers who accompanied the party, observing that without their knowledge of the country and the local language, he did not know 'what I could possibly do':

> The nature of the country is such that foot soldiers with a heavy flintlock and belts have little chance of coming up with the natives. Their decoutrements also make the attempt to surprise at night almost a certain failure, and should I be unsuccessful in the now proposed push into the heart of their country I must regret to state that in my opinion that a military force, except employed as a guard at the outstations of the settlers, is at present totally useless in this settlement.[37]

The military may have been more effective had all the soldiers been mounted, as Grey had suggested when issuing Hugonin his orders. The reason they were not might simply be because there were not enough horses in the district: early in 1840 there were just twelve, and those were probably jealously guarded by the settlers themselves.[38] By the middle of June 1842 Governor Grey came to the conclusion that the military were not appropriate for the task of restoring order to the district. Lieutenant Hugonin was recalled, together with most of the company that had been despatched in April, though two officers and six men remained at Port Lincoln as sentries. Henceforth the protection of the settlement would be left in the hands of the Mounted Police.

'They merely laugh at our guns'

In July 1842 Charles Dutton, a prominent pastoralist who held the station most distant from Port Lincoln, became disheartened with the anxiety of Aboriginal attacks and decided to return to Adelaide. He was not the only settler to give up at Port Lincoln for this reason. In the same month, another prominent pastoralist, Mr White, applied for exemption from port taxes so that he could leave with his property.[39] While White left by the usual sea route, Dutton, keen to preserve his valuable stock, chose to travel the much longer and little travelled overland route around the head of Spencer's Gulf. He anticipated that the journey, undertaken with his four employees, would take about a month. In after years, prominent settler Nathaniel Hailes described how he accompanied Dutton's party on the first leg of their journey. As they passed Biddle's now-deserted station, they could not help but be aware of the industry now 'wantonly destroyed in its infancy'. It was a scene of desolation which, as it transpired, evoked 'gloomy forebodings' on Dutton's undertaking.[40]

When after three months Dutton's party still had not arrived, a series of search parties was organised.[41] A party led by brothers James and Charles Hawker set out on 14 September from the Hawkers' Bungaree station in the mid-north. On 9 October they arrived at Dutton's deserted station, having found no trace of Dutton's party, but having 'ascertained through some of the natives that he and his party were killed by a murderous tribe'.[42] On their way into the district they passed 'the deserted and destroyed stations of the murdered Brown and Biddle, and here a more melancholy sight could not be imagined':

The flowers in one of the gardens were in full bloom, displaying the beauties of peaceful nature, growing up around the shattered furniture, recklessly destroyed and cast about here and there.[43]

By this time, anxiety among the settlers in Port Lincoln was rising again with fresh reports of the 'hostile intentions of the natives'. Charles Driver wrote to the Governor with these reports, enclosing another Memorial from the settlers for the 96th Regiment to be augmented, and for provision of 'a few stands' of firearms for settlers' use. He enclosed a statement from Schurmann, who had been informed by his friend Yultalta that the Aborigines of the district had not been intimidated and that in the summer they would return to seek revenge.[44] Yultalta and Schurmann were named as specific targets for the help they were giving to the government. The Coffin Bay and Port Lincoln Aborigines, Driver wrote, 'had coalesced for the express object of murdering all the whites in the settlement – that they merely laugh at our guns and say their spears are much better expressing the utmost confidence that before many moons are passed they will not leave a white person alive in Port Lincoln'.

Grey responded to the settlers' pleas by despatching the Police Commissioner 'with instructions to secure if possible the natives who were concerned in the late murders'. Mindful now of the ineffectiveness of the military for this task, he cautioned that he could not 'comply literally with the prayer of the memorial ... although the government may unfortunately on some occasions find it indispensable to call on the military to aid the civic power in reprising the aggressions of the natives, it is nevertheless upon the latter force that reliance for internal security should literally be placed'.[45] Port Lincoln was by now a shattered community. When Police Commissioner Thomas O'Halloran arrived in the town a few weeks later he described the town as 'a deserted place': 'more than half the houses have been abandoned, and the remainder are barricaded to protect the occupants against the attacks of the natives'.[46]

In October 1842 Edward Underwood sent a letter to the *Register* from Port Lincoln describing the state of the district. 'Consternation', he wrote, 'was the order of the day. What with the loss of Dutton and party, and an expected invasion of the natives, the settlers seem truly to be pitied'. He reported the rumours that 'our declared enemies' were 'now coalescing' to 'make one grand attack on the white settlers of Port Lincoln'. 'Revenge', he wrote, was the object; and before 'three months, and perhaps much sooner, blood would be running again in Port Lincoln'. He concluded by observing that it 'is well known that by promiscuously destroying the natives when the soldiers were sent out against them,' friends had become declared foes.[47]

The capture of Ngarbi

In early November, before Major O'Halloran arrived with his men, Charles Driver organised a fresh expedition to go in search of those believed responsible for the recent murders. His party comprised six police constables, Charles Hawker, still in the district after his unsuccessful search for Dutton, Clamour Schurmann, and his Aboriginal guide Yultalta.[48] On the third day out they encountered a large Aboriginal camp which included, Yultalta said, several of the murderers. When they rode into the camp Yultalta indicated by surreptitious signs four of the guilty. Two fled but two others, Merltalla and Naltia, were captured.[49]

Merltalla and Naltia were tried in the Supreme Court in March 1843 and both were sentenced to hang, although Merltalla's sentence was later commuted to life imprisonment.[50] The Government Resident selected the location of the murders on James Rolles Biddle's station as the site of Naltia's execution. Schurmann was asked to assemble as many Aborigines as possible, 'especially those of Naltia's immediate tribe,' to witness the event. The sentence was carried out on 6 April 1843.[51]

Perhaps because of the large police presence, the district was quiet over the summer. However, on 10 May 1843 about 40 or 50 Aboriginal men appeared at McEllister's station. They called out to him that they were Biddle's murderers. Ngarbi, the young man implicated in the murders on Biddle's station, was said to be among them, and they claimed they would kill McEllister if he didn't leave. McEllister retreated into his house and fired, sure that he had shot at least one man, but the attackers retreated with the coincidental arrival of two soldiers. Ngarbi was captured the following morning.[52] So ended a year-long campaign to bring to justice those believed to have been the leading players in the killings of five settlers in the previous year. Ngarbi was the prize; he was allegedly involved in the initial attack on Brown's station, was reportedly among the party that attacked McEllister's station just a few months before, and most seriously from the settlers' point of view, he had killed a woman who had shown him kindness.

Ngarbi, alias Little Jemmy, was tried in the Supreme Court in July 1843 and found guilty of murdering Elizabeth Stubbs.[53] After his arrest Schurmann spoke with him and Ngarbi freely confessed his guilt, claiming that his people had obliged him to commit the murder.[54] Shortly after the sentence was handed down, Schurmann wrote to the Protector of Aborigines urging mercy on the grounds that Ngarbi was merely carrying out the directions of his elders:

> Whatever a majority of the older natives decide upon must be carried out if practical by the younger men. The whole of the tribe agreed to attack Mr Biddle's station. It was with them a tribal (national) decision and he could not have prevented the attack had he been so disposed.[55]

The appeal had no influence and, despite his desire to be executed at Port Lincoln, Ngarbi was hanged in Adelaide Gaol on 1 August 1843. His last words were: 'By and by I will be a white man'.[56]

By the close of 1843 the numerous police and military expeditions that had operated in the Port Lincoln district appear to have served their purpose and for the next few years there were relatively few reports of violence. An exception was the killing of Charles Darke, who had left Port Lincoln to explore the interior and been fatally speared in October of 1844.[57] But for the most part, according to the reports of Government Resident Charles Driver, Aboriginal 'crime' around the township of Port Lincoln was now of a kind to annoy rather than seriously intimidate the settlers. These cases Charles Driver dealt with through a style of discretionary justice sanctioned by Grey's early instructions of 1841.[58] In September 1845, for instance, an Aboriginal prisoner Yailgalta, who had been charged with robbery, was sentenced to eighteen lashes, and the sentence was carried out by two other Aboriginal men who had been enlisted to the task. Driver reported that since his punishment, Yailgalta had remained in the settlement and proved to be 'an active willing and useful character'. In February 1846, an Aboriginal boy of 'eight or nine years of age' was brought in to the township, having been shot in the back and shoulders with buckshot. He had been stealing wheat from the threshing floor at the station of the township's doctor, George Lawson, who pursued him with a fowling piece. Driver reported that he himself had picked the small shot from the boy's back and shoulders, and considered the case closed. On the same day that he had shot the young boy with buckshot, a drunk Dr Lawson had also assaulted a Native Constable in his own camp. Charles Driver fined him 20/. It is little wonder that he 'had some difficulty in making the natives comprehend the nature of a punishment so dissimilar to what would have been inflicted on them'.[59]

Although Governor Grey had considered such a discretionary system of justice appropriate when he first issued the Government Resident's instructions in 1841, his successor Governor Robe now discouraged it. He observed that the flogging of Aboriginal prisoners was 'entirely unwarranted by law', and that in shooting at the Aboriginal boy Lawson 'had taken the Law into his own hands'.[60] The letter of the law should be followed more closely in future. The Government Resident conceded, but noted that the system of effecting corporal punishments for Aboriginal transgressions was one that had been beneficial in deterring 'Europeans from taking the law into their own hands, which they have the greatest facilities for doing without the risk of detection'.[61]

Despite these doubts about how the needs of the law should be met, it seemed as though the years of crisis that had defined the district were now passed, and that a new era of prosperity was ahead. Reporting on a policing tour of the district in March 1846, Sub-Inspector of Police Alexander Tolmer noted that the settlement was 'advancing rapidly – Many thousand sheep have lately arrived and many more are still expected.' He made comment on 'how contented, and cheerful the inhabitants appeared to be compared to the alarmed state they were in' not long previously. 'The natives I am happy to state, are now very peaceable'; and the country to the north, he concluded, held only promise: 'it is well adapted for sheep ... the grass is abundant and in many gullies I found several springs of beautiful water'.[62] Yet this state of relative peace was only secure so long as the pastoral frontier expanded no further.

Of all the frontiers of South Australia, the violence that occurred on Eyre Peninsula in the early 1840s came closest to conforming to a stereotypical European notion of warfare. The Aboriginal attacks on the settlers were co-ordinated, widespread, carried out by large bodies of fighting men, and sustained for a long period of time. Nearly every station in the district was attacked and many of them abandoned for a period of time as the settlers took refuge in the town. Individuals prominent in reprisals against the Aborigines – James Rolles Biddle, Sgt McEllister, Charles Driver, the soldiers stationed at Pillaworta, and even Clamor Schurmann and his Aboriginal guides – were specifically targeted. During this period, the Battara had a numerical advantage as well as a geographical one over the Europeans; the Europeans were confined to the narrow coastal end of the peninsula, while the inland country of the Battara enabled them to mount attacks and then retreat into the hinterland. We also have greater insight into their motives than the European historical record usually allows, especially their oft-expressed desire to drive out the Europeans. That we know these things is not necessarily because the actions and motives of the Battara were so different to those of other Aboriginal groups facing European incursions into their country, but because of Clamor Schurmann's presence, a missionary sympathetic to their plight and familiar with their language who recorded what he was hearing.

Almost 50 years later, when the South Australian frontier was extending into central Australia, colonist John Bull wrote extensively of the violence in the Port Lincoln district during the 1840s. He saw a lesson in it. Experience in 'every part of Australia, he wrote, proved that the safety of Europeans was secured where 'in the first instance of occupation large and concentrated bodies of whites had settled down'. Alternatively, where the Aborigines succeeded in killing 'a few individuals venturing to occupy lonely places' the 'safety of succeeding parties has not been secured until a dread has been created in the minds of the offending tribe by speedy and severe punishment inflicted on the offenders'. 'It cannot be denied', he concluded, 'that there has been no safety for the lives and properties of the whites until such a dread has been established.'[63] The establishment of just such a 'culture of terror' against Aboriginal people,[64] as anthropologist Barry Morris has described it, eventually became part of the lore of the Australian frontier, but for a short time at Port Lincoln it was the Europeans who felt some of its effects.

Chapter 4

THE TRIALS OF THE CRIMINAL JUSTICE SYSTEM

As the first few years of British settlement in South Australia had demonstrated, use of punitive force was a method called upon by colonial governments to suppress Aboriginal resistance to incursions upon their lands wherever the pastoral frontier had stretched. Yet the principle that Australia was 'settled' rather than 'conquered', and that Aboriginal people were British subjects rather than nations 'at enmity with ourselves', was impossible to forget. This, after all, had been promoted in the recommendations of the 1837 Select Committee, and was the cornerstone of the colony's founding proclamation. The idea that a steadfast adherence to the rule of law would provide Aboriginal people with protection continued to be voiced by South Australia's governors, even as punitive police or military expeditions were being despatched. Ultimately, the principle that Aboriginal people were British subjects was easily declared but not so easily established, and the realities of cultural difference made extending the rights and privileges of that status much more problematic. In the coming years, as new pastoral frontiers emerged across the colony, it became repeatedly clear that although a rule of law could readily be declared which placed Aboriginal people 'as much under the safeguard of the law as the Colonists themselves', making this count in reality was altogether a different matter.

Throughout the 1840s, and indeed for several decades to come, the colonial authorities in South Australia struggled, just as they had in earlier Australian colonies, with a series of difficult questions about the amenability of Aboriginal people to British law. Where was the justice in making Aboriginal people amenable to laws of which they had no knowledge? How could Aboriginal people – judged to be 'heathens' – give evidence in Courts that required witnesses to swear an oath before God? How would the issue of language interpretation be dealt with, especially when Aboriginal interpreters themselves were judged to be incapable of taking an oath? Would the judicial system be able to overcome settler solidarity when 'their own' were before the courts? Finally, how could the courts deal with *inter se* cases, cases involving crimes committed among Aboriginal people themselves? Did the courts have the jurisdiction to deal with such cases, especially when they entailed the application of Aboriginal custom and law?

Amenability to British law

Not long before taking up his post as South Australia's second Governor, George Grey wrote a set of suggestions on the 'moral and social' improvement of the Aborigines of Australia.[1] It so impressed the Colonial Office that copies were despatched to all the Australian governors. Central to Grey's argument was the proposition that Aboriginal people must be brought under the aegis of British law. This, he clearly stated, entailed the injustice of imposing upon Aboriginal people punishment for offences of which they had no knowledge; but this in his view was a necessary injustice. While the Aborigines were as 'apt and intelligent' as any other race he knew, Grey argued, 'the peculiar code of laws of this people' were such that would never see them 'emerge from a savage state'. From the moment Aborigines were declared British subjects, Grey wrote, they should be taught that 'British laws are to supersede their own'. There could be no room for legal pluralism – the continuation of traditional law beneath the umbrella of British law – because Aborigines could not be expected to become civilised while held 'in thrall' by their 'savage and barbarous laws'. The necessary benefit of imposing British law upon them would be that it would

> give them a knowledge of the leading points of our criminal code, acquaint them with our judicial forms, awaken their moral faculties, and form another link in that chain by which they may eventually be led on to Christianity and civilization.[2]

Others within the judiciary were less idealistic about assuming that Aboriginal people could be so readily regarded in law as British subjects. In particular the colony's Chief Judge, Charles Cooper, struggled with deep reservations. Judge Cooper's judicial career in the colony had begun with a baptism of fire when he was asked to provide Governor Gawler with advice on how to respond to the murder of the twenty-six survivors of the *Maria* shipwreck on the Coorong in 1840. Cooper's advice – that the court had no jurisdiction over Aboriginal tribes which had had no contact with Europeans – justified Gawler's decision to invoke martial law against the Milmenrura. Cooper expanded on his legal opinion in an address to the grand jury at the last Criminal Sessions of 1840. His advice on the *Maria* case was founded on the opinion that such only of the native population as have in some degree acquiesced in our dominion can be considered subject to our laws, and that, with regard to all others, we must be considered as much strangers as Governor Hindmarsh and the first settlers were to the whole native population, when they raised the British standard on their landing at Glenelg.[3]

As early as 1839 Cooper had found two Aboriginal men guilty of the murder of Europeans and sentenced them to hang, but the distinction in those cases was that by their association with the settlers they had brought themselves under the jurisdiction of British law. With this argument he established a principle that was to guide the treatment of Aboriginal people before the courts for the next decade. In the 1842 trial of Kertameru for stealing and killing a calf, Defence Counsel Charles Mann maintained that 'the uncultivated state of his client' made it 'difficult to determine upon felonious assault', but the judge insisted that Kertameru's prior association with Europeans was evidence that he had some understanding of European ways and was therefore liable to British justice.[4]

The distinction in law between those Aborigines who had no previous contact with Europeans and those who did determined the outcome of the trial in 1845 of Wira Maldira and Wekweki for the murder of a shepherd, McGrath, on the Coorong. According to the evidence of Protector Moorhouse, Wira Maldira, otherwise known as Peter,

> was the chief instigator in the affair: he had lived for nearly two years with Europeans, and knew our habits and some of our laws, and, in consequence, was more culpable than Wekweki and others who were with him, as no stations had ever been formed in his territory at the time.[5]

Both men were found guilty of the charge and sentenced to death, but the Governor commuted the sentence in the case of Wekweki, presumably on the grounds that his 'uncivilised' nature made him less culpable.[6]

The problem of trying Aboriginal people deemed to be entirely ignorant of British law, and often for whom no one was capable of interpreting in court, continued to trouble Cooper. One of his strategies was to adopt a variation of the maxim 'justice delayed is justice denied'; for Cooper, 'justice delayed' was sometimes 'injustice avoided'. In May 1846 three Aboriginal men came before the Supreme Court charged with murdering a shepherd at Mount Arden in the mid-north. At their arraignment it was revealed that 'they belonged to a tribe who had previously had no intercourse with

Europeans, who were presumed to be altogether ignorant of our Law and Customs, and whose language was in no degree known by Europeans'.[7] The judge remanded them for three months in the hope that their language could be learned, or that they might be sufficiently instructed to stand trial. Even then, he held strong doubts 'of their being fit subjects for the jurisdiction of the Court', and questioned 'whether they should be put on their trial at all for an offence arising out of their collision with the first Europeans ever entering their territory'.[8] Cooper expanded on these difficulties in a letter to the Governor in March 1847. He discussed the difficulties of trying offences involving Aborigines who had no contact with Europeans 'until the moment of the commission of their alleged offence'.[9] Under such circumstances, Cooper considered it improper to try people according to British law because they could not be 'deemed cognizant of our assumed dominion over their country or themselves'.[10]

Cooper's doubts went to the heart of one of the implicit ideals of the rule of law: that citizens subject to it have an investment in it. As legal scholar Martin Krygier has put it, for the rule of law to function meaningfully it has to be 'knowable and generally known'; citizens need to 'appreciate its authority' and its 'relevance to their encounters,' and be 'prepared to invoke it'.[11] In Cooper's view, Aboriginal people would only become truly amenable to British law through education of it, ideally through the agency and advocacy of the Protector of Aborigines.[12] The Protector Matthew Moorhouse did in fact endeavour to do this over the coming years. On occasions when he was required to visit remote districts to investigate disturbances or crimes, he would organise a distribution of rations and speak through an interpreter to the Aboriginal people who assembled about the nature of British law, which, he told them, was committed to protecting their lives as well as the lives and property of Europeans. The task of educating Aboriginal people in the law was also expected of the Sub-Protectors who were appointed to remote posts over the 1840s and 1850s.[13] It is another question entirely as to how meaningful such law lectures on the frontier might have been.

The problem of Aboriginal evidence

Alongside the problem of Aboriginal defendants understanding, let alone accepting, the terms of British law was the problem of the inadmissibility of Aboriginal evidence. In 1843, writing from Moorundie on the River Murray where he had been appointed Sub-Protector of Aborigines and Resident Magistrate, Edward Eyre outlined the 'legal disabilities' Aboriginal people were exposed to as British subjects:

> In declaring the natives British subjects, and making them amenable to British Laws, they have been placed in the anomalous position of being made amenable to laws of which they are quite ignorant, and which at the same time do not afford them the slightest redress from any injuries they may sustain at the hands of Europeans.[14]

The root of the dilemma in Eyre's view was the fact that Aboriginal people could not give evidence in a court of law. The consequence, he argued, was that Aboriginal people were regularly punished for offences from which Europeans always escaped. Despite his reservations, Eyre argued not against the essential principle that Aboriginal people should be 'made' British subjects, but rather that the law should be amended to allow Aboriginal evidence to be more readily accepted. This was an issue that both the imperial parliament and colonial legislatures were endeavouring to address. At a meeting of the Executive Council on 30 September 1840, in the midst of the *Maria* controversy, Governor Gawler tabled a bill to allow Aboriginal testimony to be received in a court of law. Yet perhaps caught in the cross-fire between conscience and duty, Gawler damned his bill with faint praise. In his closing remarks, he observed:

> being in its object of admitting the evidence of persons unconscious of the obligation of an oath or solemn declaration, a very great departure from constitutional principles, I apprehend it may be necessary to suspend its operation until it shall have received the royal sanction.[15]

The inadmissibility of Aboriginal evidence in courts of law had long been recognised across Australia's colonies as a profound problem in treating Aboriginal peoples equitably before the law. As the Aborigines Protection Society in Britain had complained in 1839, the inadmissibility of their evidence rendered Aboriginal people not only disadvantaged by the law, but 'virtually outlaws in their Native Land'.[16] Despite this recognition, proposed acts for the admission of Aboriginal evidence were rejected in New South Wales (which included the later territories of Victoria and Queensland within its jurisdiction) in 1839, 1844 and 1849.[17] In Queensland, Aboriginal people were unable to take the oath and therefore give a statement in court before 1876.[18] In this regard South and Western Australia appeared more liberal: in both colonies, acts were passed in the early 1840s to allow Aboriginal evidence to be accepted without the sanction of an oath.

South Australia's Aborigines Evidence Act was passed in 1844, although it would take another two years for it to receive formal assent from London.[19]

Further questions relating to Aboriginal evidence arose around the court's ability to accept unsworn Aboriginal interpreters,[20] leading to the Aborigines Witnesses Act of 1848 which allowed an 'uncivilised' person to act as an interpreter without having to take the oath.[21] However, although the courts could now receive Aboriginal evidence, the effectiveness of the Act was limited by two provisos: that the court retained discretion to determine what 'degree of weight and credibility' could be attached to Aboriginal evidence, and that no conviction could be made on 'the sole testimony of any such uncivilized persons', but would require the corroboration of European evidence.[22]

Despite these efforts to accommodate Aboriginal witnesses and interpreters within the judicial system, a more difficult problem to overcome – one arising from the very nature of the frontier – was that few people could be found to act as competent interpreters for the court. Given that the most troubled phase of first contact in many districts passed within a short matter of years, there was little opportunity to develop a capacity for available translators of Aboriginal testimony. In the very phase where the humanitarian ideal that British justice could protect Aboriginal people mattered most, the judicial system was at its most impotent.

Judges of the colonial court were painfully aware of this dilemma. During the 1840s Judge Cooper, consistently faced with an absence of competent interpreters, would hold prisoners on remand for months on end until interpreters could be found or trained. A corollary of this was that Aboriginal witnesses were held in custody for inordinate periods of time. In the end, it was often easier for the judge to abandon the case. On other occasions when attempts were made to hold trials using poorly prepared interpreters, the proceedings were reduced to farce. In 1846, for instance, when Kudnutya came before the Supreme Court on a charge of murder, 'Charley', a member of a neighbouring tribe, translated his testimony while the Protector of Aborigines Matthew Moorhouse translated Charley's testimony into English; as a consequence it was often 'ten minutes before a single answer could be obtained'. Even when an Aboriginal person who knew the requisite language was entrusted with the task of interpretation, the Aborigines Evidence Act, which regarded Aboriginal evidence as insufficient unless corroborated by European evidence, meant that the veracity of the interpretation might be considered questionable.[23] In 1847, when an Aboriginal man interpreted in court, the Advocate General advised that 'there being no means of testing the accuracy of his communications it would be unsafe to admit his interpretations'.[24]

When two Europeans, Henry Jones and Thomas Morris, were tried for the murder of an Aboriginal man, Melaityappa, in September 1849 it may have seemed that the fate of the Europeans accused was cast. Melaityappa had been shot three times, and before he died of his wounds, he had given a full statement to the Protector of Aborigines identifying the accused. His companion, Perria, was a material witness, and corroborated his account. Most directly, the bullet Moorhouse had removed from Melaityappa's chest before he died matched Jones' gun. The presiding judge Charles Mann told the jury that the 'circumstances so strongly corroborate the testimony of the native witnesses that your duty, is, it seems to me, clear'.[25] Before the trial, he had interviewed Perria and his Aboriginal interpreter, and found their responses clear and persuasive. Yet as the case progressed, he viewed the evidence of Perria with growing dismay. Bewildered by the proceedings, Perria had pointed to the wrong man when asked to identify the accused. The interpreter's responses were not clear to the court. As historian Skye Krichauff has shown, an attempt to save the case by putting Melaityappa's dying testimony into evidence was rejected by the judge on the basis of a strangely clumsy concession to cultural difference:

> Judge Mann would not admit it as Moorhouse had earlier said 'the natives do not admit they are in danger of death'. According to Mann 'it is only the consciousness of approaching dissolution and a belief in future rewards and punishments, that give solemnity and force to a dying declaration'.[26]

Reluctantly, Judge Mann directed that the only safe course was for the jury to acquit the prisoners, which they did 'without hesitation'. After the trial, Judge Mann took the unusual step of writing to the Governor with his concerns about the language problems that had scuttled the trial. He 'could not help feeling that [the] effect was prejudicial; that it tended to lower the opinion of the judge in the estimation of the Public and to induce a conviction that neither a native Interpreter or Witness could be depended on'. He offered the opinion that the present system was not 'requisite for the ends of justice', and nor would it be until Aboriginal languages could be sufficiently acquired by trained interpreters.[27]

On the other hand, if Aboriginal testimony was necessary to secure the conviction of Aboriginal people for offences against Europeans, the perceived reliability of their evidence magically improved. Protector Moorhouse drew attention to this double-standard in a letter to the Chief Secretary shortly after Jones and Morris' trial. At around the same time as Jones and Morris went on trial for the murder of Melaityappa, two cases against Aboriginal men for the murder of Europeans on Eyre Peninsula came before the courts:

one against Malgalta and Mingulta for the murder of shepherd John Hamp, the other against Ninalta and Kulgalta for the murder of pastoralist James Beevor. In both cases, the Aboriginal men were found guilty on the basis of Aboriginal evidence. The Protector of Aborigines was concerned that if the defendants had been Europeans, 'the juries would not from the evidence produced have brought them in guilty'. In the first place, he argued, 'the chief evidence against them was given by natives, a kind of evidence that a few days before had been rejected as dangerous and unsatisfactory when given against Europeans'. In the second place, the efforts of the police corporal during one of the trials to address the witnesses in their own language and to translate their answers were 'unintelligible' and altogether unsatisfactory. Moorhouse complained of the 'prejudicial feeling existing in the minds of the juries', and concluded that if 'mercy and forbearance be not entertained' for these Aboriginal defendants, 'I must say that I shall have much difficulty in believing the declaration that the Natives enjoy the protection of British Law'.[28] Moorhouse's entreaties were ignored and all four men were hanged at the site of their alleged murders.

Europeans on trial

If it was difficult for courts to accommodate Aboriginal people either as competent witnesses or defendants, how did Europeans experience the justice system when charged with the injury or death of Aboriginal people? In clarifying that Aboriginal people were to be regarded as British subjects and would enjoy the protection of the law, Governor Hindmarsh's Proclamation of 1836 had emphatically stated that 'all acts of violence or injustice' attempted against them would be punished 'with exemplary severity'. Chief Judge Sir John Jeffcott made the same assertion at the first sitting of the Supreme Court. Alan Pope has shown that in the period of most intense frontier conflict in South Australia, from foundation to the early 1860s, 66 Aboriginal people were tried for the murder of settlers, and 22 executed.[29] Over the same period, only 7 Europeans in 5 separate cases were tried for the murder or manslaughter of Aboriginal people, and of these most were acquitted. Perhaps surprisingly, despite the foundational principle that Aboriginal people would receive the full protection of the law, the numerical discrepancy between Aboriginals and Europeans executed for murder in South Australia's first decades was considerably greater than was the case in other colonies over that period.[30] Although this discrepancy of numbers may not be surprising in hindsight, what does it tell us about the obstacles faced by the legal system in providing equal protection to Aboriginal people, if not 'exemplary' shows of justice? In fact, the small number of Europeans tried for the murder of Aboriginal people does not reflect the larger number of cases that were investigated. All suspicious deaths required an investigation; this was a form of legal surveillance, it was hoped, that would ensure the protection of Aboriginal people as British subjects. Yet as Barry Patton notes, the impact of such legal requirements could only be tested against 'the success of prosecution and sentencing as a deterrent to future frontier violence'.[31] The failure of the law to bring Europeans to trial for Aboriginal murder, let alone to secure convictions against them, must be seen in the context of a wider set of difficulties that obstructed the implementation of the rule of law at each stage, from the discovery of the offence and the collection of evidence through to judgment in the Supreme Court.

In theory, there was a clear line of legal process in the investigation of offences, even those that occurred a long way from the settled districts. Local Magistrates and Justices of the Peace were appointed from amongst 'respectable' settlers to be the law's representatives in remote locations where a permanent police presence and local courts did not yet exist.[32] Where a magistrate was not available, the agreement of two or more Justices of the Peace carried the same authority.[33] These functionaries constituted the first point of inquiry into suspected offences, and filtered the cases that would come before the court. They gathered evidence for further police investigations by taking witness depositions, they issued warrants for the apprehension of suspects, and they could requisition police constables to 'act under the Magistrate's immediate orders'.[34] In the event of a suspicious death, they would conduct a coronial inquest, to be attended by a medical practitioner (if need be), a constable and a specially summonsed jury also comprised of settlers deemed worthy of that responsibility.[35] If appropriate, the accrued evidence would lead to a committal and thence, if necessary, to court. But although this line of legal process was quite clear, it almost never led to the prosecution of cases involving settler offences against Aboriginal people.

What were the forces that would explain this gap between the principle of legal process and its practice? In cases of frontier collisions entailing Aboriginal deaths, the ideal of the rule of law most frequently broke down at the very first stage of evidence-gathering. 'Insufficiency of evidence' was a repeated phrase in official reports that encapsulated a whole raft of difficulties in securing criminal charges against Europeans. Underlying these, not surprisingly, was the tyranny of distance: the remoteness of places where 'affrays' took place, the time lag in investigating reported deaths, and the insufficiency of police resources. Most importantly, perhaps, obstacles to legal investigation were posed by the culture of the frontier itself. A secret culture of violence on remote frontiers of settlement was frequently suspected – even assumed – by authorities, but often proved almost impossible to investigate. In 1846, regretting the insufficiency of police resources to actually prevent frontier collisions, the Police Commissioner noted with resignation that Aboriginal people would 'pay by the loss of life' wherever 'the settlers are left to be their own judges and redressors'.[36]

The distance between new pastoral districts and the seat of government supported a frontier culture that seemed almost to ensure an 'insufficiency of evidence' for cases to proceed against Europeans suspected of crimes against Aboriginal people. Investigations were abandoned because evidence-gathering was obstructed by settlers unwilling to impeach members of their own community, or because suspects disappeared before an investigation could be completed. In 1846, for instance, when David Morgan was investigated for the murder of Pannenum, the Advocate General considered the evidence 'pregnant with suspicion', but the absence of willing witnesses rendered it inadequate to 'fix the charge on the accused'.[37] On the Eyre Peninsula in 1849 and again in 1851, separate investigations against shepherds Patrick Dwyer and Hugh Fuller, in which several Aboriginal people died after eating arsenic-laced flour, were dropped because the suspects left the colony on the first available vessels.[38] Local Justice of the Peace Henry Price noted the 'dangerous' feeling of settlers in that district who, 'scattered thinly over a wide extent of country, [had] ready means at command for working their will, almost without a chance of detection'.[39]

If the problems of distance and the solidarity of settlers created one set of obstacles in bringing charges against Europeans even to the committal stage, the potential unreliability of the officials entrusted to facilitate investigations created another. While we now conceive of the legal system as a monolith of formal rules and procedures presided over by well-trained functionaries, this was not so in the nineteenth century. The few Magistrates and Justices of the Peace tasked with prosecuting investigations in remote areas usually had no legal training and often acted in an honorary capacity. They were also usually landholders, potentially subject to the same culture of solidarity that influenced other settlers. These functionaries were more than once reproached by the Advocate General for failing to properly investigate suspected offences against Aboriginal people. In 1843, a shepherd named Shelton admitted shooting dead an Aboriginal man he had caught in the act of stealing a sheep from the fold during the night. Local JP George Hawker, who owned the neighbouring station, duly took the shepherd's deposition, but considered no criminal charge against him was warranted, since it was a shepherd's 'duty to defend the sheep'.[40]

The Advocate General was not satisfied with Hawker's efforts. On the basis of the evidence, 'the Homicide is clearly proved', and in 'such cases no magistrate is entitled to discharge on his own impressions of the guilt or innocence of the party, whereby the gravest crimes might escape judicial inquiry'. He required that an investigation proceed, adding that 'Magistrates ought to take the examinations of, and bind by recognizance, all persons who know the facts and circumstances which are to be forwarded to the proper officer'.[41] In the event, Shelton was committed for trial, but when the principal witness disappeared in the bush, the case stalled and Shelton was 'set at large'.[42] This shooting occurred on the station of pastoralist J.B. Hughes, who considered himself the primary victim of this incident: he complained to the authorities about the inadequacy of police protection against Aboriginal attacks on his stock, in the absence of which 'in simple self defence we shall be compelled to shoot more of them'.[43] Within the next decade Hughes would himself be appointed as a magistrate.[44]

While colonial authorities did sometimes make sincere efforts to bring violent acts against Aboriginal people out of obscurity into the light, it did not follow that they were willing or even able to prosecute those acts with 'exemplary severity', because the limits imposed on settlers of 'self defence' and 'justifiable homicide' were never clearly defined.[45] Writing to Governor Grey in 1842, Secretary of State Lord Stanley himself noted that although it was necessary to 'visit with severity' those settlers who 'overstep the legitimate bounds of self-defence', it was actually 'very difficult to define what are those legitimate bounds'.[46] At stake, in Stanley's mind, was the problem that if settlers were routinely prosecuted for injury to Aboriginal people in the course of protecting their stock, they would lose faith in the law. At the other end of the scale, if Aboriginal people who committed the crime of stealing settlers' property were not seen to be adequately punished by the law, it would 'lead the settlers to take the law into their own hands'.[47] Stanley's words exactly articulated an implicit inversion of the principle of Aboriginal protection through legal process: on the one hand, the inherent ambiguity of the line between legitimate acts of self defence and illegitimate acts of retaliation gave protection to settlers who caused Aboriginal death in the recovery of stolen stock; on the other hand, Aboriginal protection from illegitimate acts of retaliation was seen to be best served by the vigorous prosecution of *their* 'crime' in the eyes of settlers.

Self defence appeared so often as a justification for acts of violence against

Aboriginal people that it became a cliché which could stretch to just about any event. In 1843, after hutkeeper Gregory shot dead an Aboriginal woman who had 'struck' him while resisting his attempt to bring her in to the station for questioning about scattered sheep, he was tried for manslaughter and acquitted on grounds of self defence.[48] The justification of self defence could be extended to defence of property. When shepherd Joseph Rilka shot dead 'one or two natives' in an affray while recovering stolen sheep in 1847, no criminal charge was considered warranted.[49] During the previous month, a police constable had visited the area after hearing that 'the natives proposed to attack the sheep,' and had 'cautioned them of the criminality' of such an attempt. Notwithstanding the constable's warning, they had subsequently driven off about 400 sheep, leading to the affray. The Commissioner had himself examined the case because 'there was no magistrate in the District', and found that 'no criminal charge could be sustained against any individual concerned in the death of these natives' because 'they had been previously warned of the consequences ... The owners had a right to recover their property, by force if necessary, and they had a right to resist the offenders in the act of committing a felony'. Under these circumstances, he concluded, 'I presume the verdict of a Jury would be justifiable Homicide'.[50] The Advocate General concurred.[51] Similarly in 1852 when two station workers killed 'several' Aborigines in a clash while recovering stolen stock, it was concluded, despite the Protector's sense that there were 'flaws' in the men's testimony, that no crime had been committed because the men had fired on those refusing to give up stolen property.[52]

Self defence and justifiable homicide were reasonings that not only protected settlers' investment in their stock, but also protected police when supporting settlers to retrieve property. In August 1847, Corporal Robins reported shooting dead an Aboriginal man in the 'last extremity' while helping Mr Baker to recover stolen sheep on his station in the south east.[53] Interestingly, the Commissioner of Police found 'the conduct of Corpl Robins to be perfectly justifiable, he having legal authority'; and although any Aboriginal death must be 'deplored', 'it becomes a question whether under the peculiar circumstances ... the aggregate amount of injury done to the natives is not less when inflicted under some form of Law, than when left to the settlers themselves, who are known from experience to lose no opportunity ... to take the law into their own hands, knowing the difficulty which exists in producing evidence against them in cases of this kind'.[54] The Police Commissioner's comments are revealing of just how compromised the workings of the law could be, when the principle of Aboriginal protection could be reduced to an 'amount of injury... inflicted under some form of Law,' in comparison to a form of settler revenge in which evidence would always be elusive. With its implied hope that 'injury to the natives' inflicted by police would help to deter settlers from taking the 'law into their own hands', the Commissioner's observation was also a candid acknowledgement that settlers routinely lost 'no opportunity' to do so, and usually got away with it.

Although the law required a coronial inquiry into all cases of violent or unexplained death, very few formal inquests were held into Aboriginal deaths in frontier districts. In part, as Mark Finnane and Jonathan Richards' work on inquests in colonial Queensland illustrates, this could be because their legal requirement was 'mediated by the realities of distance, denial, cover-up and subversion of justice'.[55] There were also a number of practical obstacles that prevented inquests being held. Sometimes the required number of settlers needed to constitute a coronial jury could not be gathered,[56] or the expense of conveying a jury across 'great distance' was considered too high.[57] The lapse of time between a reported death and the investigation of it might render an inquest 'inexpedient'.[58] More typically, even if fatalities were reported there might no body on which to hold an inquest. After frontier 'skirmishes' the protagonists would retreat into their respective territories, making it impossible to recover the bodies of the deceased, or for that matter to trace Aboriginal witnesses. After a party of police and station hands were involved in a clash with Aboriginal people in 1847 attempting to recover stolen sheep, for instance, two and possibly four Aboriginal men were killed, but returning to the scene the next morning, the corporal reported, they found that the bodies of the deceased had been taken by their compatriots.[59] Depositions were taken from the Europeans involved, but there the matter was left to rest.[60]

There were however two cases, both in the Flinders Ranges in the early 1860s, where formal inquests were held into cases where Europeans shot and killed Aboriginal people in what might be described as frontier clashes. In November 1863, an armed party of men on Mr McKay's station tracked a flock of stolen sheep to an Aboriginal camp; when the Aboriginal men resisted their efforts to recover the property, McKay deposed, his men opened fire, killing three people. Within days of the clash a police corporal and doctor visited the scene and examined the bodies of the deceased. A month later, local Stipendiary Magistrate G.B. Smith conducted an inquest at nearby Mount Remarkable before a coronial jury. The jury found that the European party was 'justified in firing and shooting at the natives in their own self-defence'.[61] The investigation into this incident fulfilled all of the expected requirements of the law. As this so rarely occurred, it begs the question: why in this case and not others? By 1863, pastoral settlement in the southern Flinders Ranges was reasonably well-established. The Aboriginal group which clashed with McKay's men appear to have been an ochre collecting party from the north, travelling south to Parachilna.[62] Whereas most frontier clashes of this sort occurred when Europeans first intruded into Aboriginal lands, in this instance Aboriginal people from further north were travelling through country where European properties had been operating for over a decade, and the infrastructure of government had at least a nominal presence.

Less than a month after this incident on McKay's station, an Aboriginal man, Pompey, was shot and killed by a prominent settler, Samuel Stuckey, on his run in the northern Flinders Ranges. As in the McKay case, the local Stipendiary Magistrate G.B. Smith presided over a formal coronial inquiry. According to the evidence, Pompey, described as a 'troublesome and dangerous character', had led an Aboriginal party that robbed an outstation, threatened a white woman and killed one of Stuckey's Aboriginal station workers. Stuckey claimed that he endeavoured to take Pompey into custody. When he attempted to flee, Stuckey fired with the intention of disabling him, but killed him instead. The coronial jury, reported in the press as being comprised entirely of Stuckey's 'personal friends and servants', returned a verdict of justifiable homicide.[63] Perhaps dissatisfied with the constitution of the local coronial jury, the government ordered a second inquest to be held at the Police Court in Adelaide in May 1864. In the event, the evidence at the second hearing was little different, although more was made of Pompey's established notoriety. The three Justices who heard the case confirmed the original finding of justifiable homicide. In summing up, the presiding Magistrate added that since 'Mr Stuckey was looked up to as a chief settler, whom both the whites and the blacks regarded as a protector, he was quite right, both in that capacity and as a good subject of Her Majesty, to take the extreme step which he did for preventing the escape of the native prisoner'.[64]

Publicly commenting on the case days after the coronial inquest, the editor of the *Register* stated that although he would be sorry if 'lynch law' were adopted by settlers, he considered the jury to have made the right decision in acquitting Stuckey. There were districts, he wrote, in which 'no police troopers are to be found', and where the choice lay 'between the summary chastisement of native offenders, and their escape from justice altogether'.[65] While in the case on McKay's station the coronial jury found for self defence, in Stuckey's case the coronial juries found for justifiable homicide on grounds that a known felon was eluding arrest. This was a defence more often employed by the police, whose instructions allowed for use of deadly force in cases where suspects were escaping arrest. Given that Stuckey was an armed settler without the legal latitude of police, the Justices in this case gave even more scope to the reasoning of justifiable homicide than had been allowed in those cases where Aboriginal people had been killed in settlers' defence of private property. More than that, as a 'chief settler' and a 'protector' to his servants, Stuckey had been a 'good subject of Her Majesty'.

In the end, if holding a properly convened coronial inquiry constituted an 'exemplary' show of justice, clearly it did not alter the usual outcome which deemed Aboriginal fatalities at settler hands to be justifiable homicide. As Finnane and Richards suggest in their study of colonial Queensland, where the number of inquests held into Aboriginal deaths was categorically higher than in colonial South Australia, the holding of inquests in itself did little to produce legal accountability on the frontiers of settlement, where securing the interests of settlers was the first task of the rule of law.[66]

If a raft of circumstances prevented investigations against Europeans from ever reaching the Supreme Court, another set of obstacles obstructed the successful prosecution of those cases that did. Principally, again, these were the enduring difficulties surrounding Aboriginal evidence and interpretation. In 1849, the same year in which Henry Jones and Thomas Morris were acquitted for the murder of Melaityappa, two other cases against Europeans were foiled by the same reasons. In early July 1849 sheep were driven off Anstey's station and the owner's overseer, George Penton, led a party of station workers who tracked the stolen sheep to a coastal encampment near Hardwick Bay.[67] When the posse of half a dozen Europeans approached the Aboriginal camp, and allegedly fired over their heads, the group fled into the water. But one man, Nantariltarra, returned to fetch a young child who had been left behind. According to witness testimony, one of the European party, George Field, shot Nantariltarra as he held the child, killing him instantly and causing the child to fall from his arms into the water where she drowned. Sergeant McCullock interviewed two Aboriginal men who had been with the European party when the shooting occurred. Their evidence made it clear that Field had shot an unarmed and fleeing man, and left the child to drown. George Field was arrested and committed for trial. Yet the defence counsel argued that the unsworn testimony of the Aboriginal witnesses was insufficient to sustain the case unless corroborated by other evidence. In the absence of that corroborating evidence there was little likelihood that a conviction would be secured, and the case was dropped.[68]

On 1 March 1849 James Brown was committed to trial for 'the murder of unknown aboriginal natives'. He was alleged to have shot dead a family group of nine Aboriginal people on his station in the south east. In a letter to a friend in Adelaide, the magistrate who committed him observed that there was 'no question of the butchery or of the butcher'.[69] The Protector went to the district and was taken by an Aboriginal witness to the site where the bodies had first been buried and, at a later point, exhumed and burnt in an effort to destroy any evidence. Yet when the case was brought before the Supreme Court in June 1849, the judge was not convinced that the evidence satisfied the criteria spelled out in the Aboriginal Witnesses Act of 1848. It was the Court's responsibility, he noted, to judge the 'weight and credibility' of unsworn Aboriginal testimony, which in serious cases was deemed insufficient unless corroborated by European evidence. The 'vague and general statements' of the Aboriginal witness in Brown's case, he commented, 'do not appear to have that degree of confirmation upon which a charge so serious can be supported'.[70] He gave the prosecution more time to prepare the case, and released Brown on bail of £500.

The Advocate General made every effort to procure more evidence, but with little success. A European witness who had allegedly seen the crime committed 'denied all knowledge of the matter'. Brown's accomplice, his hutkeeper Eastwood, had left the colony aboard a whaling vessel, while another material witness had left for the Port Phillip district. The principal Aboriginal witness had disappeared and was 'supposed to have been made away with'. The Advocate General noted that all other potential witnesses 'seemed determined to give no evidence' that would impeach Brown.[71] By November, the case had disappeared from the court calendar, and Brown settled into the life of a wealthy pastoralist. Possibly in response to the case, the Act was amended again to allow a person to be convicted on the sole testimony of an Aboriginal person.[72]

The only incident that resulted in the sentencing and execution of a European for the murder of an Aboriginal man occurred in the lower south east in 1846. On 1 September Thomas Donnelly came onto the Mayurra station, inland from Rivoli Bay, and quarrelled with two of the European station workers before storming off. A short time later the workers heard someone calling out 'White man coming, white man coming' and then a gunshot. The men, having armed themselves, went to investigate and found an Aboriginal station worker, Kingberrie, on the ground with a gunshot to his abdomen. The gunshot having raised the alarm, Donnelly panicked and fled. Kingberrie died the following morning. Corporal McCullock pursued

Donnelly as he made his way toward the border, eventually capturing him on 12 December 1846.[73] Donnelly was tried for murder, found guilty, and hanged on 29 March 1847.[74] The press was full of self-congratulation at this apparent evidence of the impartial administration of justice in which 'no difference shall be made on account of the colour or nation of the individual'.[75] Yet, in truth, Kingberrie was an innocent by-stander; Donnelly's intended victim was one of the European station workers. Under these circumstances, the station workers had no incentive to protect him. Although one of the witnesses at the trial revealed that 'certain parties told me I was not to speak the truth', the station workers did give evidence against him, breaking the spirit of solidarity that usually offered settlers a protective shield. As the exception that proved the rule, Donnelly's case provides the only example in colonial South Australia where the legal process worked to punish violence against Aboriginal people 'with exemplary severity'.

Despite the fact that so few Europeans were ever tried for crimes against Aboriginal people, the ineffectiveness of the legal system for dealing with frontier conditions, coupled with the legal fiction that Aboriginal people were protected as British subjects, seemed to create a sense amongst settlers that they suffered most from the law's inadequacies, and that persistent Aboriginal aggressions went unpunished. An indication of the settler community's sentiment in this respect was a vituperative letter published in the *Register* in 1849. The correspondent sneered at the sentimental schemes hatched to protect the 'poor benighted savages' while settlers were being 'plundered, assaulted and mutilated with impunity'. Rejecting 'the anomalous nature of all our colonial legislation', he suggested a well-tried solution:

> the best and only means of teaching refractory aborigines the sacred nature of the protection afforded to life and property by British jurisprudence, is to give them a severe lesson when their depredations sanction and demand extreme measures. I could give numberless instances where a little cold lead, well applied, affected a perfectly amicable understanding between the races.[76]

Only weeks earlier, another correspondent to the same paper made his opinion equally clear that settlers were far more efficient than the government in redressing their perceived grievances against Aboriginal sheep stealers: 'we can do more towards the suppression of such crimes in one month than a mounted police force of a hundred men could do in eighteen months'.[77] Throughout the nineteenth century settlers regularly complained that the courts never provided them with the justice they required. When the Government Resident at Port Lincoln was reproached by the Governor in

1846 for acting beyond the law with his discretionary methods of punishing Aboriginal crime, for instance by flogging, he responded that such methods were at least beneficial in deterring settlers 'from taking the law into their own hands.'[78] It was critical, he later wrote, that in a remote district like Port Lincoln 'the settlers may feel that they are as far as possible protected by the Government … that as little as possible may be left to private revenge'.[79]

In so far as colonial authorities attempted to implement a rule of law on the frontiers of settlement, difficulties beset the legal process at every stage – from the gathering of evidence to the prosecution of cases in the courts – which prevented it from being fulfilled. These difficulties were shared by and debated in earlier settled Australian colonies: the problems of distance between districts of settlement and centres of law, which made implementing the law difficult if not impossible; a culture of settler solidarity which meant that settlers did not testify against each other; and ambiguities within the law itself about settlers' rights to protect their lives and property. Even in cases where the law functioned as it should – for instance in holding coronial inquests into Aboriginal deaths, and admitting Aboriginal evidence – Europeans failed to be punished 'with exemplary severity' for violent crimes against Aboriginal people. The fact that Donnelly's case was held up by the South Australian press as an example of the law's impartiality only helped to veil the reality that on no other occasion did legal process work to protect Aboriginal people by punishing violent crimes against them. In this respect, South Australia's case differed little from earlier-settled Australian colonies where the 'rule of law was tested at each stage of [British] expansion, and nearly always failed'.[80]

This may be unsurprising, given the pattern of early colonial encounters wherever the settler frontier spread. What is more surprising is that South Australia's stated principle to legally protect Aboriginal people – a principle driven in large part by Australia's earlier frontier experiences – seemed actually to produce the opposite effect. The relatively small number of Aboriginal executions in New South Wales (and Port Phillip under its jurisdiction) prior to the mid 1840s indicates amongst other things continuing doubts about the law's jurisdiction over Aboriginal people as British subjects.[81] In South Australia, where Aboriginal people were explicitly declared British subjects from the outset, the number of Aboriginal people executed over the first 30 years of British settlement was considerably higher.[82] This suggests that rather than protecting Aboriginal people, the law was enlisted most effectively in punishing them. Perversely, in order to deter settlers from unsanctioned 'acts of hostility' against Aboriginal subjects, government officials were anxious that they could demonstrate the law's capacity to protect settler investments. As the Secretary of State himself acknowledged, settlers would 'take the law into their own hands' if Aboriginal 'criminality' was not seen to be adequately punished.[83] This was also understood by the colonial officials who represented the law on the ground; as one local magistrate put it in 1847, if Aboriginal crime was seen to go unpunished, settlers would act for themselves 'on the principle of self-preservation'.[84] Ultimately, it seemed that the foundational faith in the law's capacity to treat European violence against Aboriginal people 'with exemplary severity' became inverted. Only by treating Aboriginal people with exemplary severity, it seemed, would settler excesses be reined in.

Jurisdiction in *inter se* cases

Behind the difficult questions of Aboriginal people's amenability to British law was the issue of the law's applicability to *inter se* cases. The 1836 *R. Vs Murrell* case in New South Wales, where the court decided it had jurisdiction to prosecute an *inter se* murder case (though refrained from finding a guilty verdict), had failed to establish a clear precedent amongst colonial justices elsewhere, who continued to doubt the law's jurisdiction in interfering with Aboriginal customary law.[85] In South Australia, the question of the court's jurisdiction in cases involving Aboriginal people only was first addressed in 1846 when an Aboriginal known as Larry came before the Supreme Court charged with the murder of Ronkurri. Larry's defence counsel argued that the court had no jurisdiction in such a case, and he entered the following plea:

> that the prisoner owed no allegiance to British laws. That we had set ourselves down in his country. His offence might be punishable or might not by the laws of his own people, and were we to try him, he might be subject to a second trial by them. This was not a conquered country, nor were there any laws by which we, coming into it, could, without the consent of the natives, try offences among them; though perhaps the law of Nature might justify our doing so for aggressions on ourselves.[86]

The judge refused to countenance the plea, insisting that such cases must be tried like any other, and furthermore that bringing such cases before the court 'would impress upon their minds their amenableness to the law, and teach them the consequences of crime'.[87] Yet despite the judge's insistence on the court's jurisdiction to try the case, no suitable interpreter for the defendant could be found, and Larry's case was dismissed.[88]

In 1851 three Aboriginal men from Yorke Peninsula, Takkarm, Ngulta Wikkania and Kangar Wodli, were charged with murdering Multalta. The case first came before Judge Cooper in the Supreme Court on 12 May 1851. In his address to the jury, the judge pointed out the problems involved in indictments against Aborigines involving offences committed amongst themselves, but stressed they must be treated like any other British subjects. The grand jury was disturbed by its responsibility and made a presentment to the judge. The jury foreman observed that they had found true bills to answer in two cases in which Aborigines were being tried for murdering other Aborigines. The first case was that of Multalta, who, it was claimed, the Aborigines had treated as a spy might be treated in a European country. The second case was of a woman seriously assaulted by a suitor – but in a fashion said to be customary in Aboriginal society.[89] In reference to the judge's direction to treat the defendants as British subjects, he foreman stated:

> That in so doing many of the Grand Jurors have done violence to their own natural feelings of equity and justice; since, without entering upon the abstract question of the rights which possession once obtained, the superior and more powerful people may justly exercise over those subjected to them – the Grand Jurors conceive that if the subjected tribes be uncivilized men, it is morally incumbent on the superior people, in the first instance, to confine their interference to the mutual protection of both races in their intercourse with each other, and not to meddle with laws or usages having the force of laws among savages, in their conduct towards their own race.[90]

The jury argued that within their distinct communities the Aborigines upheld laws 'for their own protection and government'; the limited contact with Europeans since settlement was insufficient to expect knowledge of European laws and usages to be communicated, or to justify 'breaking up their own internal system for the punishment of offences to which all their previous traditions and habits give force and sanction'.[91] This, the jurors continued, raised the real possibility that the imposition of British justice could result in someone being punished for a crime 'which, in the minds of the persons punished, was simply the enforcement of their own mode of justice'. The jury argued a point that had repeatedly been raised since the colony was first established: that if Aborigines are to be amenable to British laws, they should first be made aware of them:

> That to compel such conformity (the result in our own social condition of centuries of progressive civilization, under the benign influence of

Christianity), during the second decade of our residence, upon a race probably the lowest among mankind, both as to physical and intellectual position, would be an outrage on common sense, as well as a direct act of injustice.

The jurors finally asked the judge to 'define the limits within which it shall be the province of British law to interfere between the aboriginal natives in their own social relations'.

Judge Cooper responded by insisting that two separate issues were involved: offences committed by Aborigines against Europeans, and offences committed among Aborigines. The former had to be treated like any other case under British law, for he could not see how Europeans could be made subject to the law and not Aborigines. Cooper noted that in the past he had made it a rule 'not to try persons by our mode of trial who were not cognizant of our existence as a nation'.[92] Regarding the second issue Cooper simply stated that if the court 'had power to punish the aboriginal natives for offences against Europeans, the question of jurisdiction was settled, and it could try them for offences committed amongst themselves'. The judge repeated the necessity of instructing the Aborigines as to their standing under British law, and concluded:

> there was no more powerful means of civilization to instruct barbarians than teaching them practically the punishments that awaited them at the hands of Europeans for deeds of violence; and therefore the government should avail itself of every means of making all cases of punishment known amongst the natives.

When the case was actually heard, on 19 May 1851, defence counsel Fisher argued that the prisoners 'had no notion of our laws respecting murder, and ... considered themselves justified, if not bound in duty by their laws, to put strangers to death'.[93] But the judge, consistent with his previous address, refused to question the court's jurisdiction and directed the jury to make their judgment 'as in an ordinary case between Europeans'. The jury took fifteen minutes to find the three accused guilty of murder and the judge sentenced them to be hanged. Yet perhaps uncomfortable with the verdict, a fortnight later the Governor exercised his prerogative of mercy and commuted the sentences.[94]

In a letter to the Governor, Cooper expressed his unease at trying Aborigines for crimes committed among themselves. He mentioned that he had spoken to the Chief Justice of New South Wales, James Dowling, who told him that he never interfered in cases between Aborigines, and that this was consistent with accounts from other colonies. Cooper saw the problem in this way:

> As settlers generally occupy the Country the natives are driven into narrower circles; but they pursue for the most part the same wild and rude kind of life as heretofore; their customs remain the same and so long as they do not trespass against the persons or property of the white race, they are not interfered with. Such I believe has been the manner in which they have been generally treated.[95]

There is no question that judges of the Supreme Court had moral qualms about trying Aboriginal people for offences committed amongst themselves, but the letter of the law required them to be tried. However, as Pope demonstrates in his analysis of *inter se* cases in South Australia prior to 1862, judges had other ways of salving their consciences: most of the cases were dropped before they went to trial or abandoned on legal technicalities, and in the few instances where convictions were recorded, even for murder, the sentences were usually commuted or the prisoners were pardoned.[96]

Inter se cases tell another story about the nature of frontier conflict. In South Australia's south east region, for instance, the phase of most intense frontier violence lasted from 1844 to 1849 and involved attacks on Europeans, their stock and property, and a cycle of retaliatory violence. During this period no Aboriginal people were arrested for offences committed among themselves. This is hardly surprising; police had little interest in what was occurring on the other side of the frontier when their understood task was to protect settlers' lives and stock. By the early 1850s, coinciding with the labour exodus brought about by the goldrush and the sudden demand for Aboriginal labour, we finally see a string of arrests for offences committed within the Aboriginal community. A similar pattern can be seen elsewhere in Australia's colonies. Ann Hunter has shown that the question of *inter se* offences arose in New South Wales and Western Australia during the 1830s and 40s as a reflection of the emerging value of Aboriginal labour within the colonial economy. Prior to this, 'both courts and the colonial government [realised] that Aborigines could not really be treated as British subjects, nor could British law effectively be applied in relation to *inter se* matters'.[97]

Legal interest in *inter se* offences in South Australia's southern districts from the 1850s can be read as an indicator of changed social relations, as a marker that the 'frontier' period was ending and that European authority had effectively been established. This was a pattern that would repeat itself as each new frontier opened up. Although during the frontier phase of settlement offences committed among Aboriginal people, such as killings for breaches of tribal law, were sometimes known to the authorities, they were deliberately not pursued. What this picture tells us is that the status of Aboriginal people as British subjects was accepted as a legal fiction until such a time as European occupation was effectively secured in practice; it also tells us that on the frontiers of settlement, Aboriginal people continued in practice to exercise a de facto sovereignty.

Chapter 5

'THE SECRECY WITH WHICH THESE TRANSACTIONS HAVE BEEN CLOAKED ...': THE CULTURE OF THE SETTLER FRONTIER

As South Australia's first decade as a British province drew on, pastoral settlement expanded rapidly, fanning out to the west and to the south east, which grew initially as an extension of the western Victorian frontier.[1] As had become typical of the Australian frontier elsewhere, settlers arrived to capitalise on the potential of new country in the absence of any larger colonial infrastructure, and without the permanent presence of police. In terms of its climate and geography, the south east was quite unlike any other region of South Australia. Reasonably high rainfall and poorly draining soils meant that much of the land was swampy during the winter months. For the Buandig whose land it was, the environment shaped the nature of their occupation. In the winter months, their camps were on the high ground focused around Mount Gambier, and a low range that stretched along the coast. In the summer months, they shifted toward the coast where there was an abundance of fish and summer fruits. The country that was most attractive to the Buandig was equally attractive to the European settlers. It is notable that most of the attacks on European stock and property occurred during the winter months, when traditional resources were at their most scarce. As competition for diminishing resources increased, so did the violence between Aboriginal people and settlers. But as the dearth of cases against Europeans to come before the court indicated, although the authorities frequently had cause to suspect a culture amongst settlers of covert violence against Aboriginal people in such remote districts, it was often most difficult to prove.

Amongst the first settlers to arrive in the south east were the Leake brothers, Robert and Edward, who with their overseer John McIntyre established the Inverary run at Lake Leake in April 1843. In early June 1844, Robert Leake wrote to the authorities describing his trouble 'with the natives'. Over the course of the last month, he wrote, his flocks and men had been attacked on eight separate occasions; sheep had been speared and others driven off.[2] He also described 'two battles' with the Aborigines, during which he believed one Aboriginal man had been fatally shot and two others wounded. As it happens, Leake was meeting a legal responsibility to report a frontier fatality. By law, anyone who knew of an expected death, even at the furthest reach of the colony, was obliged to report it to the authorities at the risk of incurring a £10 fine.[3] But Leake's decision to report the shootings had little if anything to do with fulfilling the requirements of the law. His letter was motivated by a desire to impart to the government that he and settlers like him were victims of the government's failure to protect settlers' valuable stock from Aboriginal theft. Like most of his contemporaries, Leake's sense of the role of police did not include belief in the principle that Aboriginal people were due legal protection as British subjects; patently, for them, Aboriginal people were not British subjects but a 'criminal' class whose threats to settlers' property – regardless of whether produced by hunger, political resistance or any other conceivable motivation – it was the government's responsibility to suppress. In short, Aboriginal people had become imagined as the invaders, while settlers were the stoical defenders of the colony's economic future.

Yet while he wanted to urge upon the government the material necessity of providing settlers with police protection against the loss of precious stock, Leake would also have been aware that in his description of clashes with Aboriginal people, he would need to be circumspect. He was, he claimed, in 'constant dread of myself and men being murdered'; and if settlers were compelled to repel Aboriginal attacks on their property themselves, it was because the government's failure to provide adequate protection left them with little choice.[4] The Commissioner observed that given the remoteness of this newly opening district, it was 'utterly impossible' to provide the police support Leake requested. He asked instead that the recently arrived local magistrate Evelyn Sturt, brother of the explorer Charles Sturt, investigate the clashes on the Leakes' station.[5] In the depositions taken by Sturt, Leake stated that during the previous May one Aboriginal man had been shot in self defence while he and his men were attempting to recover their stolen property: 'had we not succeeded in defeating them on this occasion, the lives of the men would have been endangered'.[6] Reading Sturt's report, the Commissioner of Police was suspicious that there was more than met the eye.

He considered that the accounts provided by Leake and his men were 'inadequate' and that Leake and his men were bound to put their own actions 'in the best light', but that distance and the lapse of time made further investigation impracticable.[7] As further inquiries would show, he had good reason to be suspicious, but little grounds of proof.

Shortly afterwards, the Commissioner despatched Sergeant Major Alford to the south east to inquire into the state of the district. Alford spoke with Leake's overseer McIntyre, who revealed that in one clash between Leake's men and Aborigines, not long after they established themselves in the district, 'eight natives had been shot'. This was quite a different account than the two or three men reported shot or wounded in Leake's original letter requesting police protection. Alford's report, which the Commissioner of Police summarised for the Colonial Secretary, went on to detail other concerns about settler actions in that district:

> The Sergeant Major learnt from another person on his way home as a rumour, that the natives of the Rivoli Bay District and Glenelg have generally been treated in a manner which can only be called atrocious if true. It was stated to him that damper poisoned with corrosive sublimate was given them. Another method of ill-treatment which can be vouched for is that of driving the natives from the only watering places in that neighbourhood. The native women appear likewise to have been sought after by the shepherds whilst the men were driven from the station with threats.[8]

Although the Sergeant Major thought further investigation into the activities of Leake and McIntyre was warranted, a good deal of time had passed and 'in the absence of the bodies of the slaughtered it may be impossible' to establish the truth, especially given 'the secrecy in which these transactions have been cloaked'.

The following year, Robert's brother Edward Leake wrote again to demand police protection for their stock, and described another 'affray' over lost sheep. In May 1845, he wrote, Aborigines had driven 165 sheep off the newly established SA Company run at Rivoli Bay and 'many more' off the Leakes' run. He and the station workers had tracked the sheep to an Aboriginal camp where, faced with resistance in recovering them, they had fired three volleys upon the group. Although he did not detail whether there were any deaths, he noted that 'two or three natives were seen to crawl away'.[9] Once again, the Commissioner of Police was suspicious; he worried that settlers in the south east were leading themselves into 'acts of unjustifiable hostility' against Aboriginal people, and conceded that the time was right for police to be despatched.[10] Two Mounted Constables were posted to the district in November 1845.[11]

Whether or not the presence of small numbers of constables would make a significant difference to the nature of the remote frontier was another matter. Certainly, by the end of the decade, Protector Moorhouse was expressing the view that the level of police protection was not a good measure of whether or not the district remained peaceable.[12] Despite the presence of the two police, Aboriginal attacks on the settlers and their stock did continue, following the contours of rapid European settlement: 19 runs had been taken up by 1845, an additional 30 in 1846 and another 20 in 1847.[13] For the first few years of settlement in the district, the eyes and ears of the government were those of the local magistrate Evelyn Sturt. In August 1846, months after the arrival of a permanent police presence in the region, he reported the deaths of five Aboriginal men at settlers' hands, all in separate incidents. He expressed his belief that 'a wholesale system of murder is being carried on, which it is most difficult to obtain any evidence of'. The culture of secrecy around violence against Aboriginal people, he added, made it 'almost impossible to get at the truth'.[14] He related how one amongst the 'nest of ruffians' in the district, Owen Curran, had an Aboriginal man's head 'hung on a nail in his hut'. He advised against Curran being granted a depasturing licence, especially in a part of the colony 'so remote as this, where a man has so much power to do evil'.[15]

The remoteness of new pastoral districts and the difficulty of providing adequate police resources to them seemed almost inevitably to produce a hidden culture of settler reprisals against Aboriginal people. If some settlers felt driven to report these clashes – even in modified form – in order to gain the authorities' ear, others recorded them only privately. The journal of Edward and Robert Leake's neighbour Edward Arthur records an escalating series of 'troubles' with Aboriginal people over the course of 1844. Sheep were regularly driven off, shepherds and hutkeepers threatened and horses speared. In his journal, Arthur wrote of the 'hostilities' that ensued when he and his men attempted to 'driv[e] off the Blacks':

> a fight ensued; nor did they retreat until they had left many stretched on the grass – at a rough calculation, I should think about thirty fled; we then destroyed their camp, and took possession of their implements of warfare.[16]

Although Edward Arthur was prepared to note privately that 'many' Aboriginal people were left 'stretched on the grass' after this clash, no report of it ever reached the authorities in Adelaide.

If sometimes the details of violent reprisals against Aboriginal people were kept to the privacy of settlers' journals or circulated as local knowledge within the settler community, at other times they came to the notice of authorities by chance, or because settlers sought legal redress in seeing Aboriginal sheep stealers further punished. A case that demonstrates both circumstances was a violent clash between Aboriginal people and shepherds that took place on John Hallett's station in the mid north in July 1844 in which two Aboriginal people were killed. Local JPs Henry Price and George Hawker took statements from two of the five shepherds involved and issued a warrant for the arrest of an Aboriginal boy known to have been present, but saw no reason to press forward an investigation into the deaths, despite a statement from shepherd William Carter that he had shot an Aboriginal man and woman.[17] When reports of the event finally reached the Advocate General's office, he was annoyed that the 'origin and extent' of the affray were 'still in obscurity,' and reminded the JPs of their requirement to undertake a full investigation.[18]

As details of this case unfolded, it proved to be one that exemplified the many difficulties of bringing effective legal process to the obscure culture of frontier violence. For a start, the incident only came to the authorities' notice by chance, through the coalescence of two things. Firstly, the Protector of Aborigines Matthew Moorhouse happened to be visiting the district when he was told by local Aboriginal people that, some three months earlier, Hallett's shepherds had 'committed a daring outrage upon a group of natives'.[19] Secondly, the station owner John Hallett, who wanted to see the Aboriginal sheep stealers further punished, brought charges against two Aboriginal men known to have 'partaken' of the stolen sheep, one of whom, Pari Kudnutya, would later provide an account crucial in raising suspicion against the shepherds.

Wanting to pursue the Aboriginal reports, Moorhouse visited several stations in the district pulling together a picture of the incident. When he reached Hallett's station and questioned the shepherds involved, he discovered that Carter had changed his account; 'having originally made a very brutal disclosure to Mr Price … [that] he had killed a man and woman… he now swears that he saw no dead natives nor believes that any were killed'.[20] On receipt of Moorhouse's report, the Advocate General felt the case to be 'far from satisfactory', not least because Carter's first incriminating statement had not been certified and forwarded by the JPs to his office.[21] When finally Pari Kudnutya was committed for trial in Adelaide on the charge of stealing Hallett's sheep, Moorhouse interviewed him and gained clarifying testimony.²² Pari Kudnutya told Moorhouse he had been present when Hallett's men attacked the Aboriginal group and wounded four people; a man had died of sword wounds and a woman from bullet wounds. Two others had been shot but had recovered.²³

Now required by the Advocate General to take statements from the other shepherds involved, the local JPs duly forwarded three more depositions which, they said, 'fully corroborate' the other shepherds' statements. To these local Justices, apparently, the authorities' fuss over the incident seemed excessive, and they rejected the Advocate General's concerns about the 'origins and extent' of the affray. Far from 'resting in obscurity', they wrote, its origins and extent were clear: it had been caused 'by the blacks refusing to give up the sheep', and their resistance had been met by the shepherds 'who all through appear to have acted with great moderation'.²⁴ As for Carter's varied statements about the Aboriginal deaths, 'it is a point that we have been unable to discern, and ... is at variance with [our] unanimous opinion'.²⁵ The Advocate General was not satisfied. He considered that the Justices' failure to discern a discrepancy in the shepherd's statements was 'extraordinary', and their approach to the affair had been altogether lax: they had assumed that evidence was to be taken merely 'to warrant a commitment' against the Aboriginal prisoners, rather than 'to inform the Crown of the truth of the matter'. In short, there was good reason to consider 'the whole affair an extremely suspicious one'.²⁶ Protector Moorhouse was sent to the district again, with a police Sub-Inspector and Pari Kudnutya as guide, to see if the Aboriginal bodies could be recovered. Pari Kudnutya took them to two graves, but the bodies had been removed and burnt.²⁷ The efforts to gather sufficient evidence to bring the shepherds to trial continued into the new year, and were delayed in part by the unwillingness of the station owner John Hallett to answer questions put forward by the police magistrate.²⁸ Finally, the case collapsed after Carter absconded on a ship to England, and the Grand Jury found that the other shepherds had no case to answer.²⁹

Despite the authorities' efforts to bring the circumstances of this event to light, they were hampered by a whole range of difficulties that repeatedly beset them in effectively providing Aboriginal protection through legal process: the lapse of time before the event came to official notice, which in this case it did almost accidentally; the shepherd's contradictory statements, which left the circumstances veiled in obscurity; the laxity of local JPs, who were also neighbouring landowners, in pursuing an investigation until prompted; the station owner's reluctance to co-operate in an investigation; the obstruction of evidence in the burning of the bodies; and finally, the opportunity for the key suspect to disappear. Pari Kudnutya, the Aboriginal witness in the case, was only able to provide his testimony and guide the Protector to the gravesites because he had been brought to Adelaide and incarcerated on a charge of sheep stealing after Hallett's shepherds had killed two of his countrymen. It is little wonder that Aboriginal people themselves did not appreciate the protective function of British law.

Meanwhile on the west coast, despite the apparent peace that had followed the first wave of violence at Port Lincoln in the early 1840s, violence flared again as settlers sought new and even more distant runs. By 1848, pastoral settlement had extended 150 miles to the west, toward Venus Bay, and 50 miles to the east, toward Franklin Harbour.[30] As settlement spread, so did the potential for conflict. In June 1848, shepherd John Hamp, who worked on William Pinkerton's Stoney Point station on the western extreme of this new frontier, was waddied to death.[31] In the following month on the same station, shepherd Charles Goldsmith was attacked as he tried to protect his sheep. He fired upon his attackers, reportedly wounding one man, and his attackers retreated.[32] Wherever Aboriginal attacks occurred, settlers or their shepherds would be sure to retaliate. The local magistrate at Port Lincoln was Henry Price, who had recently arrived in the district from the mid north. Price warned the authorities in Adelaide that settlers' confidence in the government to protect their lives and property through the law was something they 'do not possess', and without that confidence, settlers would continue to administer 'justice' in their own way. He also cautioned that 'this feeling is fast spreading amongst the settlers themselves – Nor is it to be wondered at. Each fresh outrage committed by the Natives irritates and hardens them, and unfortunately in such instance some person peculiarly inoffensive from age or known disposition seems selected as the victim.' For as long as government resources were limited in policing Aboriginal people and protecting settlers' property, he concluded, Aboriginal people would suffer 'continued loss of life'.[33]

In May 1849 two murders of Europeans in quick succession revived the sense of crisis that had gripped the district just a few years before. On 3 May 1849, Captain James Beevor, whose Tornto station lay about 80 kilometres north-west of Port Lincoln, was killed by two spear wounds through the heart.[34] Just four days later, while the police were out in pursuit of Beevor's killers, another murder occurred on E.B. Vaux's Lake Hamilton station adjoining Beevor's run. Annie Easton, the wife of one of station's shepherds, was alone in the hut with her baby when Aborigines killed her and rifled the station stores. Her baby was left unharmed. This latest spate of murders shocked the local community. Beevor was an 'old and much respected settler', while Easton was a woman and a mother; the fact that she was killed on her bed gave rise to unconfirmed suspicions that she was raped.[35]

Commentators in the press made little effort to investigate the motives for such attacks, typically ascribing them to the 'treacherous and cunning' character of Aboriginal people. One correspondent, for instance, pointed out that Beevor was a war veteran, renowned for his courage and strength. That he had been murdered 'in so treacherous a manner', wrote a correspondent to the *Register*, 'makes the blood in me rise'.[36] However, an event that was uncovered during the murder investigations suggests a more concrete motive. The bodies of five Aborigines were found near a mine about 30 miles from Port Lincoln, not far from the location of Beevor's and Easton's murders. They had died of arsenic poisoning. Suspicion fell on the hutkeeper Patrick Dwyer. Dwyer's hut had been plundered on several occasions and it seemed he laced flour with arsenic and deliberately left it for the Aborigines to take. Based on Clamor Schurmann's autopsy, the Commissioner believed there to be a connection between the poisonings and the murders of Beevor and Easton:

> The supposition of their being connected is also strengthened by their known and natural propensities to retaliate and revenge the wrongs sustained by members of their own peculiar tribes and if eventually proved to be correct, tends to point out the imprudence to say the least of it of resorting to unlawful methods of punishing the Aborigines, a practice rendering the innocent on both sides liable to the consequences of the sins of the guilty.[37]

Before an investigation could be completed against Dwyer, he fled the district and the colony.

For as long as new pastoral frontiers expanded, it seemed the cycle of violence, of resistance and retaliation, would persist. Governor Robe's insistence to the Government Resident at Port Lincoln that discretionary punishment of Aboriginal people must be abandoned and the letter of the law henceforth be followed had no sympathy from settlers who felt themselves to be insufficiently protected by the government. The day after Annie Easton's murder, a Port Lincoln settler wrote to the *Register* bemoaning the ineffectiveness of the legal system: 'I say the present system will not do now, and it never will, until the race of blacks – I mean Australian blacks – are exterminated'. They were constantly 'prowling' about the stations for the purpose of plunder and 'assassinating our shepherds', always contriving to attack when the police were nowhere to be seen. His solution was to 'let us punish them ourselves'.[38] On 16 May 1849 the Clerk to the Government Resident John Brown reported to the Governor that in the aftermath of Beevor and Easton's murders there were 'three separate parties of volunteers out in the pursuit, as well as all the available police force from Port Lincoln'; a fourth volunteer party was anticipated.[39] Brown was concerned about what these parties might do. He had, he told the Governor, advised the Corporal of Police to 'prevent, in as much as possible, the indiscriminate slaughter of the natives which the exasperated state of the settlers had rendered probable'.[40]

Decades later, stories began to circulate in the district of a massacre of Aborigines near the cliffs at Elliston in retaliation for the murders: 'hundreds', it was claimed, were driven over the cliffs to their death. If there is truth in these stories, its origins probably lie in these punitive expeditions, which were organised not just in response to the settlers' deaths but also for more minor attacks on local stations. Thomas Cooper Horn led one such expedition three weeks after Easton's death, after his Kappawanta run was robbed and a shepherd threatened. Horn's party tracked the alleged offenders to the Waterloo Bay cliffs. As the Aborigines scrambled down the cliffs to escape, Horn and his men fired upon them, killing three, and capturing five others.[41] It is powerfully ironic, and revealing of the historical echoes of the culture of secrecy, that later stories of a massacre at this place, dismissed by many because never proved, served to mask the genuinely disturbing violence of this era which all too often occurred out of sight and out of mind.

Chapter 6

'THE NATURAL WORKING OF AN UNSOUND SYSTEM': ADMINISTRATIVE RESPONSES TO FRONTIER VIOLENCE

'The difficulties attending any attempt to secure permanent peace'
The period between 1847 and 1851 witnessed the most intense period of frontier conflict on South Australia's southern frontiers; not only was there a disturbing renewal of violence on Eyre Peninsula and a peaking of violence in the south east, but there were outbreaks of violence on the newly opening frontiers of Yorke Peninsula and the mid north. These events gave government officials reason to reflect on the causes of conflict and to consider how it might best be suppressed. Port Lincoln's Government Resident Charles Driver, writing with a world-weary sense of resignation, eloquently observed that the succession of murders was 'merely the natural working of an unsound system, only rendered prominent here from the circumstances of the district which from its extent of unavailable land will never carry a sufficiently large European population to overawe the natives'.[1]

The principle of 'overawing the natives', as a necessary pre-requisite to their subjugation, was becoming one of the key tenets of frontier settlement. Shortly before Driver penned this observation, another resident of the district wrote to the *Observer* criticising the government yet again for not providing sufficient police protection, 'without which there cannot be that effective combination of force and rapidity of action necessary to overawe the natives, whom it is the universal opinion here nothing will keep quiet but the most severe measures'.[2] Writing in the aftermath of alleged poisonings on Vaux's station in 1851, Justice of the Peace Henry Price was frank about how the cycle of violence worked. On the 'hostile feelings' station workers entertained toward the Aborigines, he speculated:

> They are – directly – greater sufferers than their masters – Their lives alone are in danger – and in numberless instances – now too common to be even mentioned or reported the huts are stripped of their clothes and blankets and

rations not always to be replaced. The death of a native becomes to them a matter of triumph as the death of an enemy. I fear that the transition from the mere rejoicing in to the actual accomplishing of their destruction cannot in every instance be difficult or distant.[3]

Without confidence of being 'cared for and protected by the Government' to allay settlers' distrust, he found it difficult to imagine a means 'for securing *permanent* peace.'[4] Henry Price's words on the 'reckless' character of station labourers were strikingly similar to Edward Eyre's words on the worst excesses of the Australian frontier when he speculated on the first outbreak of violence at Port Lincoln in 1840. As Eyre had stated, even the most well-intentioned settlers became drawn into a cycle of violence because of the injudicious behaviour that characterised the pastoral frontier. The Protector agreed. In 1849 he observed that if 'the settlers are injudicious in exposing their property, and the shepherds determined to hold intercourse with the women, it is impossible to prevent collisions'.[5] After the renewed wave of troubles at Port Lincoln in 1851, he wrote again: 'Common prudence would accomplish more, than at first sight, it would appear to do, and if it had been exercised at Port Lincoln latterly, it is more than probable, the late distressing occurrences, would not have taken place.'[6]

But more immediately, although Aboriginal aggressions in the Port Lincoln district might have begun as a concerted resistance to invasion, they became as time passed a response to starvation. Many Aboriginal people in the district, Corporal Geharty wrote, 'were absolutely on the point of starvation'. When questioned as to their 'reasons for injuring the white men, they state that they were refused food'.[7] Archdeacon Matthew Hale, who had established the Poonindie Mission in the district, was of similar mind, observing that Aboriginal people 'are almost driven by destitution to resort to *any means* in order to procure food'.[8] The presence 'of the foot of the white man upon their soil' had not only deprived them of their land, but also kept them from their water sources and prevented them from procuring 'the necessities of life'.

The Commissioner of Police understood this also. The 'root of the evil', he wrote, was the deprivation Aboriginal people were suffering through their loss of land and resources:

> We see the Native driven from his hunting grounds and his food, by the lawful intrusion of the White man, starving, and in want of water; we see the White man, in possession of food and water in abundance, that, indeed,

which the native requires to keep body and soul together, we see this inestimable prize, this unendurable want, I regret to say, in many instances, ill-protected, and in some cases left quite exposed, and results are murder and robbery.[9]

Asked to respond on the need for increased police protection in Port Lincoln, the Commissioner himself doubted that more armed forces would be beneficial. No increase in police numbers, he stated, would 'have the effect of *preventing* the murders and aggressions', when Aboriginal acts against settlers were driven by desperate want; it is then 'but a bare act of Justice' to alleviate that want 'with an equivalent for that food of which he has rightly or wrongly been deprived and the want of which, I feel inclined to believe, has instigated him to the commission of Crime'.[10] The Protector of Aborigines also argued that Aboriginal aggressions against settlers were occasioned by deprivation aggravated by drought, and he suggested that many of the attacks against settlers might have been prevented with government provision of food supplies:

> I may observe that nine tenths of the murders committed by the natives, have been committed in the autumnal season or say from the last days of January to that of June. It appears that want in the Port Lincoln territory has been the cause of the recent outrages, that the late drought compelled the tribes to leave the interior for the coast and it is probable that had provision Depots been in operation, the evils might have been avoided.[11]

By the end of the 1840s no one seemed particularly satisfied with the rule of law in managing frontier collisions: neither the government officials who attempted often in vain to implement it, nor the settlers who regarded it as inadequate to their needs, and certainly not the Aboriginal people for whom its imposition incurred the worst punitive effects. While mounted police had so far been the government's principal instrument in dealing with Aboriginal resistance on the colony's remote frontiers, they did not and could not resolve the underlying problems of Aboriginal starvation and dispossession. By the late 1840s, the government turned to other, more conciliatory approaches in an attempt to prevent the seemingly unremitting cycle of violence.

The Protectorate
When the position of Protector of Aborigines was conceived, it was imagined as one of the strategies, along with the accommodation of Aboriginal rights to land and the impartial application of the rule of law, which would help to

avert in South Australia the sort of violence that was occurring in the earlier settled colonies. The Protector was to be responsible directly to the Governor and thereby, it was hoped, remain aloof from the self-interest of settlers. His instructions stipulated that he was to teach the Aborigines the 'arts of civilization' and the 'fundamental truths of CHRISTIANITY'. He was to 'observe their means of subsistence' and, while 'leaving them … to their own exertions', ensure that they did not 'fall into destitution'. Finally, considerable stress was placed on the fact that he was to work in the field: 'a great part of his time must be spent among the natives'; he must 'make himself acquainted with their language and dialects' and their 'peculiar districts' and he 'must visit frequently all the tribes in the Province to which the Europeans have access'.[12] To support his task, he was given the powers of a magistrate and coroner.

In a province incorporating tens of thousands of Aboriginal people, speaking dozens of languages and as culturally diverse as the nations of Europe, these were utopian demands, but through the years of the 1840s and early 1850s Protector Matthew Moorhouse did the best he could. He oversaw the operations of the Native Location and the Native School in Adelaide, he supervised the implementation of a colony-wide system of ration distributions, and he was periodically called upon to conduct coronial inquiries and organise interpreters for the court.

The general view of the settler community was that Moorhouse held a cosy sinecure in his comfortable Adelaide compound, where a handful of Aboriginal children were taught the alphabet while in the frontier districts the very people over whom he should have been exercising control were killing settlers' stock and spearing their shepherds. As each new frontier crisis was reported in the press, the question was invariably asked, 'where is the Protector?' While his given role was the advocacy and protection of the Aboriginal population, there was an implicit sense in the settler community that his real task should be ensuring Aboriginal compliance to the needs of settlers. In the neighbouring Port Phillip Protectorate, Moorhouse's counter-part George Augustus Robinson at least had the assistance of four Sub-Protectors who each supervised districts of relatively modest size. Protector Moorhouse, charged with the supervision of Aboriginal people in a vastly more extensive, and seemingly ever-expanding territory, rarely had more than one Sub-Protector operating under his control at any one time.

Despite the perception that he was an office-bound bureaucrat, Moorhouse travelled extensively through the colony endeavouring to instruct Aboriginal people about the new regime that was being imposed upon them.

Between 1847 and 1851, he travelled to each of the colony's frontier districts in the south east, the Eyre and Yorke Peninsulas and the mid north. On each occasion he distributed rations as a show of good faith and, through an interpreter, endeavoured to explain the law. A more abiding legacy of his tenure of Protector was the establishment of an extensive system of ration distribution.

The Systematic distribution of rations

The origins of a system of ration distribution lie in 1841, when Edward Eyre was posted to Moorundie in the aftermath of the Rufus River massacre. As Sub-Protector of Aborigines, Eyre was instructed to assemble the local Aboriginal population on 'every other full moon' and issue them with a present of flour on the condition of good behaviour. Governor Grey believed that such assemblies would provide Aboriginal people with the chance to air their grievances, and for the Protector and police to address them. Distributions of flour were also attempted at Port Lincoln in the early 1840s, although on an *ad hoc* basis, and intended primarily for the elderly or infirm. In March 1847 Governor Robe, at the prompting of the Commissioner of Police, asked Protector Matthew Moorhouse to investigate the establishment of a broader system of ration distributions. The earlier systems at Port Lincoln and Moorundie were held up as examples of how rations could be successfully used to 'pacify' the Aborigines.[13]

By the late 1840s, both the Protector and the Commissioner of Police had sufficient experience of the colony's frontiers to appreciate that a significant motive for stock theft was deprivation caused by settlement, as Aboriginal people lost access to traditional resources. Rations were conceived as a form of compensation, and a means of drawing Aboriginal people away from the runs of settlers. Moorhouse made the following recommendations:

> The distribution of flour should take place once a month (at the full moon), that at outstations 4 lb should be issued to each adult, and 2 lb to each child, under twelve years of age, & a registry kept of all who attend.[14]

In addition to the sites already operating at Moorundie and Port Lincoln, Moorhouse recommended the establishment of seven new ration depots, mostly housed in established police stations and all in areas of considerable Aboriginal population which had seen marked conflict: Bungaree and Mt Remarkable in the mid-north, Lake Bonney and Wellington on the River Murray, Guichen Bay and Mt Gambier in the south east, and Encounter Bay in the south. It was decided that the police already operating in these districts would manage the distributions. For the police, ration distribution would, for a time, provide them with one form of control and surveillance over Aboriginal people.[15]

As the frontier spread further into the interior, new depots were established as need dictated. In the early 1850s, in the aftermath of attacks on newly established pastoral stations in the southern Flinders Ranges, the government decided on the Protector's recommendation to appoint a new Sub-Protector and establish a new 'feeding station' in the north. As Protector Moorhouse explained, the 'settlers are all short of men to attend their flocks & the Natives are much disposed to take advantage of it' and a 'feeding station would be a means of keeping them quiet'.[16] The depot was established on 1 February 1853 at Mount Brown and Henry Minchin, a local magistrate, was appointed Sub-Protector. Moorhouse summarised Minchin's role: 'His aim will be to induce the wild natives from the hills to live at his station, and by keeping them some time in contact with himself and the police, so far civilize them, as to render them not only harmless, but useful to the settlers'.[17]

Over the course of the 1850s, the practice of distributing rations to Aborigines from police stations became formalised. Rations of flour, tea and sugar, occasionally supplemented with other goods such as blankets and medical supplies, were issued to those Aboriginal people regarded as being most in need. They were restricted to 'the sick, the old, the infirm, orphan children and women with infants under twelve years old', for the able-bodied were expected to find work or to subsist by fishing and hunting; in reality, the rations issued to dependents would have been shared among the family group.[18] Yet it is unlikely that ration distributions ever had much effect in suppressing frontier violence. For Aboriginal people, attacks on settlers' stock and property were both a means of subsistence and a form of resistance. More often than not, it was only when the phase of frontier conflict had largely passed – when European dominance was more firmly established and Aboriginal people made refugees in their own land – that people came in significant numbers to the depots.

In 1863 the newly-appointed Protector James Walker added an innovation to the ration system by arranging for them to be distributed on selected pastoral stations. Distributing rations from pastoral rather than police stations would be both more economical to the government and more practical, since numbers of Aboriginal people already coalesced near the pastoral stations. Having government rations to issue eventually proved to be an unexpected advantage to station owners. The Protector of Aborigines noted in 1868 that settlers were often disappointed when he refused to grant them rations for distribution to Aboriginal people, and that 'great jealousy exists between those who have Aboriginal depots and those who have not'.[19] There are a number of reasons for this. In the first instance, rations could be used to obtain some control over the Aboriginal people in the district; as one settler put it, they would keep Aboriginal people near the station and within view, where 'they would not do so much damage'.[20] More importantly, as the phase of frontier antagonisms passed and Aboriginal people became the principal source of labour in the pastoral industry, government rations constituted an inducement for them to work on a station, and for their bosses, a way of subsidising the cost of labour. From Aboriginal people's point of view, rations could provide a source of support when their own resources were diminishing and a means of retaining important connection to their land, albeit in a transformed socio-political environment.

The Native Police

Another government response to managing the frontier in this period was the establishment of a Native Police force. For a number of years, the police had employed Aboriginal people on an ad hoc basis for their skills as trackers and for their ability to speak the language of the local Aboriginal population. The principal now was to establish small Aboriginal forces under the command of a European officer to operate as units throughout the colony. The model was the Native Police force operating in the Port Phillip district which was principally used to track and capture other Aboriginal people, and operated under the command of a European officer. In 1850, Protector Matthew Moorhouse was asked his opinion about the organisation of such a force. Following the Port Phillip model, he agreed that Native Police should not operate autonomously, or have the same powers as ordinary police; they should not be involved in the capture of Europeans, serve summonses, take charge of prisoners, or prosecute inquiries into crimes. They should be located in remote districts and assist European officers in tracking and recovering stolen sheep and cattle, and in the 'detection of native offenders'.[21] Not everyone agreed with this approach: in 1854 Sub-Protector Henry Minchin suggested that the Native Police at Port Augusta should perform their duties under his authority, 'exclusive of the European police,' because the latter, he feared, would 'attempt mastery' over them, leading to ill-feelings. The Commissioner of Police was unconvinced, writing that 'Mr Minchin cannot be everywhere and the NP couldn't be trusted alone'.[22] The Native Police never operated autonomously.

Towards the close of 1852, a detachment of twelve Native Police was established in the Port Lincoln district under the command of Corporal John

Cusack. Its duties were 'to patrol the country and follow with expeditions, in case of need, the perpetrators of any outrage, accompanied however by and under the orders of a European constable'.[23] The Native Police would be paid £18/5/0 per annum with clothing and rations, with the expenditure to be charged to the Aborigines Land Fund.[24] In early 1854, newly appointed Police Commissioner Peter Egerton Warburton expanded the Native Police force, overseeing the establishment of additional corps at Wellington, Moorundie and Port Augusta under European officers. Many of these constables would operate as Mounted Police and all were armed with a sword, a carbine and a pistol.[25]

On the surface, there was a certain administrative elegance in the plan: by 1854 there were four separate detachments of Native Police scattered throughout the colony, all armed and most of them mounted, led by a European officer, and under the command of a regional Police Inspector who was also a Sub-Protector of Aborigines. Yet in comparison to the fearful reputation such forces would garner elsewhere, most particularly in Queensland over the coming decades, once established these Native Police corps became virtually invisible in the historical record. Comment is occasionally made in police reports about their good or bad conduct, but rarely do police reports highlight their involvement in patrols. Indeed, there is no record that any of these Native Constables actually fired a shot in anger. This might be partly explained by the fact that these corps were established at a time when the worst of the violence in those districts had passed, and perhaps also by the fact that most Native Constables were outsiders in the districts to which they were posted.

By 1856, the usefulness of the Native Police corps was being questioned. Writing to the Commissioner of Police that year, Inspector Holroyd argued that the Native Police were useless as 'trackers or aides of Justice in a country that does not belong to them – they know nothing of its waterholes, they do not know where to go to look for a wild native, and from being always mounted and well clothed, they lose the chief quality wanted in them, namely tracking'. He found it difficult to justify retaining them.[26] At about the same time, Corporal Mason, Inspector of the Native Police on the southern Murray River, wrote to inform the Commissioner that his Native Constables had all left to work the harvest and had not returned; he was instructed not to enlist any more.[27] Soon afterwards, the Native Police corps were disbanded. Although Aboriginal people would be employed as trackers throughout the force for many years to come, a dedicated Native Police force would not be established again until the expansion of the Central

Australian frontier in the mid-1880s. Unlike their counterparts during the 1850s, the Native Police in Central Australia would come to earn a reputation for violence of a kind largely unmonitored by the police administration a long way to the south.[28] At this stage, Central Australia was another newly evolving frontier, subject to the same problems of implementing the rule of law that had been experienced on earlier settler frontiers across Australia.

Aboriginal Rights on Pastoral Lands

One of the more surprising administrative innovations of the early 1850s – a Colonial Office intervention – was a decision to enshrine in law Aboriginal access rights to pastoral leases of the Crown. In the 1840s squatters, principally in New South Wales, agitated for more secure tenure than the existing annual depasturing licences in the form of a system of pastoral leases. The Colonial Office was wary about the extent to which the control of Crown lands should be surrendered to private individuals. Another concern, however, was the impact these changes might have on Aboriginal people. In 1846, Port Phillip's Chief Protector George Augustus Robinson wrote:

> The claims of the Aborigines to a reasonable share in the soil of their fatherland has not, I regret to say, been recognised in any of the discussions which for so great a length of time, have agitated the public mind on the question of rights of Squatters, to the occupancy of the lands of the Crown.[29]

As Robinson put it, Aboriginal people would soon have 'no place for the soles of their feet'.[30] The British government was responsive to these concerns. In 1848 the Secretary of State, Earl Grey, made it clear that these leases were exclusively for the pasturage of cattle and were 'not intended to deprive the natives of their former right to hunt over these Districts, or wander over them in search of subsistence'. The Order-in-Council, authorising the introduction of fourteen-year pastoral leases, instructed the Governor to insert whatever conditions he thought necessary 'for the protection of the Aborigines'. As South Australia's Governor Young was entering into discussions with the Crown Lands Commissioner about the form which that protection might take, events on the west coast coincidentally underscored the need for it.

In November 1850, an Aboriginal group stole 800 head of sheep from Henry Beard's station at Cape Radstock, 175 miles north-west of Port Lincoln, and plundered his shepherd's hut. Henry Beard went in pursuit of his flock, and was speared to death bringing the sheep back.[31] Before establishing his run, Beard had been warned by police that the Streaky Bay Aboriginals were 'on very bad terms with the whites from the bad treatment they receive from the whalers', but he had ignored the caution. Referring to Beard's murder in a report to the Colonial Office, Governor Young observed that the settler had been 'reckless' in establishing a run in such a remote region, and without a licence to occupy the country.[32] Sergeant Geharty tracked the sheep stealers and in attempting to take prisoners, he reported, 'it became necessary to fire on them in self defence'.[33] The Police Commissioner George Dashwood and Protector Moorhouse were despatched to the west coast to investigate Beard's murder and the subsequent shooting of Aboriginal people. They spent almost a month in the region, speaking with Aboriginal groups as they travelled along the coast, and learnt that Aboriginal people broadly held a 'fear of passing through the runs of the settlers, which we regret to find can seldom be done by the natives with impunity'.[34]

Meanwhile a draft of the conditions spelling out Aboriginal access rights was published in the *Government Gazette* for public comment. One of the few to offer comment was Archdeacon Matthew Hale, who had recently established the Poonindie Mission near Port Lincoln. While he had no objection to the provisions, he reminded the Governor that Aboriginal use of the land, such as the practice of using fire to hunt game, was 'diametrically opposed to the interests of the white occupiers of land'. Their rights of access needed to be clearly spelled out, including access to watering places. In response to Hale's recommendations the Commissioner of Crown Lands Charles Bonney suggested simply withdrawing the access provisions and providing Aboriginal people with 'provisions and clothing' as compensation for deprivation of 'their means of securing food'. The Governor, however, would not be dissuaded. He instructed Bonney to ensure that reservations were made for Aboriginal people to 'follow their usual customs in searching for food', to 'dwell upon lands held under lease', and to ensure rights of access to watering places. In a subsequent letter to the Chief Secretary, Bonney explained the logic of the new provisions:

> whether it may be found expedient or not to allow full exercise of these privileges, I think such reservations should be inserted in the leases as will give the Government complete control in the matter.
>
> I am of opinion that the knowledge that the Government is in possession of this power and that the runs are liable to be resumed for the use of the natives, will be sufficient to ensure the forbearance of the white people, and to render them rather desirous of conciliating the natives in order that no necessity may arise for the exercise of these powers.[35]

A new system of fourteen-year pastoral leases came in to operation on 1 July 1851, and included the clear direction that Aboriginal inhabitants of the province and their descendents would continue to have 'full and free right of ingress, egress and regress' upon the lands leased by the Crown. They 'may at all times during this demise use occupy dwell upon and obtain food and water' upon those lands, 'unobstructed' by the lessee. They may erect such 'dwellings as they have heretofore been accustomed to make,' and 'take and use as food birds and animals ferae naturae in such a manner as they would have been entitled to do if this demise had not been made'.[36] Not only were the 'occupiers of runs' to be made aware that they risked forfeiting the runs if they breached the conditions of the lease, but if so forfeited, the land would be 'resumed for the use of the natives'.

What is astonishing is that there was barely a murmur of protest from pastoralists acquiring these new leases, a fact explainable by the coincidental drama of the Victorian gold rush and the sudden demand for Aboriginal labourers. By 1852, the Victorian gold rush was drawing away South Australia's labour force as thousands of people, from pastoral workers to police, resigned their jobs to try their luck at the Victorian diggings. Sub-Protector Edward Bates Scott at Moorundie on the River Murray reported that large numbers of people were streaming past his station: 'for some months past the line of road ... has been well defined by extensive caravans'.[37] Some fears were voiced that Aboriginal people would rise up against undermanned and isolated stations. In February 1852, J.B. Hughes, recently appointed a Special Magistrate at Bundaleer in the North, wrote to the government complaining about the withdrawal of police from Mount Remarkable:

> The gradual migration of Europeans ... from the country north of this has impressed the Aborigines with a strong belief in the truth of a philosophy they profess to have received from their old men to the effect that the white men would leave their country as suddenly as they entered it ...[38]

The Aborigines, he wrote, were boasting that 'the time would come when they would retake possession of their country and drive away the last of the white fellows'.[39] In a letter to the *Observer* in February 1852, a settler wrote that with the 'adult male population rapidly draining away; town, hamlets, farms, and out stations almost deprived of protection and the savages openly exulting in the desolation – may not their cry soon be "up and be doing?"'[40] Yet despite these fears, the most significant consequence of the labour exodus was to create a demand for Aboriginal labour. Settlers who only a few years before had been driving Aboriginal people off their pastoral stations were now offering them rations to work as shepherds. Protectors' reports throughout the 1850s frequently noted the importance of Aboriginal labour. Of the northern districts in 1854, Sub-Protector Minchin wrote:

> It is well known by the whites, that such blacks as are employed, and receive sufficient food and clothing, are not only invaluable for their services, but indispensable at present: the work on many stations being chiefly carried out by the natives, and to a great extent among the sheep farmers.[41]

In the south east in the same year it was reported that most of the shepherding was being done by Aboriginal people. As the disruption caused by the gold rushes began to subside and white labourers resumed their places, the demand for Aboriginal labour declined. Yet a beach-head of sorts had been made: it was realised that Aboriginal people could be a valuable source of labour in the pastoral industry.

By 1851, when the conditions of pastoral leases clarified Aboriginal rights of access to land, the worst of the covert violence against Aboriginal people had significantly passed in the pastoral country south of Goyder's line. In retrospect, this was perhaps due more to the evolving pattern of frontier relationships than to government intervention. Although colonial authorities had attempted to respond to violence on the frontiers of settlement with administrative innovations, such as the systematic distribution of rations and the establishment of a dedicated Native Police force, there was little sign that these measures had a significant effect either in diminishing Aboriginal attacks on settlers' stock and property in times of want, or in checking settlers' unlawful acts of punitive violence against Aboriginal people. Rather, the reduction of violence is more likely to be explained by the coincidence between the gradual establishment of a colonial infrastructure in the colony's more southern pastoral districts and, with the exodus to the gold fields, the new demand for Aboriginal labour.

Nonetheless, by the early 1850s, the authorities may well have felt some confidence that the frontiers of settlement had become largely 'pacified'. The northern districts, however, were yet to expand with settlers seeking land. As these districts opened up, the same sequence of conflict would begin afresh which governmental interventions seemed powerless to prevent. Underlying this cyclical pattern of the frontier was the problem, again, that the rule of law proved inadequate to the task either of preventing Aboriginal resistance to occupation of their lands, or of protecting them as British subjects. As experience of the southern frontiers had demonstrated, and as the frontiers opening to the north would repeat over the coming decades, the legal status of Aboriginal people was defined by what they were expected to become, rather than what they were. Aboriginal people were effectively 'provisional' British subjects, and they had to be policed into subjecthood.

Chapter 7

'THESE WAR-LIKE PREPARATIONS': THE MOUNTED POLICE AND THE TYRANNY OF DISTANCE

Travelling north

George Goyder was appointed Surveyor-General in 1861, when the colony was entering a terrible drought that would last much of that decade. During the 1860s, Goyder mapped the line separating the drought-ravaged country from the region with reliable rainfalls; its ragged boundary, he found, stretched from Mount Remarkable in the north to Streaky Bay in the west. The importance of his discovery lay not in plotting the southern limits of a transitory drought, but in establishing that there was a more abiding boundary between land fit for agriculture and land 'only fit for pastoral purposes' – its marker was saltbush.[1] The character of the country beyond Goyder's Line determined a type of settlement that would shape the nature of relations between Aboriginal people and Europeans in the decades to follow. The carrying capacity of the land north of Goyder's Line required Europeans to establish significantly larger runs than were characteristic of the more temperate southern districts. For Aboriginal people, at least in less drought-affected years, this meant more room to manoeuvre as European settlement spread. But in times of drought, conflict amplified as the two communities competed for scarce and diminishing resources. These conditions produced a frontier that was more permeable, and a phase of conflict that was longer-lived, than anywhere else in the colony.

In the early 1850s, the fledging pastoral sector extending into the north was struggling to establish itself in the face of the exodus to the Victorian goldfields. Labour was hard to attract, and hard to keep. Police numbers thinned as troopers resigned the force to try their luck at the diggings. Until 1856, Melrose in the southern Flinders Ranges remained the most northerly police post, while settlement moved yet further north. The northern stations were sprawling and sparsely scattered, and their owners complained regularly to the government about the need for more police to protect them against Aboriginal attack. At the same time, the dearth of police meant that some settlers were able to pursue a sense of frontier justice in their own way.

In 1851 brothers Thomas and Robert Brown were establishing their sheep run near Mount Arden. This was prime country on the edge of Goyder's line, 70 kilometres north of the Mount Remarkable Police Station. The family had established a productive property south of Adelaide, and the expansion of settlement into country to the north provided an opportunity for the sons to strike out on their own. The seasons had been good and the stock was flourishing, but the labour shortage on the land produced by the goldrush continued to be felt. The parents sent their other two sons – John, their eldest, and 17 year-old James, their youngest – to help out. Less than three months later, on 19 September 1852, James Brown was killed by Aborigines and his sheep taken. His body had been ritually mutilated, his genitals cut off and stuffed into his mouth, suggestive of payback for a sexual crime that he or his companions may have committed against an Aboriginal woman.

Neighbouring settlers responded to James' murder decisively. Three separate parties comprising nearly twenty 'well equipped men' were formed to pursue the suspects and recover the stolen sheep. PC Phillips, the only policeman available in the district, accompanied one of the parties.[2] On their third day out, having travelled 80 or 90 kilometres, they found the missing sheep in the hills near Lake Torrens. Afterwards, PC Phillips reported that they encountered four Aboriginal men and two boys hiding near the sheep, who pelted the Europeans with stones, calling out 'blackfellows got no butter white fellow plenty butter. Only one white fellow tumble down'. In his deposition of what occurred next, PC Phillips claimed that he called upon the men to put down their spears and talk, but they began making threats. The settler party began firing, and two Aboriginal men were shot. In a second round of firing, the two others were killed. Benjamin Raglass, who was amongst those in the punitive party, claimed in his deposition that in the absence of sufficient police strength in the district, the Aborigines had become 'more daring'. When they attempted to retrieve the sheep, he stated, they were met with spears and stones, and had to retreat because their only firearms were a brace of pistols. Of the depositions relating to the settler party's actions on this day, none were signed.

In later years, Thomas Brown left a written account of the punitive expedition against the Aborigines in the wake of his youngest brother's death. 'Almost before the first shovel full of earth had been put upon the grave', he relates, 'every man was in the saddle' ready to pursue the murderers. As the party set out, an 'old hand' called out, 'The government can't hang you for what you're going to do'. When their party caught up with the Aboriginal camp, Brown writes, the Aborigines tried to escape into the mulga scrub. A call was raised to '"Cut them off who can!"', and the men on the best horses rode to the crest of the hill, cutting off the Aboriginal men 'who lagged behind to the last to cover the retreat of the women and children'. The results of that day, Brown writes, 'need no telling', though he describes the 'report and ping of the passing bullets' from the rifles on the rocks. He does not specify any number of Aboriginal deaths or injuries; only that they received a 'severe but necessary lesson'. 'I feel quite clear,' he concludes, 'that we only fulfilled God's command that "Whosoever shall shed man's blood by man shall his blood be shed". I can only say that in this case we carried out God's decree and I can further declare and swear that not one woman or child was injured'.[3]

What of the police constable who took part in this expedition? In spite of the legal status of Aboriginal people as British subjects, the role of police on the pastoral frontier was implicitly understood to be one of support for the settler. When the police rode together with aggrieved settlers into an Aboriginal camp, the events that might follow joined police and settlers in a sometimes difficult, and sometimes unholy, communion. In his account of the retaliatory raid in the wake of James' death, Thomas Brown's description of chasing down the Aboriginal camp casts doubt on PC Phillips' report that the party had only shot four Aboriginal men in self-defence. Yet Brown had felt confident enough to say that 'in all we did there was no concealment or action outside the law' because a mounted constable was present amongst them.

Major Warburton and the Mounted Police

On this northern frontier, as on the colony's earlier frontiers, entrepreneurial settlers set out first to test the capacity of the land, and police presence followed. From the 1850s a style of frontier policing evolved that was considered suitable to the isolated districts of new European settlement, and at its heart were the Mounted Police. As new pastoral frontiers opened up and Aboriginal attacks on remote settlers began, the government typically responded by posting to the region a pair of Mounted Constables, usually assisted by an Aboriginal tracker. On receiving a report of Aboriginal aggression, such as the driving off of sheep or attacks upon a settler, the Mounted Police would travel to the station and, with the assistance of station workers, set off to track down the alleged offenders. In the vast region of the north, the period of most intense conflict between Aboriginal people and settlers lasted from the early 1850s until the end of the 1860s; this period coincided with the term of the colony's longest serving Police Commissioner, Major Peter Egerton Warburton.

Appointed in 1853 and Commissioner of Police until 1867, Warburton had previously served in the British army in India, and he brought a distinct military flavour to the organisation of the police and the management of the frontier. He introduced reforms that would improve morale and make police service a more attractive vocation. Under his watch police numbers almost doubled and new administrative districts were created. New uniforms were introduced, regarded as more appropriate to the climate. On the grounds that the standard issue muskets and pistols were 'clumsy antiquated articles', he was given authority to purchase new carbines and revolvers – weapons that were lighter, more accurate and considerably more deadly. He introduced new ranks within the force, and encouraged men to seek promotion. His attitude to the status of the Mounted Police, who were now referred to as 'troopers', is a good indicator of his military thinking. In an 1856 report he expressed the view that a mounted officer's 'clothing and equipment should plainly show that he was a cavalry soldier', and that the Mounted Police force as a whole should be regarded as a 'military body'.[4] One day, he speculated, it might form the basis of a national army.

With regard to the role of the Mounted Police in dealing with Aboriginal people, Warburton's surprisingly frank and sometimes bellicose letters and reports reveal the fine line he walked in trying to reconcile Aboriginal people's legal status as British subjects with the realities of frontier warfare. Writing in 1855 with reference to the recent violence in the Port Lincoln district, Warburton observed that should the Aborigines

> show any disposition to renew their atrocities it will be both wise and merciful, I think, to put them down with a strong hand. The technicalities of British law are unsuitable to such savages, and summary justice should be dealt on the spot to those who are convicted of murder. I would not advocate the spilling of blood on account of a few sheep or bags of flour stolen; but where life has been taken, those who do not know its value should be made to feel and see how sacred we hold it.[5]

Although the official view was always that the law would protect Aboriginal people as equally as Europeans, the primary role of the Mounted Police was undoubtedly to provide protection to settlers in the outlying regions. By the mid-1850s, new stations were being established in the central

Flinders Ranges, in the vicinity of Beltana and Blinman, and Warburton was of the view that police protection should be provided to them. When William Borthwick wrote to the Commissioner in 1856 to request a small party of police to reside on his new run, considering an early application the 'best and safest' course to follow,[6] Warburton was keen to comply. 'I am most anxious to meet Mr Borthwick's wishes,' he wrote to Inspector Henry Holroyd. 'I hope you will so arrange the distribution of the force under your orders as to leave one Trooper available for this duty'. The implication that Mounted Police might serve almost as a sort of private security force for individual stations was suggested by his recommendation to the Chief Secretary that, if possible, all advanced posts of settlement should receive police protection in the economic interests of the colony: 'the purchasers of land are constantly pushing the stockowners outside the protected lines, and as the welfare of the Province is so closely connected with the prosperity of the latter class, policy alone might render it proper to embrace them all within Police ranges'.[7]

Certainly, Warburton's approach to the problems of Aboriginal resistance to European occupation in the northern districts was indicative of a culture of frontier policing which did not easily regard Aboriginal people as equal British subjects deserving of protection. In fact, the primary consequence of maintaining the official view that Aboriginal people were British subjects was that their attacks on settlers' property would always be treated as 'criminal' rather than political activity. In 1856, a party of Aborigines killed James Mitchell, a shepherd working at an outstation of Baker's Angipena property. The Mounted Police went in pursuit of the alleged murders and in late December captured Putaba Bob, one of the alleged ringleaders, after severely wounding him. The Police transported the prisoner to Mount Remarkable where he died of his wounds. The Bishop of Adelaide, when on a missionary tour of the North, heard details of this event and wrote to the press complaining of Putaba Bob's treatment: he claimed that despite 'receiving two pistol-shots and three swords cuts', which were left 'undressed and fly-blown', he was marched in chains 240 kilometres south to Melrose where 'death released the poor wretch from his misery'.[8] Warburton responded to the Bishop's criticism with outrage. In a letter forwarded to the press, he informed the Bishop that the 'poor wretch' was an 'atrocious ruthless ruffian; he had murdered an Englishman, and would have killed two police officers had they not been armed'. The police, he added, required fortitude in their role; he often found himself censuring officers for being too 'soft-hearted'.[9]

In 1858, the Attorney-General initiated an inquiry into police use of deadly force after two Aboriginal men had been shot and killed in response to an attack on John Jacob's station at Mount Serle in June. Aboriginal men had come to the shepherd's hut and thrown stones at the three stockmen there. While rock throwing may seem trivial, it was commonly used in the region of the Flinders Ranges where the landscape was strewn with rocks that had been weathered away from the surrounding ranges; some settlers referred to it as the 'stone country'. The Aborigines had retreated after being fired upon, but concerned that they would return one of the stockmen was despatched to a nearby station to get help. While he was away, the attackers returned, rushing the hut and spearing both of the men before throwing a firestick onto the thatched roof. The hut burned down, but the men survived their wounds and managed to escape and report the attack. Corporal Burtt, Police Trooper Simpson, an Aboriginal tracker and four station workers went in search of the assailants, eventually tracking them to Arkaroola Creek. In his report, Corporal Burtt stated that he called upon them to stand, but when they responded with more rock throwing, the Europeans fired upon them, killing two men. Receiving this report, the Attorney-General observed that such cases 'must be expected from time to time to occur in the remote districts', but he nonetheless questioned the necessity of using deadly force.[10]

Major Warburton was asked for a copy of the instructions he had issued to police in September 1857 regarding the use of 'deadly force'. Those instructions are absent from the Commissioner of Police's General Order books and their wording unrecoverable; but the Chief Secretary's response made it clear that they were overly military in intent, and legally unacceptable. The police, he wrote, 'were not an army to be used against enemies who are to be put out of the way, or deprived of the power of resistance'; they were a 'Civil Body', 'employed to preserve the peace by preventing violence, when possible, and to protect life & property by such means as may secure the legal punishment of offenders':

> When the latter cannot be accomplished without the employment of force, then force – even to the taking of life – may be employed. It should, however, be understood, that this is not to be done as a matter of course, or indiscriminately, but that the Police Officer who so takes life, must show that he did it in self-defence, and that there were some peculiar circumstances which rendered the taking of life inevitable ...
>
> The Chief Secretary is therefore of opinion that the Instructions should be modified, at least to the extent that under any circumstances the use of

firearms is to be avoided, if possible – but that if it become necessary, it should strictly be confined within the limits of that necessity.[11]

Two days later, the Commissioner printed new orders incorporating much of the language and tone of the Chief Secretary's letter, but not substantially restricting the degree of license to use firearms on suspects resisting or eluding arrest. Even within the letter of the law, the open-ended nature of police instructions did, in fact, allow police in remote locations to fire upon Aboriginal people almost with impunity.

Policing and the tyranny of distance

Not surprisingly, the men who policed Australia's frontiers faced a complicated network of difficulties which did not apply to the settled districts, at the heart of which was facilitating the expansion of pastoral settlement in the face of Aboriginal resistance to it. The conditions under which they executed their duty were hard. They were stationed at the most remote locations in the colony, accommodated in makeshift police huts or camps. In these isolated postings, they were responsible for protecting relatively small numbers of Europeans running sheep and cattle over vast tracts of country. Expected to travel over hundreds of kilometres for weeks without respite to locate suspected felons, secure them, and transport them great distances as prisoners, they were usually under-resourced. Technically, any crime required the police to respond by making arrests where possible and, if a charge went forward, to take it before a Court. But the difficulties of distance encouraged a margin of flexibility in the interpretation of the law.

The first problem the police faced was the difficulty of apprehending Aboriginal suspects in often unfamiliar and difficult country. Inspector Henry Holroyd and Sergeant Geharty, long-serving officers in the Port Lincoln district, knew these issues only too well. On 1 June 1855 Aborigines killed Peter Brown, a shepherd employed on Dr McKechnie's run near Franklin Harbour on the west coast of the colony. Holroyd and Geharty were out for three weeks searching for the suspects but gave up when their horses became 'knocked up' and their provisions ran out, having failed to find 'the slightest trace of the Blacks'.[12] In explaining their lack of success, Geharty pointed out that five days had elapsed before the shepherd's disappearance was reported, meaning that the tracks were no longer distinct. Another officer, Trooper Woods, was earlier on the scene but, as Geharty condescendingly observed, he had only 'recently joined the force' and 'it would be the last thing he would think of to take natives with him' as guides

Letters Patent erecting and establishing the province of South Australia and fixing its boundaries, State Records of South Australia GRG2/64.

Colonial Secretary Robert Gouger's draft of a proclamation, popularly known as 'the Proclamation', as read by Governor Hindmarsh at Glenelg, announcing the establishment of the government. State Records of South Australia GRG24/90 GRG24/90 (Miscellaneous records of historical interest, item 401).

Charles Hill, Australia, 1824-1915, 'The Proclamation of South Australia 1836', c. 1856-76, Adelaide, oil on canvas, 133.3 x 274.3 cm, Morgan Thomas Bequest Fund 1936, Art Gallery of South Australia, Adelaide, [0.893]

Alexander Schramm, Australia, 1814-1864, 'An Aboriginal encampment, near the Adelaide foothills', 1854, oil on canvas, 89.0 x 132.0 cm, South Australian Government Grant 1976, Art Gallery of South Australia, Adelaide [761HP1]

E.C. Frome, Australia, 1822-1886 ' "Pilgaru" – two natives hung for murder, September 1840', 1840, Adelaide, watercolour on paper, 11.1 x 19.0 cm, South Australian Government Grant City Council & Public Donations Fund 1970, Art Gallery of South Australia, Adelaide [709HP43]

'Overlanders attacking the natives, 1846',
Pen and ink drawing by George Hamilton, SLNSW Call No. V89.

W.A. Cawthorne, 'A fight at the Murray', 1844. SLNSW PX*D 70/f.32.

Edward Eyre distributing rations at Moorundie, ca. 1844.
Reproduced from F. Dutton, *South Australia and its Mines*, London 1846, opp. 331.

List of arms and ammunition in the possession of settlers at Port Lincoln in 1842. State Records of South Australia GRG24/6 Chief Secretary's Office, Inward correspondence, file no. 124 of 1842.

George French Angas, Australia, 1822-1886, 'Messrs Arthur's sheep station with volcanic well, Mt Schank in the distance', 1844, South East, watercolour on paper, 15.8 x 25.8 cm, Bequest of J. Angas Johnson 1902, Art Gallery of South Australia, Adelaide, [0.625]

John Magill, 'Barracks of the 96th Regiment', Flinders Street, Adelaide, view from the mess room, 1844. Rex Nan Kivell Collection NK2037/B. NLA Record ID NBD5836942.

John Magill, 'Barracks of the 96th Regiment', Flinders Street, Adelaide, Rex Nan Kivell Collection NK2037/A. NLA ID NBD5836943.

Boston Bay 1840. SLSA B 9483/3.

The Marauders, watercolour by S.T. Gill, SLNSW. No. PXA 1983/f. 44.

'45 Natives driven to the Police Court by the Police for trespassing, 1845'.
Watercolour attributed to W. A. Cawthorne, SLNSW SV/97.

Edward Snell, 'Blacks on the way to Adelaide in custody, Yorke Peninsula, 22 June 1850'. SLNSW Call No. SV/88.

Police Commissioner, John Egerton Warburton, c. 1874. SLSA B 7938.

Mrs (Christina) Smith, c. 1865, SLSA B 3384

Protector of Aborigines, Dr Matthew Moorhouse, c. 1870. SLSA B 10848

Herbert Cole, 'Without the smallest repugnance or concern he began piling up dried wood, dead black men, and defunct sheep in a heap together', from Simpson Newland, *Paving the Way: A Romance of the Australian Bush*, Drexel Biddle, Philadelphia, 1899.

Herbert Cole, 'Darkie saw his pursuers grow less and less', from Simpson Newland, *Paving the Way: A Romance of the Australian Bush*, Drexel Biddle, Philadelphia, 1899.

Bethesda Aboriginal Mission Station, Killalpaninna, SA, late 1880s, Lutheran Archives, M00708 00359.

Blinman Police Station 1868. State Records of South Australia GRG5/2 Police Commissioner's Office, Correspondence files, file no. 649 of 1868.

Mounted Police on Parade at the Adelaide Barracks, c. 1890. SLSA B 18966.

G. Meissel, Watercolour painting of the Moravian Mission at Kopperamanna, no date, Lutheran Archives, P03011 05992

Mounted Police, Innamincka, c. 1890. SLSA 48237.

Aborigines at the Adelaide Jubilee International Exhibition, 1887. SLSA B 10212/27.

Tree Planting at the Old Gum Tree, 1887. SLSA B 7094.

Reading the Proclamation, float in South Australia's Centenary 'Pageant of Progress', 1936. SLSA B8334/95.

The Advertiser Centenary Issue, 1 September 1936, Cover

Recreation of Sturt's expedition landing at Goolwa, 1951. SLSA B 21731.

Bitter Springs Film Poster, c. 1950, Canal+ Image UK Ltd.

Acknowledgement of traditional custodians at the Melrose Police Station Museum.
Photo: A. Nettelbeck.

Section of the Exhibition at the Wadlatta Interpretive Centre, Port Augusta. Photo: A. Nettelbeck.

Memorial Plaque at the Melrose Police Station.
Photo: A. Nettelbeck.

Melrose Police Station and Post Office, c. 1876. SLSA B380.

Aboriginal, Australian and British flags flying at the Melrose Historical Precinct.
Photo: R. Foster

and trackers. Making matters worse was the fact that the country was covered in dense scrub 'where the native gets his living' and through which he could travel, unlike Mounted Police, without ever having to move into 'open country'.[13] Not only did Aboriginal people's knowledge of the country make their capture difficult but, as Holroyd pointed out, they 'know all the moves of the Police but too well'.[14] Speaking from fifteen years' experience, Geharty wrote that Aboriginal suspects were only to be taken 'by stratagem':

> That is by tracing by another native in the scrub, and teaking [sic] them in their wurleys at night or seeing their fires from some rising ground in the scrub at sundown when they retire for the night.[15]

If securing Aboriginal suspects was difficult enough, holding them as prisoners proved no less a challenge. After weeks of searching, Police Troopers Cooper and Woods eventually captured five men suspected of involvement in the murder of Peter Brown. After a week's travel through 250 miles of scrub, the troopers arrived at the Salt Creek Police station. PT Cooper was on guard that night but, 'literally worn out with fatigue', he fell asleep and four of the prisoners broke their handcuffs and escaped.[16]

The sheer monotony of reports concerning escaped Aboriginal prisoners during the 1850s and 1860s drove Commissioner Warburton to distraction, leading him to issue ever-more detailed instructions as to how they should be secured. After the prisoners escaped from Cooper's custody at Salt Creek, Warburton made the following suggestions to Inspector Holroyd:

> I would request your attention to the modes of *securing* native prisoners — the ordinary handcuffs are almost useless for such a purpose, unless used as fetters, but as an additional precaution I think a chain should be passed round their necks being secured at each man's throat with a pair of handcuffs; when any number of prisoners have to be secured for the night, they should be linked together hand to hand, the outer hands of the two end prisoners being so fastened to fixtures as to prevent any one man getting both his hands together.[17]

He concluded by observing that 'as the Natives are slippery to a degree almost inhuman, it behoves the police to be proportionately careful, so that they may not be outmatched'.

Even seemingly secure lock-ups built of stone and mortar seemed inadequate. In May 1855 eight Aboriginal prisoners serving a sentence at Port Lincoln gaol escaped from their cell. According to the police, one of their friends passed them a small iron bar through their cell window which they used to cut away 'about 2 feet square of the wall'. According to one of the constables on duty, the noise of their digging and scraping was drowned out by the sound of the prisoners 'singing and corroberying in their cell'. To affect their escape they managed to 'wrench open the patent padlock which confined them by neck irons' to the wall.[18] All the clichés of the prison-break seemed to conspire to torment Commissioner Warburton; several years later at the Mount Remarkable lock-up a prisoner used a piece of soap that he had secreted in the pocket of his prison uniform to help him slip off his handcuffs and make good his escape.[19]

Warburton took the issue of Aboriginal prisoners escaping custody very seriously. He was willing to show leniency to officers who took every reasonable precaution to prevent escapes, but where he believed they had failed in their duty he responded harshly; troopers faced pay cuts, demotion and even dismissal if their actions were judged negligent.[20] Warburton had introduced these sanctions to improve discipline within the ranks, but they had created a vicious circle: Aboriginal prisoners, knowing the treatment that awaited them, were keen to escape, while police officers, fearful of the sanctions they might face if prisoners escaped, resorted to ever more severe methods of securing them.

An equal difficulty facing Mounted Police was finding and keeping witnesses, without whom a case was unlikely to be sustained. Often the only witnesses were Aboriginal people, unwilling participants in the British legal system. Aboriginal witnesses – variously puzzled, afraid or affronted – often sought the first opportunity to escape. The response of police was to treat their witnesses in the same way as their prisoners. When in 1867 an Aboriginal prisoner arrested on suspicion of murder and the Aboriginal witness escaped together from the Blinman police station, the police trooper fired at them both before they disappeared into the scrub. Reading his forwarded report, the Protector of Aborigines complained that had the trooper's bullets killed the witness, he would 'have committed a very serious crime'.[21] The Protector drily noted that the witness's treatment, 'handcuffed and chained to the supposed murderer was not calculated to give him a very exulted idea of white man's justice, and was very likely to provoke the attempt he afterwards made, at all hazards, to escape.' He observed that the 'troopers in the far north are too ready with their firearms in their dealings with the natives; and I trust that the Commissioner of Police will warn them of the very grave responsibility they thus incur'. Required to respond, the Commissioner of Police wrote a memo advising police to show more caution in distinguishing 'between culprits and innocent persons, it is bad enough to manacle and confine the witness and treat him as a guilty man, but it is worse to shoot him'.[22]

The dilemma of how to secure Aboriginal witnesses troubled Warburton as much as the problems of capturing and securing Aboriginal prisoners. If a suspected felon was committed for trial on a serious charge, he was manacled and transported to Adelaide for a trial before the Supreme Court, the witnesses travelling likewise in chains. Once in Adelaide the prisoner was remanded to Adelaide Gaol while the witness, in all likelihood, shared an adjoining cell. The Commissioner of Police occasionally pondered alternatives, but nothing proved satisfactory. Leaving the witness in the care of the Protector of Aborigines was a possibility rejected because 'he has no proper means of securing him';[23] the Destitute Asylum was another option, but it was 'fearfully overcrowded' and afforded 'no security as a place of custody'.[24] It was simply more effective to incarcerate the witnesses. The Commissioner more or less conceded that this practice was improper, if not illegal, but he defended it on the grounds of utility: 'In former years the practice of committing Native Witnesses obtained, and though no law justifying such commitment exists; still as a matter of necessity it is I think the best mode of proceeding'.[25]

Gathering European witnesses to take cases to trial could be just as problematic. Sometimes a case could not proceed because station owners worried that to release station workers to appear as witnesses in court would leave their isolated property vulnerable to Aboriginal attack. In 1858, for instance, after John Jacob's station was attacked, Mounted Constable Burtt spent weeks searching for and then escorting the Aboriginal suspects 400 kilometres south to the magistrate at Mount Remarkable.[26] The magistrate was not convinced that the evidence was sufficient to sustain a case so he ordered the Constable to return to the station and secure witnesses. Jacob, however, refused to send down his station workers as witnesses for the hearing, in the belief that if the Aborigines who had attacked the station became aware of its diminished numbers, they might attack it again.[27] Burtt was then required to travel south to Mount Remarkable once again to report this to the magistrate, who then promptly released the prisoners.

The frustrations of having to transport prisoners and witnesses hundreds of miles, as well as the belief that if punishment was not immediate then it was not effective, led some police to consider that the ends of justice might best be served in other, more pragmatic ways. Summary punishment of Aboriginal 'offenders' was one strategy sometimes employed by officers of the law. In 1853 the Sub-Protector of Aborigines and local magistrate

Henry Minchin, in the company of a police corporal, had an Aboriginal man suspected of robbery tied to a tree at the Port Ferguson Police station and flogged.[28] In 1867, after a series of 'depredations' on Umberatana and Mt Fytton stations, the owners were loathe to enter the long and expensive process of prosecution but instead asked the police inspector 'to flog them and let them go'.[29]

Settlers also were known to resort to this strategy. In his reminiscences of the Flinders Ranges in the 1850s, pastoralist Frederick Hayward describes holding a 'drumhead court-marshall' for cattle-killing: he tied his Aboriginal prisoner up and flogged him with a stockwhip.[30] Hayward's actions were motivated by a previous experience where he had apprehended a suspected sheep-stealer and taken him before a magistrate, only to see the prisoner released because of a lack of convincing evidence. Samuel Stuckey, the pastoralist whose fatal shooting of Pompey had been taken as 'justifiable homicide', recalled making 'a useful man' out of one Aboriginal man by chaining him to an iron casting for three days before releasing him.[31] Reports of this sort of summary punishment arose commonly in other frontier districts. After sheep were stolen from James Thompson's run on Eyre Peninsula in October 1861, the owner gathered a group of six or seven Aborigines together with the promise of a 'big breakfast', but instead of being given food they were surrounded by station workers and beaten with sticks. An ex-policeman who reported the incident claimed that one man was held by the overseer and 'beaten until he was nearly dead'.[32] In December 1863 two station workers named Barton and Miller on a property near Venus Bay thrashed an Aboriginal man so badly that he died. The men were put on trial for the death, but the jury returned a verdict of not guilty.[33]

The difficulties of effectively applying the legal system to the conditions of the frontier led some government officials to advocate a provisional code of law to deal with Aboriginal 'troubles' in outlying districts. The employment of such a provisional legal code had in fact been recommended in the 1837 Report of the Select Committee on Aborigines when the colony of South Australia was first established.[34] In 1857, on the grounds that the 'requirements of British Law' were inapplicable to Aboriginal people, Commissioner of Police Warburton recommended to the government that they should no longer be considered subject to British law but rather subject to their own traditional law, albeit under the umbrella of colonial authority. Such a system would relieve the police from their current dilemmas in frontier policing, and would be less expensive to the government. This was a legal system, 'easy of execution and sound of principle', that pertained in other British colonies like India, where Warburton had previously been posted, and he saw no reason why it should not be equally appropriate to Australia.[35] Against the government's tenacious insistence that Aboriginal people were British subjects, Warburton argued that Aboriginal people comprised independent communities, were governed by their own laws, and would resist incursions upon their land to the extent that they were able. In his view, the repeated dilemma of the police was not that they had to police Aboriginal people as British subjects, but that they had to police them into becoming British subjects.

Not surprisingly, Warburton's recommendation of a provisional code of law found no purchase with the government in 1857, since it could hardly acknowledge the existence of any alternative legal system, even under the umbrella of British law, when the official position was that Aboriginal people were British subjects. In 1860, at the Select Committee of Inquiry into the condition of Aboriginal people in the colony, Warburton raised the concept again in different terms. What was needed, he argued, was a system of justice suitable for application to Aboriginal people that could be delivered immediately and locally. The Committee subsequently recommended allowing the Protector of Aborigines the power to 'hold a court, and dispense justice summarily, in all matters of dispute between the natives themselves, as also between Native and Europeans', with the exception of capital offences.[36] Although the recommendation was not put into practice, the discussion of it was symptomatic of the vexed, ongoing debate amongst police and government about how to effectively police Aboriginal people in remote areas. The police, as the Commissioner was only too aware, were few in number and responsible for patrolling vast districts; they had little in their armoury to prevent Aboriginal attacks on settlers' property, beyond retaliatory raids for punitive effect.

By the early 1860s, as European settlement expanded in the north and Aboriginal attacks on stations escalated, Warburton increasingly came to the view that the rule of law, as it pertained, was patently inadequate to the realities of the frontier. This was also understood by the ordinary police who patrolled the pastoral frontiers, like Corporal James Wauhop, who observed that wherever the settlers expanded into a new district, Aboriginal people would be 'sure to show resistance'.[37] In mid-1863, Corporal Wauhop led a police party in response to an Aboriginal attack on Mudnowadna station, in which station workers had been threatened and cattle were killed. Having tracked the suspects, Corporal Wauhop's party eventually confronted a group of about 40 Aborigines near Mount Deception. In his report, Wauhop stated that his men had fired upon the Aboriginal group because the police party was threatened. He could not say how many people had been shot, but had no doubt some had fallen. He concluded by offering the view that 'Breech loading rifles are the only weapons that would intimidate such a determined lot of natives – for they appear to take no notice of pistols'.[38]

Warburton elected to take 'active and effectual measures' to suppress Aboriginal attacks on pastoral stations in the north.[39] He arranged a redistribution of troopers in order to increase the available strength of police at the far northern police station at Angipena, and bolstered supplies of arms and ammunition for them. On receipt of this information, the Protector of Aborigines James Walker was alarmed: 'a considerable addition has been made to the Police force at Angipena, and I was informed this morning at the Armory that a supply of breech-loading rifle carbines with ammunition, is about to be sent to the same station'. Aboriginal people, of course, were technically British subjects, and Walker called for caution against the police taking 'such war-like preparations' against them.[40] Warburton responded with contempt:

> I have the honour to inform the Chief Secretary that the Police have no desire to use force, if it can be avoided, against the Natives – should the peaceful provisions of this Protector be first tried upon them and succeed in turning them from their evil ways, I shall then have great pleasure in restoring the 'warlike preparations' to the place from whence they were taken – As matters at present stand – black is white and white black – the Settlers require Protection and the Savages punishment.[41]

Only a week earlier, Warburton had written to the Chief Secretary about his frustration with the gap he perceived between the ideal of legal process and the realities of the police's role in the frontier districts. The '*legal* punishment' of Aboriginal offenders, he wrote, was 'next to impossible' when police were required to pursue Aboriginal people who were not in any practical sense bound by British law. What is more, the practical difficulties of responding to the crime of stock theft, well after the event, often made legal requirements impossible to fulfil. Reporting on troubles around Lake Hope, he added:

> no one sees who kills the Cattle, and no one can prove before a Court who did it – no apprehension can be made without almost certain loss of life and when this has been done the Police may be convicted of Murder because they can not *prove* what in the eye of the Law would be sufficient participation in crime …

> These savages could not be made to understand our Laws whatever pains we might take to teach them – they know none other than that by which their own conduct is regulated; the Majesty of our laws is nothing in their eyes – they will not yield to the covenants of the Law whilst they have the least power of resistance, and every instance of successful resistance only incites them to further acts of violence ... From 15 to 20 Troopers at hand would be required to protect our frontier stations – they should be well armed, and (in my opinion) directed to use their arms.[42]

Whereas in 1858 Warburton had advocated providing police protection on all newly established stations, by the 1860s he began urging settlers to take more measures to protect their property and defend themselves. As the 1860s progressed and the great drought set in, Aboriginal people were forced to compete ever harder for diminishing resources, and a constant complaint to police from settlers was the theft of goods and provisions from their huts. On the earlier frontiers further south, station owners had regularly employed hutkeepers to watch the stores during the day while shepherds were out on the run. This precaution appears to have been largely dispensed with in the more marginal country in the northern and western regions of the colony. Police troopers investigating thefts often reported not only that shepherds' huts were left unattended, but also that doors were left open or merely fastened with a piece of string. When urged to employ hutkeepers, the station owners' typical response was that 'it will not pay', but they nonetheless expected the police to pursue the thieves and recover the property.[43]

The Commissioner had some sympathy for Aboriginal people in these circumstances: 'the practice of leaving huts with provisions in them open and uncared for obtains a great deal too much – it is not fair to tempt hungry and uncivilized men in this manner'.[44] He had less sympathy for the settler who not only left his provisions unprotected, but often his stock as well: 'if he does not like' to take the precaution of employing sufficient men, Warburton complained, 'he ought to be prepared to part with a few head'.[45] On a number of occasions the Commissioner threatened to withdraw police from a district as a means of forcing settlers to better protect themselves.

In October 1863, when a settler in the northern district requested more police support after his unprotected huts had been plundered and the cattle driven off, the Commissioner reported to the Chief Secretary that it was futile for the police to 'fire into a mob' of Aboriginal people *'after the Sheep are stolen & killed'*. Instead, he was willing to allow that settlers should use their own firearms in preventing Aboriginal attacks on their property in the first place. He advised that

> owners of Stock should increase the number of their Servants in charge of their property, and that they should supply them all with serviceable arms for the defence of their lives or property ... supposing more Police were to be there are *they* to shoot the Natives like dogs? Or are they to be sent there to relieve the Settlers from the necessity of taking care of their lives and property?'[46]

The great drought

Buoyed by some years of good rainfall, the pastoral frontier had begun moving north of the Flinders Ranges into the Lake Eyre Basin. This was even more marginal country, suitable mainly for cattle. But by 1864, the great drought was beginning to take hold. In the spring of that year, George Reynolds, an employee working on the Lake Hope run, wrote to the station owner's brother William Dean about the state of the country. He had just returned from a trip south to Blanchewater, noting that even the 'stone country' was in poor condition: 'I assure you it was quite a treat to see something for the horse to eat. We want rain very badly'.[47] In another letter written a week earlier, he commented that at Lake Hope, the Aborigines had 'had a turn at the cattle', but had been quiet for a while. He personally felt little cause for alarm: 'I think the niggers will leave *us* alone, they do not like our rifles, and we have a knack of shooting pretty straight'.[48]

By the following year the drought had taken stronger hold. In good years the Aboriginal people of the district could keep their distance from settlers by moving to smaller water sources, but in times of drought they had no choice but to fall back on the principal waters in the district, which by this time had become the jealously guarded life-blood of the stations. In April 1865 John Jacob's station near Mount Fytton was again raided, the sheep driven off and the shepherd John Jerrold killed. Rumours were abroad that the Aborigines were mustering at Umberatana. In a letter published in the *Register* Jacob observed that if 'the police cannot come up, a muster must be made of the settlers, and the country thoroughly secured'.[49] Police Troopers Gason and Poynter did come up, although not until September. They tracked the suspects for the raid on Jacob's station – Parrallana Jacky, Parrallana Tommy and Parrallana Jacky's wife – to a location near Mt Freeling, and Tommy was shot and killed while allegedly fleeing from the police.[50]

Jonathan Hughes, a settler who had been in the district at the time, wrote to the *Register* with a different version of events. The Aboriginal people, he said, had approached the shepherd asking if they could take some sheep. The sheep they were given were so emaciated from the drought that they had no 'butter' on them, which is why they killed some others. This was how the struggle had occurred in which Jerrold died. Hughes wrote:

> They see our people settle in their country, occupy it all, and wantonly destroy the animals on which the natives have depended for food. They cannot prevent or obtain redress for this; but when they are reduced to the verge of starvation, and, following the example of the white men, seek it from the flocks and herds of the white man, they are hunted, captured and chained.[51]

Writing again the following month, he observed that the drought had become so severe that the game on which the Aborigines depended for food had 'become almost extinct in many localities'. 'No wonder', he added, that 'in their extremity' Aboriginal people should take the 'flocks and herds of the settlers'.[52] A doctor at Nuccaleena wrote to a friend in Adelaide in early December praising the Aborigines of the district for their forbearance; they were, he wrote, 'on the brink of actual starvation', and yet 'bear their destitution with great patience'.[53]

In November 1865, Henry Dean wrote to his brother about the difficulties he was facing on Lake Hope station, and his letter was forwarded for publication in the *Register*. Dean described the impact of the terrible drought which was gripping the district, and the trouble they were having with Aboriginal people: 'The blacks have been playing up with the cattle since I left the station. They have been killing them by wholesale. I am going at them in a day or two, just to let them know that I am home again'.[54] He expressed the view that the 'down-country blacks ... are spoiling our Lakes blacks by putting them up to all sorts of mischief'. How it would end he did not know, 'but for the protection of our lives and property stopped this must be'. A few days after Dean's letter was published, Thomas Elder, a part-owner of the Lake Hope property, addressed the parliament on the subject of the drought and its devastating impact on the pastoral industry. To underline the gravity of the situation he read out Dean's letter, including a passage that had been omitted in its published version. After noting that the Aborigines had been 'killing cattle by wholesale', Dean had written:

> A few days ago a lot of blacks stuck up one of our men; he saw them killing a cow, and as soon as they discovered him they faced and tried to drive him back. They then all got round and sent their boomerangs at him until he was obliged to fire upon them to save himself from being murdered, and one of the natives was killed, of which we have sent notice to the police.[55]

The remainder of the letter is identical to the published version. It appears the *Register* was concerned enough to publish the section indicating Aboriginal aggressions, but was unwilling to report the news that the stockman had fired upon and killed 'one of the natives'. Dean and his men did 'go at' the Aborigines. In a biographical sketch of Henry Dean which draws on his wider correspondence with Elder, Rodney Cockburn relates how Dean 'used forcible methods in order to establish the authority of the white man': 'He burned down three of their camps', and 'sent out a party of station hands to clear the country northwards'.[56] In the course of his campaign to drive the Aborigines from his run, his own party of nine men was attacked as they slept beneath a dray. Charles Neumann was killed and six of the party were wounded, including George Reynolds who the previous year had bragged of his 'knack of shooting pretty straight'. Dean himself suffered four spear wounds. Dean's party 'made a spirited defence', shooting several of their Aboriginal attackers.[57] In a letter to Thomas Elder, Dean related the circumstances:

> The blacks caught me asleep at last, and all but killed me. They had been giving us a great deal of trouble for some time, and seemed determined to do as they liked with us and our property until we were compelled, for the preservation of our lives and property, to put a stop to the slaughter of our cattle and attacks on our men ... the blows came so thick and fast that they would not give a man time to rub his eyes. So soon as I got the spear out of my ear I shot a black though the body with my rifle. It was something awful.[58]

Official reports record that four Aborigines had been shot dead and several others wounded in this clash.[59] None of the official police reports give any information about Dean's earlier attacks on the Aboriginal camps, actions which would surely have motivated an Aboriginal attack. Police Trooper Poynter was the first to investigate the attack on Dean's party. Reporting to Inspector Roe, he requested that since he only had 'sixty rounds of cartridges' with him, he wished to be forwarded another 'one hundred rounds as I have no doubt I shall want them'.[60] With Samuel Gason, Poynter led a party of 15 men in pursuit of Dean's attackers, but apparently only 'succeeded in meeting with a few natives, the majority having decamped'.[61] However, in a letter to Thomas Elder, Dean made it clear that the state of conflict with the Aborigines at Lake Hope was not over: 'We must have more men and more arms to defend our position and our property, otherwise this country will have to be abandoned by the settlers'.[62] Another member of his party was even more direct:

We want some large sized revolvers, as those we have are too small. We shall not be able to settle the up-creek country until we are stronger handed, as I am afraid it is now open war between the blacks and us.[63]

The continuing cycle

When Corporal James Wauhop reported his clash with around forty Aboriginal people on Mudnowadna station near Mount Deception in 1863, leading him to recommend breech loading rifles for Mounted Police, he noted that the Aborigines involved in the incident were members of the 'Lake Hope Tribe' who had come down as far as Brachina 'to procure a kind of red earth that they use in painting themselves'.[64] Brachina is a long way from Lake Hope – hundreds of kilometres south. What the Corporal's observation alerts us to is that the settlers in the district of the Flinders Ranges contended not only with local Aboriginal tribes resisting the invasion of their country, but also with distant Aboriginal groups who regularly travelled through the region to collect ochre from Parachilna in the southern Flinders, in the vicinity of Brachina Gorge.

The nineteenth century anthropologist Alfred Howitt noted that parties of Diyari men numbering as many as eighty would set out in the winter of each year from the region of Lake Hope to travel the 400 to 500 kilometres south to Parachilna. It was here that they collected the sacred red ochre that motivated their long journey. As Philip Jones points out in his book *Ochre and Rust*, the ochre network was considerably more complicated; many other groups from the north, and quite probably the south, journeyed to Parachilna to collect it. The ochre mine was one of the most important sites in the region, and the regular journeys to it were effectively pilgrimages. During the course of the journey, Aboriginal groups would of course sustain themselves by hunting: prior to the arrival of Europeans, their principal diet would have been the kangaroos, wallabies, and the small mammals of the region; after the arrival of Europeans, sheep and cattle provided their sustenance. Many of the violent confrontations reported by settlers in the region during the 1860s were with members of these ochre expeditions, and settlers gradually came to realise it. Settlers often made reference to the presence or approach of the 'Saltwater Blacks', so named because they appeared from the vicinity of Lakes Blanche and Gregory, inland salt lakes north of the Flinders Ranges. The Aboriginal people of the Flinders Ranges, the Yura, were sometimes colloquially referred to as the 'Hill Blacks'. Pompey, who had attacked John Jacob's station in 1858 and was shot dead by Samuel Stuckey in 1864 while allegedly stirring up revolt among his Aboriginal station workers, was considered a 'Saltwater Black'.

Jones suggests that the violence settlers meted out to these groups in retribution for loss of stock may have been well in excess of what official records might indicate. In November 1863 an ochre party of forty to fifty men stole sheep from Captain McKay's station near Beltana, forcing the station workers to seek shelter in the kitchen while a messenger was sent to get help. McKay, the overseer and another man tracked the stolen sheep to Wariotta Creek. The Aboriginal party allegedly attacked them with waddies and boomerangs, forcing them to employ their firearms. Mounted Constable Wauhop investigated the 'affray' and reported that he had seen the remains of three Aborigines who had been shot; he believed that 'more' had been injured.[65] Two decades later, the owner of the Blinman mines, T.A. Massey, recalled this episode: in his account, '11 blacks were killed on the spot, and it is said that 40 to 50 others died of their wounds before they reached their own territory'.[66] It is possible that Massey's account is exaggerated, but its existence casts doubt on the official record.

Shortly after the event on McKay's station, Commissioner Warburton suggested a plan that he thought might remove the need for the northern Aboriginal groups to make the ochre journey through country now occupied by settlers: that is, to provide it to them nearer to home.[67] While this plan was first mooted in 1864, it was not attempted until a decade later. In 1874 the government paid for four tons of ochre to be mined from a site south of Adelaide and carted to the Killalpaninna Mission in the Lake Eyre district to be distributed among the Aborigines there. As Jones points out, the experiment was a failure: the cultural significance of the Parachilna ochre and the ritual journey to collect it could not be replaced with a cartload of ochre from just anywhere.[68]

With the dramatic expansion in the government system of ration distribution over the 1860s, the era of conflict between Aboriginal people, police and settlers in the northern districts was already waning when in October 1866 a party of German Lutherans from the Hermannsburg Missionary Society set out from the Barossa Valley with the plan of establishing a mission in the north.[69] At Blanchewater Station they met Sub-Protector Buttfield, who informed them that another missionary party, Moravian brethren from Melbourne, had arrived just before them.[70] Like the Lutherans, the Moravians had chosen this missionary field partly because of the stories they had heard about how the Aboriginal people of the district had helped the stranded Burke and Wills expedition at Coopers Creek.[71] The Moravians established themselves at Kopperamanna, about 70 kilometres north-west of Lake Hope, while the Lutherans chose Lake Killalpaninna, a further 15 kilometres distant.

Within two months of the missionaries' arrival, Aborigines began gathering in large numbers at Perigundi, and rumours spread that they planned to kill all the Europeans in the area, including the missionaries. Aside from any political motives for wanting to attack the intruders, Aboriginal people must have been appalled that these newcomers were occupying two of the most important water sources in the district, and that during the middle of a drought. This was the same region where, just the year before, Henry Dean's men had endeavoured to 'go at' Aboriginal people at Lake Hope, only to be attacked in return. In early March 1867, a large Aboriginal gathering was preparing for a corroboree within telescope distance of Kopperamanna. Believing this to be a prelude to a planned attack, the Moravians sent a message to their brothers at Killalpaninna to be prepared. On 14 March, as a large tribal group began gathering at Killalpaninna, the missionaries started to make plans to flee. As it happened, a police party was on patrol in the district and arrived at Killalpaninna to dispel the tension, although in spite of the presence of the police, an attempt was made on the life of brother Vogelsang as he set off from Kopperamanna to return to his mission at Killalpaninna.[72]

The powerful message to the missionaries was that their presence was not wanted. The very people they had come to 'save' were trying to drive them away. Corporal Morton and Constable Gason visited all the Aboriginal camps in the district and spread a message that the missionaries had come 'to instruct and protect them'; that if they interfered with the missionaries in any way, 'the Police would take them to Adelaide or shoot them down'.[73] For their own safety, Morton recommended, the missionaries should augment their numbers; otherwise they required a permanent police presence, for Aboriginal people would know 'that they would not protect themselves with firearms'. In a letter to their brethren in Germany, Reverend Goessling summed up the missionaries' dilemma: 'What shall we do? If we defend ourselves and shoot heathens it will kill the mission prospects forever ... If they kill us ... this is not a desirable end. The Lord must assist'.[74]

In the short term, the missionaries retreated to the protection of Bucaltininna station, but their presence presented the police with an ongoing problem. In particular, their pacifism left the newly-appointed Police Commissioner, George Hamilton, with a dilemma: how could he best protect them when their very attitude 'emboldened' the Aborigines and might lead them to 'rob and murder them without compunction or mercy'? In a memo regarding the missionaries' unwillingness to defend themselves – they are referred to as 'non-combatants' – Commissioner Hamilton makes it very clear what was expected of police and settlers in these remote districts:

Two or three troopers supported by armed bushmen would be able to repel a large number of natives and overawe them and keep them in order while the same number of troopers could not so well protect white men who scruple to draw a trigger in their own defence or in support of their defenders and therefore a larger force than is usually sent to an outstation would be required and this would be more necessary when the natives become aware that the missionaries declined fighting for the salvation of their property or their lives.[75]

The Commissioner's memo distils the strategy of frontier policing that had taken shape during the tenure of Warburton. The task of the Mounted Police was to provide protection for settlers on the frontier, and it was also understood that settlers would use firearms 'in their own defence or in support of their defenders'. Given the limited number of available police in remote areas, it was taken for granted that armed settlers would assist them in 'repelling' Aborigines, and that an essential part of keeping them 'in order' was to 'overawe' them with displays of force. These were the things expected of 'combatants' in Australia's frontier wars.

The missionaries approached Commissioner Hamilton to provide them with police protection, and an outpost was established at Kopperamanna in October 1867.[76] Despite the presence of the police, by the end of 1867 the Moravians decided to abandon their missionary enterprise and return south. The police camp was then shifted to the Lutheran establishment at Killalpaninna, where it remained for the next five years, mostly under the control of Mounted Constable Samuel Gason. The presence of the police did not end the anxieties of the missionaries at Killalpaninna. On 21 April 1871, they found themselves in the middle of a tribal feud. In the evening, Reverend Homann was confronted by the spectacle of dozens of Aboriginal people crowding onto his verandah, imploring his protection. The kin of an Aboriginal man who had been killed a month before had formed a Pinya or revenge expedition and were camped nearby, awaiting the moment they could extract retribution. The missionary allowed them to remain, and told them he would only use his firearm if they attempted to enter the house. After an anxious night, the Pinya expedition left at sunrise the next morning.[77] Mounted Constable Gason, who had been in the region for some years now, wrote to his superiors that he had no doubt they would return in the near future with a stronger party in to fulfil their law as it required, and two more troopers were dispatched from Blinman.[78] For the time being, the augmented patrol was maintained, though the Commissioner questioned the 'desirability of incurring a large expenditure for the purpose of assisting a religious sect'.[79] By 1873, the Lutherans were told that if they remained, they 'must be prepared to protect themselves'.[80]

Most tellingly, the concerns over the Pinya expedition had raised questions about the extent to which the police should interfere with what Gason had acknowledged as Aboriginal law. Commissioner Hamilton wrote to the Chief Secretary for advice:

> I should be glad to know if the Honourable Chief Secretary wishes the police to interfere with them at a distance so far from the settled districts or if he thinks it would be advisable to embroil the Police in the quarrels of the Aborigines of Australia.[81]

The Chief Secretary's simple answer was 'no'. His reluctance to involve the police in matters relating to traditional Aboriginal law is revealing, for it highlights yet again the often unarticulated reality of Aboriginal people's legal status: although technically British subjects, they maintained a de facto sovereignty until such time as European authority could be firmly established. Bringing Aboriginal people within the authority of the Crown first required their actual subjugation. This pattern had been visible since the beginning of settlement. A telling marker of change across the colony's frontiers, as across other colonies, was that it was only once European authority was considered to be secure that police were willing to arrest Aboriginal people for *inter se* crimes.

The rule of law?

By the 1870s the worst of the violence between Aboriginal people and settlers in South Australia south of the Northern Territory border had run its course. This is not to say that there were no subsequent clashes, or indeed that there were no subsequent battles that have gone unreported, if not unremembered – but that merely reminds us of the remarkable architecture of Australia's 'strange frontier'. By the 1870s European authority had effectively been established, and it was established by force of arms. This is a point that should not be passed over lightly; dozens of Aboriginal nations occupying a region which in combination exceeded the land mass of Europe were dispossessed through force of arms. In so far as the rule of law did work on the frontier to recognise Aboriginal people as British subjects, it did so principally to punish them, indicated by the considerable figure of 22 Aboriginal people tried and executed over the first 30 years of settlement.

The clash on Elder, Dean and Hack's Lake Hope property in 1865, in which Charles Neumann died, was perhaps the last significant frontier battle to be fought in South Australia's 'land wars', or at least the last to be publicly documented. It had its sequel in 1866 in a court case which tellingly underscored the fact that even after 30 years of frontier violence, the ideal of the rule of law was hopelessly inadequate at providing the protective shield to Aboriginal people that it promised.

In the aftermath of the attack on Dean's camp, a well-armed party of 15 police and settlers under the command of Inspector Roe endeavoured to track down the Aboriginal party responsible. After weeks on the track they gave up, having met with only a few Aboriginal people during their search.[82] In all likelihood the attackers, an ochre party, had returned north. Yet some time later, two Aboriginal men known simply as 'Frank' and 'Freddy' were arrested when found in the vicinity of Lake Hope, and in September 1866 were tried for the murder of Charles Neumann. The case against them was exceedingly weak, since only one of the three European witnesses who gave evidence claimed to be able to identify them as being present during the attack on Dean's party. In the absence of any more incriminating evidence against them 'Frank' and 'Freddy' were acquitted, but what makes this particular case unusual is that it has a documented 'back story' that is usually missing in the reporting of such clashes. For whatever reason, Thomas Elder made available to the press a series of letters that he had received from Dean which detailed the events surrounding the attack, and some of the correspondence was published in the *Register* in the months leading up to the murder trial. As the editor of the *Register* observed, having failed 'to affect a peaceable removal' of Aboriginal people from his run, Dean and his men had engaged in a concerted campaign to forcibly drive Aboriginal people from it.[83]

When the trial of 'Frank' and 'Freddy' for the murder of Charles Neumann took place, then, this correspondence was in the public domain. At the closure of the trial, the Defence counsel's summing up and the Judge's directions to the jury provide us, in microcosm, with all the contradictions and flaws of a system that had been in operation for thirty years but was still incapable of dealing with cases such as these. The defence counsel's address to the jury began with a sketch of the circumstances: 'a party of armed squatters and their assistants armed themselves for the purpose of dispossessing the blacks of certain cattle they alleged the natives had taken away, and after an encounter were driven away, and the cattle fell into the hands of the whites'. It was regrettable, he stated, that rather than calling upon the police for legal redress, the leader of the settler party instead organised 'an armed party with which to meet the natives', which went out expressly 'for the purpose of shooting the blacks in the event of any resistance being offered'.[84] His simple and honest summary distilled the essence of violence between Europeans and Aboriginal people on the Australian frontier: settlers used force of arms to drive Aboriginal people from the land of which they had been dispossessed, and Aboriginal people, to the extent that they could, used force to resist that dispossession.

The Judge's summation of the case also went to the heart of the legal system's inability to deal with these simple truths of invasion and dispossession. Ever since the foundation of the colony, he began, Aboriginal people 'had been subjects of Her Majesty', but in this case he 'scarcely knew in what terms to direct the jury'. 'Equal justice', he said, should be administered to all inhabitants of this colony, regardless of their class, but it was 'almost a matter of impossibility in a case like this'. The two prisoners' lives were 'trembling in the balance,' but they 'probably did not understand a single word of the evidence', much less the nature of the proceedings; nor did they have 'the opportunity of calling witnesses on their behalf, who might describe the events of the affray from their own point of view'. How difficult it must be, he continued,

> for persons who had never known anything of the existence of English law, who had never heard that the Queen of England had any authority over them ... to realise the position in which they were placed.

Going to the particular circumstances of the case, he pointed to the nature of settler behaviour: 'this affray arose out of proceedings which never could have been contemplated unless blacks had been the persons. If a dispute similar to this had arisen, and white men had shot cattle, who would dream of arming 10 of his servants for the purpose of recovering cattle by force of arms?' These were matters that were more properly the province of government, he said, 'because he felt that the very attempt to apply our forms and processes equally as between the prosecutor and the prisoners did, in reality, involve a grievous inequality'.[85] After three decades of colonial experience, at the very point where European possession of the country had effectively been secured, the judicial system was still struggling with the issue of the equitable application of the rule of law. It was an issue only ever resolved when force of arms had rendered the dilemma redundant.

By the early 1870s, European settlement was expanding further north into South Australian administered Central Australia. The next two decades would demonstrate that the same cycle of violence would turn again, and the legal status of Aboriginal people as British subjects would yet again be put on hold as their subjugation to colonial authority was affected through force. When the recently built Barrow Creek telegraph station on the new Overland Telegraph Line was attacked by a Katyetye party in February 1874 and the station master killed, Police Commissioner Hamilton considered the Aboriginal group responsible to be 'bound by no law'. Mounted Constable Samuel Gason, who had just arrived there from his Killalpaninna posting, led four punitive expeditions over the coming months. Official reports indicate that perhaps eleven Aboriginal people were shot by police in the course of those expeditions; other evidence suggests the fatalities may have been as high as ninety.[86] In authorising these punitive expeditions, the Commissioner himself recommended 'that a too close adherence to legal forms should not be insisted upon'.[87]

By 1884, numerous sheep and cattle stations were established in the vast district around Alice Springs. Pastoralists' complaints about Aboriginal attacks on their stock led the South Australian government to establish a Native Police corps under the command of Mounted Constable William Willshire to patrol this sprawling region, despite the controversial reputation the Native Police held in Queensland. As Willshire put in, his 'duty was to see that the wild natives do not interfere with the white settlers'.[88] The Native Police operated under Willshire over the rest of that decade and into the next, earning a notoriety for violence against Aboriginal people that only ended in 1891 when Willshire was eventually charged with the murder of two Aboriginal men, and the Native Police disbanded.[89] The history of policing on the Central Australian frontier in the last decades of the nineteenth century suggests an exact repetition of the same legal dilemmas that had defined South Australia's more southern frontiers since the colony was established: it was only possible to fulfil the rule of law when Aboriginal resistance had been effectively suppressed, and Aboriginal people themselves effectively subjugated.

This lesson was one that continued to be voiced by contemporary commentators towards the end of the nineteenth century. In February 1878, a teamster named James Ellis was murdered by Aborigines at Granite Creek in the Northern Territory. In an account of the aftermath of Ellis' murder, the *Advertiser* reported that Mounted Trooper Stretton had led a combined party of police and settlers who had gone out and 'administered to the savages a lesson not at all too severe for the occasion'.[90] They had tracked suspects to an Aboriginal camp three miles from the murder scene and, although it was not clear 'whether any attempt to capture the miscreants was made on this occasion', the camp was fired upon and 'seventeen blacks bit the dust'. In their use of firearms, the writer argues, the police party had acted in accordance with their duty, for 'the blacks are British subjects, and were in armed rebellion against lawful authority'.

Yet having attempted to justify these shootings in terms of 'lawful authority', the reporter's following comments pinpointed precisely the inconsistencies in the workings of the rule of law on the settler frontier. Legal niceties, he wrote, such as evidence and testimonies in a court of law, were cumbersome technicalities that had little relevance for frontier conditions and which had all too often led to 'farcical' results. Dragging witnesses thousands of miles to a place of trial was 'costly and cumbrous', and had any Aborigines in this case been arrested and brought to trial, technical flaws such as want of an interpreter 'would probably have caused an acquittal' and allowed the culprits to 'commit fresh atrocities on the first opportunity'. In assuring his readers of the correctness of police action in this case, the reporter referred back to the lessons learnt from the early years of the province. That was a time, he writes, when 'aboriginal outrages were punished by the authorities promptly, and in a manner to strike fear into the breasts of the savages'. This early-established tradition now offered a valuable precedent for managing new frontiers in the Northern Territory, because 'when the natives find that crime is followed ... by condign and certain punishment, they learn to hold the white man and his laws in awe, and then, but not till then, kindness may be successfully employed in dealing with the sons of the forest'.[91]

In 1871, a few years before police administered a 'severe lesson' to Aborigines for Ellis' death, leading businessman Emmanuel Solomon hosted a dinner for 500 'old colonists' in the Adelaide Town Hall to celebrate the 35th anniversary of the colony's foundation. One of the speakers was John Brown, 'the oldest man present who heard the Proclamation of the colony read'. As Emigration Agent, Brown had been closely involved in the planning of the colony and, like his compatriots, had bristled at and resisted the attempts of the Colonial Office and those 'Saints in the House of Commons' to provide for the protection of Aboriginal people by insisting that the settlers negotiate for the purchase of land and that an independent Protector of Aborigines be appointed.[92] Yet ironically, in his address to the old colonists Brown adopted those very foundational principles as a point of pride. The early colonists, he said, had 'avoided one of the greatest difficulties, and one which was more anxiously anticipated than any other – that was with reference to the natives. They established relations without bloodshed, without injury, or without loss'. Although relations with 'the natives' had been 'a source of great difficulty and anxiety in England,' South Australia's pioneers, 'assisted by those in authority, and guided by justice and right feeling,' had 'managed to introduce themselves to the blacks without difficulty of collision. They did not begin by shooting the aborigines, or anything of that kind.'[93] Brown's focus on the moment of foundation, and the ideal behind it that South Australia's settlement was more peaceful than elsewhere, merely served to obscure the history of violent dispossession that ensued. Even as John Brown was toasting the founding fathers with this speech, legal violence was continuing in the colony's expanding far north. But in commemorations of foundation, a belief in South Australia's sense of difference was already becoming firmly established.

Part 2

NEGOTIATING THE PAST

Chapter 8

PAVING THE WAY BACK

With the passage of years, settlers became 'pioneers'. Although of course Aboriginal peoples have always known their history, white Australian stories of settlement put to the foreground the pioneer as a figure of origins, and in this process necessarily forgot the people whose dispossession secured the pioneer's identity.[1] Yet this process of national forgetting was never total, because the lived events relating to Aboriginal and settler encounters often remained central to pioneering accounts.[2] Despite the frequently covert nature of frontier land wars, the violence that took place in the course of dispossessing Aboriginal people of their lands did in fact figure quite prominently in the foundational memoirs of those settlers who came to define themselves as pioneers. Its telling, however, was perhaps inevitably framed by the emergent pioneer legend, which in turn was shaped by two forces that gathered momentum in the last decades of the nineteenth century: the burgeoning mood of nationalism, and the consolidation of social evolutionary thought.

A sense of nationalism was strong well before the nation was formalised with Federation in 1901. The children of the 'founders' had grown-up in the prosperous post-gold rush years. The census of 1881 showed that more than 60% of the South Australian population had been born in the colony.[3] In 1871 the Australian Natives Association, an organisation for native-born European Australians, was formed in Victoria and by the 1880s branches had been established in all the Australian colonies.[4] The Association's motto was 'Australia for the Australians', and as converts to the doctrine of racial purity, their Australia would be a white Australia. While pro-Australian, it was not anti-British; its aim was to forge 'a Greater Britain under the Southern Cross'.[5] In telling their story this generation endeavoured to find a distinctive vocabulary and set of stories that defined their experience as Australians.

By the 1880s too, the concept of the 'doomed race' was well-entrenched in popular culture and Aboriginal people were re-cast as living relics of prehistory.[6] For Edward Stirling, Director of the South Australian Museum, Aboriginal people were 'zoological survivors,' and he expressed the view that 'no people upon earth possessed a more ancient ancestry and less mixed pedigree than the aborigines of Australia, and that they more nearly than any other exhibited the characters and conditions of prehistoric man'.[7] The newspapers of the day, when discussing themes such as development, progress, race or nationalism, routinely drew on the idea of the natural evolution of civilisation as a variation on the ideal of 'survival of the fittest'.[8] The long-held belief that Aboriginal people were a 'dying race' was now attached to a powerful explanatory device. In evidence given to a parliamentary Select Committee in 1899, the anthropologist Frank Gillen described Aboriginal people as 'interesting barbarians' worthy of preservation, but added: 'Scientific investigation goes to show that the aboriginal race began to decay many years before the white man set foot in Australia'.[9] As accidental survivors in the modern world, Aboriginal people could be conceived of as existing outside of time and history.

In the arena of state-sanctioned commemoration, stories of land won through the spilling of blood were largely invisible, subsumed to the burgeoning international interest in 'primitive' cultures. Like other colonies, South Australia's contributions to the colonial and international exhibitions that proliferated in the last decades of the nineteenth century routinely included artefacts and dioramas of 'primitive' Aboriginal life, alongside displays of local produce and industry.[10] Such displays were to become part of a 'sentimental vision' of Aboriginal people as primitive 'spectacle' that would frame white Australian commemorations of settlement well into the twentieth century.[11]

South Australia's Jubilee festivities year of 1887 made reference to Aboriginal people in much the same way as other Australian colonies did in this period, feting Aboriginal 'primitivism' in public displays, while Aboriginal people themselves were becoming increasingly coerced into the age of state supervision and control. In the Jubilee year and the years leading to it, the performance of Aboriginal 'corroborees' provided a ready forum for the public consumption of a form of Aboriginal culture which, sorted and sanitised, served the master narrative of colonial nationalism. In May 1885 a corroboree, performed by Aboriginal people brought from the mission stations at Point McLeay and Point Pearce, was held for the public's entertainment on Adelaide Oval, attracting a crowd estimated at 20,000.[12] The event was so successful that two further performances were held over the following weeks, attracting crowds of several thousand, and concluding with the Aboriginal dancers re-appearing in European dress to sing the National Anthem.[13] Even as these celebrations were taking place, South Australian mounted police were still employing punitive violence in central Australia to suppress Aboriginal resistance to European settlement.[14]

By the closing years of the nineteenth century, the Proclamation Day holiday on 28 December had become one of the State's most iconic 'sites of memory'. On that day, 'Old Colonists' and their descendants would gather to commemorate the State's foundation. The Governor was usually in attendance, together with representatives of the armed services, and at noon South Australia's gun-boat, the *Protector*, would fire a 21 gun salute.[15] As the likelihood of Federation loomed, commentators referred to Proclamation or Commemoration Day as South Australia's 'national day' and it was celebrated with gusto.[16] Tens of thousands of people celebrated its 'great annual fete'; tugs would bring visitors from the Port, while colourfully decorated watercraft of all varieties would ply the gentle waters of Holdfast Bay.[17] The city itself was decked out with streamers and bunting, carnival attractions did brisk business on the foreshore, and in the nearby parks the visitors were entertained with athletic events ranging from the 100 yard dash to the 'greasy pole'. While the holiday-makers enjoyed outdoor fun, the official guests gathered in the Town Hall to enjoy luncheon and to hear speeches.[18]

Given the prominence that the status of Aboriginal people had in the Proclamation itself, and the fact that it was read aloud at every annual commemoration, it is notable how infrequently the issue of Aboriginal rights was raised in the copious editorials and lengthy speeches that marked the event in the last years of the nineteenth and early years of the twentieth centuries. Typically these would praise the enterprise of the first settlers – 'the Pilgrim Fathers of the State' – the progress of the colony and, not uncommonly, draw attention to South Australia's sense of difference.[19] In 1909, for instance, the *Advertiser* observed that 'the colonisation of South Australia was the first true attempt at the utilisation of the empty lands of the Commonwealth'. True it was that other colonies were earlier established, but 'in every case the taint of convictism was present'.[20] In 1914, the *Advertiser*'s editor noted that in South Australia 'the foundation was laid very early of those free institutions which one after another was adopted in this progressive State. The ballot, the Real Property Act, religious freedom, and land reform are some of the contributions South Australia has made to the general cause of progress'.[21] The Proclamation Day editorial in 1920 claimed that South Australia was the only State to be established with no 'birth-stain'.[22]

Among these claims to exceptionalism, discussions of Aboriginal people or issues were almost absent apart from formulaic references to how, at the genesis point, 'savage tribes faded before the advance of civilisation'.[23]

The *Advertiser's* 1890 account of Proclamation Day is particularly telling in this regard. The journalist mentioned that the Proclamation was hanging on the wall of the Mayor's parlour, that its language was 'as noble as the sentiments it expresses' and, as it had not been published for many years, 'it will doubtless be read with interest by the descendents of the pioneers'. The verbatim text of the Proclamation was reproduced, followed by a description of the events of the day:

> It was not only the white inhabitants of the colony who were taking an interest in the success of the colony; those with darker skins now roll up quite as a recognised thing, and in a staid and solemn Oriental manner appear to enjoy an outing on the beach as much as anyone. The Afghans came in considerable numbers from the neighbourhood of Little Gilbert Street under the leadership of their [Haji Mulia], and their imposing turbans of many colors, embroidered caftans, and linen [continuations] lent a very variegated air to the part of the crowd in which they moved. The Lean Hindoos in striped calico garments were also well represented; Chinamen were present – in the day time – and even a dozen aboriginals lazily wandered up and down on the lookout for a bit of 'bacey or anything else in the way of creature comforts which might come their way.[24]

There is no comment on the significance of the Proclamation for Aboriginal rights, and when Aboriginal people are mentioned they are securely anchored in stereotypes of the day, subsidiary to the greater exoticism of Afghans, Hindus and Chinese.

Yet one context of Proclamation Day celebrations that did give rise to discussions of South Australia's early relations with Aboriginal people was the part of official speeches extolling the virtues of the explorers. By the close of the nineteenth century Charles Sturt's foremost place in the pantheon of founding figures had become a repeated theme in Proclamation Day speeches. More than just signifying South Australia's discovery and settlement, he came to personify the story of South Australia's peaceful origins. When Governor Sir Henry Galway spoke at the Commemoration Day luncheon in December 1914 he observed that South Australia, 'compared with other parts of this great continent, never had any real difference with the Aborigines', something owed to the 'words of wisdom of Governor Hindmarsh in the proclamation which has just been read'. 'In fact', Galway continued, 'Charles Sturt, one of the most illustrious of South Australia's pioneers – (Cheers.) – went through all his journeyings without shedding one drop of Aboriginal blood'. Galway contrasted Sturt with New South Wales' explorer Thomas Mitchell, who had conducted his expeditions 'in the spirit of a soldier campaigning in a hostile country'.[25] At the level of such official commemorations, 'benevolent intentions' were becoming a primary motif in a developing narrative of South Australia's historical relationship with its Aboriginal subjects, though it was one that was only fitfully recalled.

The frontier in the pioneering story

In the last decades of the nineteenth century histories of the colony were increasingly appearing in print, sometimes published to coincide with landmark years or events. Their sub-titles hint at the story being told: they are about 'resources', 'productions' and 'progress'.[26] In 1876 William Harcus published *South Australia: Its History, Resources and Productions*, a history that presaged the marginalisation of Aboriginal people from the national story. 'It is a small matter', wrote Harcus, 'to supplant the aboriginal inhabitants of a barbarous country and to secure possession of their land'. The difficulties of colonisation, he argued, lay elsewhere:

> It is the battling with nature, conquering the soil, holding on against capricious seasons, fighting with the elements and compelling the earth to yield what it never yielded before – a reward for man's toil – that the real triumphs of an old people in a new land are seen.[27]

For many of Harcus' contemporaries, however, the story of how Aboriginal people were 'supplanted' and 'possession of their land' was secured was no small matter at all. In the closing years of the nineteenth century they would write about it at length. After all, for first-generation settlers this had been an integral part of their story. By the time South Australia celebrated its Jubilee year in 1886, personal accounts of the frontier experience – of attacks from and reprisals against Aboriginal peoples – were becoming a staple of the memoirs and reminiscences that were regularly appearing in the colonial press.[28] At the same time, Harcus' elaboration of the 'difficulties of colonisation' suggests the way in which that story would be told: it would be the story of the pioneer. By the 1870s, a pioneer legend was emerging nationally as the principle expression of the 'Australian experience'. In the well known words of J.B. Hirst, the pioneer legend is one that 'celebrates courage, enterprise, hard work, and perseverance',[29] and at its heart were the experiences of the men and women who had 'opened up' the country. In South Australia, the first generation of settlers were penning their experiences for the benefit of future generations in carrying on the legacy they had left. This was a time for consolidating the historical landscape through which settlers and their descendants sought, through remembrance, to secure their stories of rightful possession.[30] While a generation earlier the difficulties of the settler frontier had been subject to protracted and controversial debate – about the status of Aboriginal people as British subjects, and about the use of force in ensuring their subjugation – a generation later, it served to personalise and highlight the 'bitter experiences' endured by settlers in a burgeoning saga of pioneering life.[31]

John Wranthall Bull's popular memoir and pseudo history *Early Experiences of Colonial Life in South Australia* was first published in 1878, and he wrote extensively about the 'troubles' with Aboriginal people in the colony's difficult early years. As a successful pastoralist, Bull's approach to Aboriginal subjugation on the settler frontier was pragmatic. Where Aboriginal resistance interfered with colonial expansion, he argued, the 'irregular' but ultimately 'necessary' course to follow was the use of deadly force.[32] Bull's account of South Australia's early frontiers quickly became a source for other foundational memoirs of the period, such as Sub-Inspector of Police Alexander Tolmer's *Reminiscences* of 1884 and James Hawker's similarly named *Early Experiences in South Australia*, published in 1899. The result, by the end of the century, was the creation of a surprisingly cohesive and circular foundational history which did not disguise the violence of the frontier, but enlisted it as a sign of the hardships of pioneer life, and as a justification of Aboriginal dispossession. By the time the nineteenth century drew to a close, the frontier experience had been told, retold and circulated in published and family memoirs, fictional novels and serialised newspaper features. Well known events such as the *Maria* massacre, the Rufus River massacre and the troubles at Port Lincoln were now recounted as examples of the treachery of 'bloodthirsty savages', and of the vulnerability and courage of early pioneers.[33]

If an emergent story of pioneer struggle was one framework for early reminiscences of the frontier experience, another was the increasing popularity of colonial adventure romance fiction. A particularly Australian brand of colonial adventure romance, including novels such as *The Lost Explorer* (1890) and *The Secret of the Australian Desert* (1895), entered the popular domain in the late nineteenth century as a localised variation on the imperial romance.[34] Colonial romance fictions proved to be an inspiring influence for many South Australian pioneering reminiscences, such as 'Reminiscence of Port Lincoln' by 'H.J.C.', which appeared in *The Observer* in 1880. H.J.C. was the pen-name of Henry John Congreve, who had worked on pastoral stations around Port Lincoln in the early 1850s. Although some readers probably took his 'Reminiscence' as history, it was in fact a piece of historical fiction.[35] Certainly an air of factual authenticity frames the story: it begins for instance with an account of the writer's own arrival in the young settlement, provides detailed descriptions of the country, and is based on real events. But as historical fiction, the primary purpose of Congreve's story is to create a more generalised frontier saga in which the pioneer's experience of 'trials and hardships' is played out against Aboriginal foes. Beginning with the butchery of Captain B- (Captain Beevor, killed near Port Lincoln in 1849), a party of Aboriginal warriors goes 'in search of fresh victims to gratify the appetite thus sharpened'. Moving on to 'the next station', they find the hut where Mary, the 'young and pretty wife' of a shepherd, is discovered with her baby. As Mary raises her eyes to heaven, she is overcome by the savage 'chief' Multulti and his murderous followers. In spite of her brave efforts to save herself and her child, Mary is brutally murdered and her child's brains are dashed out against the chimney.

This is of course a reference to the spearing of Annie Easton in 1849 in her hut at Elliston, shortly after Beevor's death. Predictably, Congreve makes no mention of a possibly prefiguring event, the poisoning of Aboriginal people with arsenic-laced flour which the Commissioner of Police suspected may have motivated her and Beevor's killings, since his point is not to relate historical events but to dramatise the pioneer experience.[36] The horrific image of the baby's brains being dashed out on the chimney is for instance pure invention; the baby was left unharmed. As we know, stories of reprisals for Annie Easton's death have circulated ever since and remain strong in local social memory to the present day, most famously as accounts of 'the Elliston massacre' in which some two hundred Aboriginal men, women and children were alleged to have been forced over the coastal cliffs to their deaths. Two years after Congreve's 'Reminiscences' appeared in *The Observer*, local writer Ellen Liston published her short story about the same events, 'Doctor', in the same paper, and it is likely that Liston drew as much from Congreve's fictionalised tale of Easton's murder as much as from other circulating stories.[37] Yet unlike Congreve's tale, which focuses on the drama of Easton's death, a central theme in Liston's story is the settler reprisals that followed. In this story, the Aboriginal leader 'Coolmultie' who attacks the lone woman is as savage a villain as fiction can imagine. Yet at the story's end, after the settlers have completed their 'crusade' against the local tribe,

Liston allows her narrator to reflect on the many deaths exacted by settlers in exchange for one of their own. While Congreve drew on settler tribulations purely in the service of colonial melodrama, Liston's story identifies something of the culture of settler violence that leaves behind an echo of disquiet.

Simpson Newland's historical novel *Paving the Way*, first published in 1893, also drew on the lived experience of the South Australian frontier, and it referenced events which included not only the deaths of settlers at Aboriginal hands, such as the *Maria* massacre of 1840, but also the deaths of Aboriginal people at settler hands, most notably the Avenue Range Station massacre of 1849 for which James Brown was charged but never tried. Despite its conventional framework of colonial romance, Newland is at times openly critical of settler violence and greed for land in the campaign for Aboriginal dispossession:

> the white man was the personification of ruthless, all-absorbing power; never satisfied without the whole of the country ... Those who have seen the process must unhesitatingly though reluctantly admit that the darkest stain on Australia's fair fame is her treatment of the aboriginal race. We found them a happy, healthy people and wherever we have come in contact with them, in less than fifty years we have civilized them off the face of the land.[38]

'The time has not yet arrived'

The fact that first generation settlers wrote so frankly and openly about violence between Aboriginal people and Europeans should not surprise us. Many of the authors were 'eye-witnesses' and some of them participants in events that constituted significant crises in the colony's foundational years. The massacre of some two dozen survivors of the *Maria,* and its impact on the young colony, could hardly be ignored: it remains the largest European death toll in any one frontier event in Australia's history. Aboriginal attacks on overlanders in the early 1840s, at a time when the colony was virtually bankrupt, threatened the economic viability of the colony and culminated in a clash at the Rufus River in which at least 30 Aboriginal people died – again, this was probably the largest Aboriginal death toll in any one punitive expedition in the colony's history. The attacks on settlers in the Port Lincoln district in the 1840s were concerted to an extent that surprised the colonists, and led to repeated petitions for government protection. The European death toll was already significant and threatening to grow when Governor Grey dispatched a military detachment to the region in the expectation that soldiers would be able to quell the violence. These three events, which became centre-pieces of late nineteenth century accounts of frontier violence, were all initiated by Aboriginal people, and the punitive responses were all sanctioned by colonial authorities. There was little reason for later chroniclers to feel coy about elaborating them in detail.

However, much of the violence on the frontier was not of this sort; it was not sanctioned by the state, and it lay beyond even a pretence of the rule of law. While some writers in the late nineteenth century remembered key moments of state-sanctioned violence to justify the history of Aboriginal dispossession and feed the growing mythology of the pioneer, others alluded to a more secretive, less morally certain aspect of the Australian frontier experience, one that was less easy to tell. This was a more localised and personal experience of what Tom Griffiths describes as Australia's 'strange frontier', a frontier not easily given to a 'romance of heroes and campaigns'. Those colonists who viscerally felt the 'fear and distain' that accompanied settlement – who felt required to raise their weapons and fire upon Aboriginal people at times when there were no police, let alone military detachments to support them – often felt the need to be circumspect in their remembrance. In theory, Australia was colonised, not invaded; Aboriginal people were not 'enemy aliens' against whom war could be waged, but British subjects protected by the law. Even in retrospect, these 'founders', itching to tell of the dangers and dramas they faced as they established their lives in a new world, needed to be cautious about what they revealed.

In the early 1850s Johnston Frederick Hayward was one of the first settlers to establish a pastoral property in the southern Flinders Ranges. The historical record reveals that he was involved in a number of violent clashes with Aboriginal people, the most significant of which entailed the murder of one of his shepherds. Having made his fortune, Hayward returned to England and lived out the remainder of his life as a country gentleman. In these later years, probably the 1880s or 1890s, Hayward wrote a memoir of his time in Australia which remained unpublished until 1929. Replete with allusion, his memoir shows a palpable tension between a desire to reveal and an imperative to conceal the violence of those times. The early years were difficult and dangerous, he tells his reader, but the 'nigger hunts', as he puts it, 'gave a zest to life that was not wholly disagreeable'. Yet despite the many years that have passed, he is still loath to incriminate himself. One of the stories he tells concerns the murder of his shepherd Richardson. In the aftermath of Richardson's murder, with rumours abroad that Aboriginal people in the district were about to attack his station, he resolved 'to attack them before they commenced their raid'. He describes in detail his preparations for a dawn attack, but then concludes, 'beyond giving them a good fusillade …

I doubt we did more than frighten them awfully'. Rumours, he adds, that fifteen Aboriginal people had been killed by his men soon dwindled to five, 'and then just one'. Of the Aboriginal man arrested and imprisoned for Richardson's death, Hayward writes that when he was eventually released from prison and returned to the district, he soon received that 'punishment he so richly deserved'. Although Hayward leaves his reader in no doubt that the man was killed in retribution for the shepherd's death, he is constrained merely to imply it.[39]

In 1885, Mounted Constable Wurmbrand reported the killing of one Aboriginal man in a clash with police in Central Australia. Missionaries at the nearby Hermannsburg mission complained to authorities that they understood 17 people had been shot. When asked for clarification of his report, Wurmbrand denied the charge, and reasserted that only one man had been killed while resisting arrest. His account was accepted.[40] Many years later William Benstead, manager of Glen Helen station who accompanied Mounted Constable Wurmbrand on this patrol, referred to the incident in an unpublished memoir. Warrants were held for the arrest of those they were tracking, he wrote, 'so on this occasion we ran no risks as far as our necks were concerned; but all the same, caution was used, and whatever happened, it was usually reported as having successfully dispersed the natives; it read better.' 'What happened that day,' he continued elliptically, 'it is a thing of the past, and of little use writing up now; but I am sure that seventeen out of this lot never killed or troubled anyone else.'[41] Even years after the events they describe, settlers, writing only to an audience of family and friends but still aching to tell their stories, felt as reticent to fully confess what they had done as they had when the events had originally transpired.

This opaque aspect of frontier culture is more likely to be more transparent in journal accounts or reminiscences that were not written for publication, and that only appeared in print decades later when the eyewitness accounts of early pioneers were being sought out for publication. Alexander Buchanan's diary of his overland journey with sheep from Sydney to Adelaide in 1839 was not published until 1924, when it appeared in the *Proceedings of the Royal Geographical Society*. In the editorial introduction, Buchanan is given a place as a great pioneer of the early days of the colony. He is introduced as a man of 'great repute' and 'high character', who in his lifetime commanded 'respect and confidence' to such a degree that his name was known as 'a household word'. This reputation as a respected pioneer is apparently untarnished by his following narrative, in which he liberally gives accounts of the Aboriginal people he and his party shot during the course of their months-long overland journey. What clearly emerges from his account is that a deliberate culture of terror prevailed in subduing any possible obstacle to the overlanders' progress through the country. But despite writing daily accounts in his journal of Aboriginal people fired upon and killed by his party, Buchanan maintained the culture of secrecy. Near their journey's end, when he was asked 'if the blacks had been troublesome', Buchanan applied the necessary caution and did 'not say we had shot any'.[42]

Whether dealing with privatised violence or with well known events that involved state-sanctioned action against Aboriginal people, most settler accounts of the frontier experience engage in some way the story of conflict with Aboriginal people. For the mainly first-generation settlers who were now producing their narratives as revered pioneers, these encounters were often at the heart of their experience. Some accounts dramatise violence as a vital element of a pioneer adventure narrative, some express a moral ambivalence about Aboriginal dispossession, while others use a vocabulary of concealment that both reveals and disguises the realities of violence. Mostly, though, violence is remembered in terms that serve the burgeoning sentiment of nationalism, with its celebration of the figure of the pioneer. What these foundational accounts demonstrate is a partial kind of remembrance, one that recalls and at the same time forgets. As Simpson Newland noted in his Preface to *Paving the Way* in 1893, 'the time has not yet arrived in the life of Australia when the historian or novelist can write with an untrammelled pen'.

Chapter 9

THE GREAT AUSTRALIAN WHISPERING

The future of the past: 1900–1920s

By the beginning of the new century, and with the decline of the 'eyewitness' pioneers who had recorded their memoirs, the living memory of conflict on South Australia's frontiers retreated considerably further backstage in the building of a foundational story. Now a state within the new nation, South Australia began more consistently to nurture a pride in the idea that, since foundation, it had always been more benevolent and benign in its treatment of Aboriginal people than was the case elsewhere. Discussions in the press about Aboriginal matters became routinely couched in these terms. In 1909, for instance, an article about the need for protective legislation was prefaced with the assurance that 'Governor Hindmarsh's famous proclamation of the province of South Australia breathed a solicitous regard for the welfare of the aboriginal population.'[1] Despite the fact that concern for Aboriginal welfare – evident in documents like the Proclamation and the Letters Patent – reflected Colonial Office ideals more than settler sentiments, the idea of 'solicitous regard' for Aboriginal welfare began to be adopted more broadly as one of the state's markers of 'difference'.[2] While this foundational difference could be regarded as a source of congratulation, the place of Aboriginal people in the history of British settlement could also be seen as irrelevant to the present, rendered redundant by the passage of time and the 'inevitability' of Aboriginal disappearance. Despite the humanitarian concerns of the founding fathers, this writer continued, nothing had altered 'the practical result' that Aboriginal people had, 'with slight exceptions, disappeared from the greater part of Australia'.[3] They had no civil rights and warranted none, for 'the aborigine is a child, and needs for a long while to be treated like a child'. The ongoing neglect of Aboriginal people was justified on the basis that they were 'incapable of such social, industrial, intellectual, and moral progress as to enable [them] to take any real part in the nation.' This was the nub: with no place for Aboriginal people in the new nation's vision of its prosperous future, a presence in its past seemed to have little point.

Despite the fact that Aboriginal peoples' status as British subjects had been powerfully underscored at the point of first settlement in 1836, over the course of the nineteenth century no over-arching 'Aborigines Acts' were passed by the South Australian parliament. In theory of course, Aboriginal people continued to share the same 'rights and privileges' as other British subjects; indeed, in the 1890s some were exercising those rights by voting in colonial elections. However, for much of the second half of the nineteenth century the belief that Aboriginal people were a dying race was so pervasive that it seemed just a matter of time before they would cease to be a group about whom legislators needed to bother themselves. This era of calculated neglect changed in the years leading up to and following Federation, as most colonial or state parliaments passed dedicated 'Aborigines Acts'. The reasons for this change in Aboriginal policy are various, but central to it was the issue of 'race'. At a time when 'racial purity' was being hailed as a hallmark of national integrity, the fact that the 'half-caste' population was growing became a matter of concern.

South Australia was the last state to pass an Aborigines Act, not because the government had any doubt about the necessity of it, but because political expediency slowed the process. An Aborigines Bill, modelled on Queensland's *Aborigines Protection Act 1897*, had been brought before parliament in 1899, but objections to certain provisions saw it sent to a Select Committee for review. The pastoral lobby were its most vociferous opponents, objecting to the provisions that sought to protect Aboriginal people from exploitation, such as the requirement that pastoralists obtain permits to employ Aboriginal labour. Their objections won the day and the Bill was withdrawn. In 1908 the newly appointed Protector of Aborigines, William Garnett South, a former mounted constable who had served in Central Australia, discussed a proposed bill for the 'protection and control' of Aboriginal people in his Annual Report, emphasising that separate Acts were required for South Australia and the Northern Territory on the grounds that 'in South Australia proper the chief problem is the half-caste, who is yearly increasing'.[4] The Act would provide him with the ability to remove 'half-caste children' from what he regarded as the degrading influence of camps and the corrupting influence of older relatives. His vision was that Aboriginal 'full-bloods' would soon die out while the mixed descent population would eventually be 'merged into the general population'.[5] In 1910, on the eve of the Commonwealth's takeover of the Northern Territory, the

Northern Territory Aborigines Act was passed. South Australia's Aborigines Act, 'for the better Protection and Control of Aboriginal and Half-caste Inhabitants', was passed in 1911. The provisions contained in the 1899 bill, designed to control the employment of Aboriginal labour, remained in the Northern Territory Act but were excluded from the South Australian one.

The Act, like those already operating in the other states at this time, gave the government tremendous control over the lives of Aboriginal people. It gave the Protector power to remove children from their parents. Aboriginal freedom of movement was now strictly controlled; at the discretion of the Protector, Aboriginal people could now be confined to or removed from reserves, and whole districts could be declared off limits to them. Regulations under the Act gave the superintendents of Aboriginal institutions sweeping powers. Aboriginal people could now be removed from an institution or reserve for being 'habitually disorderly, lazy, disobedient, insolent, intemperate, or immoral'.[6] Refusal to obey a superintendent's 'lawful orders' could be punished with a fine or imprisonment. The regulations were akin to those that might operate in a prison or reform school. As Chesterman and Galligan have put it, after Federation and under the various Aborigines Acts of the early twentieth century, Aboriginal people were still technically citizens, but they were 'citizens without rights' who were systematically denied the rights and privileges routinely enjoyed by other Australian citizens.[7] With South Australia's *Aborigines Act* of 1911, the age of surveillance and control of Aboriginal people had truly begun.

In 1911, the same year as the *Aborigines Act* was passed, the Reverend John Blacket's *History of South Australia* was published in a revised and extended edition. An overview of the progress of the colony and its transformation into a twentieth century state, it takes the nineteenth century image of the hardy pioneer and turns him into the guardian figure for future generations. For Blacket, the pioneer did not belong in an age now past, but was the very character best equipped to serve the future needs of the new nation. It would be the future labour of the pioneer's descendants, rather than the decrees of politicians or lawyers, that would make the nation 'determined, energetic, masculine, and self-reliant'. The most valuable lesson to be carried down from the pioneers was that success only arises from having 'battles to fight', 'foes to conquer' and 'difficulties to surmount': for it is 'grappling with difficulties, contending with adverse circumstances, that made our pioneer fathers and mothers the men and women they were'.[8] This was a very evolutionary struggle in which, presumably as the 'losers' of progress, Aboriginal people were expected to fall by the wayside.

By the early twentieth century, then, the pioneer legend had not only become consolidated as a story of national origins, but also offered an ideal character to a nation anticipating its future prospects. As the twentieth century progressed the pioneering story would come to have increasing weight and influence, and in this story Aboriginal people would play a minor role, either as helpmates in or as obstacles to the pioneer's efforts. Of the pioneer's first struggles with Aboriginal people, Blacket had little more to say than that in the early days 'the native tribes were fierce and treacherous', and had tested the settler's patience by giving him 'much trouble'.[9] While the figure of the pioneer was coming to occupy a first place in the emergent story of a proud Australian nation, Australia in the early decades of the twentieth century was entering the age of Aboriginal policy defined by assimilation and governmental control. At the national level, as W.E.H. Stanner famously put it, a 'great Australian silence' settled like a blanket over the nation's consciousness of the history of colonisation and Aboriginal dispossession.

Although the days of the violent frontier seemed to be a barely recalled feature of the national past, in some parts of Australia they were an ongoing reality well into the twentieth century. In August 1928, in the Northern Territory now under Commonwealth jurisdiction, itinerant labourer and prospector Fred Brooks was speared on Coniston station by a Warlpiri party, apparently for abducting an Aboriginal woman, and in the following month, station owner Nugget Morton was attacked. A police party under the command of Gallipoli veteran Mounted Constable William George Murray undertook two punitive expeditions that scoured the country over several weeks. Murray's official reports of those expeditions documented twenty nine Aboriginal fatalities. Other reports suggest that Aboriginal lives taken in retribution for the station attacks were as high as 70.[10] The Coniston massacre took place almost twenty years after the *Adelaide Observer's* editor confidently observed that Aboriginal people had, 'with slight exceptions, disappeared from the greater part of Australia'.[11]

Only a couple of years before the Coniston Massacre, Rodney Cockburn published a series of sketches on the 'Pastoral Pioneers of South Australia' in the *Adelaide Stock and Station Journal* (1923–1927). It was, and remains, the most comprehensive record of those whose labour on the pastoral frontier led to the wealth now enjoyed by the state of South Australia. Those who, in their own words or by their known deeds, had recorded the 'troubles' of the pastoral frontier and documented their own violent retaliations against Aboriginal aggressions – figures such as Robert Leake, James Brown, Fred Hayward, Samuel Stuckey and Alexander Buchanan – are all present in the roll call of Cockburn's 'Pastoral Pioneers', and all receive a high place in the annals of South Australia's founding fathers.

Cockburn does not pass over their 'trouble with the blacks' in the course of listing their pioneering achievements; as in memoirs of the nineteenth century, such frontier struggles are called upon to demonstrate the pioneer's capacity for strength and resolution. Dealing firmly with 'molestation by the blacks' is a sign of the pioneer's 'bush heroism', similar to dealing with difficult country, isolation, and the occasional bushranger.[12] In the confident and nostalgic mood of the 1920s, the violence of the pastoral frontier could still be a natural wellspring for an inspiring pioneer legend.

Centennial celebrations

Through the 1930s, as Julian Thomas has shown, an historical culture emerged in Australia that was dominated by the theme of foundation.[13] Over the decade, a whole new field of historical writing was produced, including 'works of economic, political and administrative history, biography and general history, commemorative volumes and school textbooks', which in cementing a sense of the foundational past, aimed to project a sense of the bright national future.[14] At the same time, Australia was preparing for commemorations of British settlement both at national and state level. 1934 saw Victoria's centenary, 1936 South Australia's, and 1938 Australia's Sesquicentenary. On the national scale, Sesquicentenary festivities were primarily geared around presenting the image of a unified and progressive nation in which internal troubles were minimised.[15]

In this national climate it is hardly surprising that South Australia's official centennial celebrations in 1836 had little to say about the place of Aboriginal people in the foundational story, either in terms of their 'humanitarian' treatment by the colonial state, or in terms of the dramas of the frontier. Rather, commemorative activities served to celebrate not so much the achievements or failures of the past but, as Nicholas Thomas has noted, 'something of the nation' that came later.[16] Throughout 1936, the state paid honour to one hundred years of progress with a spread of special publications and activities. In November, South Australia's history as a province of the British Empire was celebrated with an Empire Pageant, performed on the Adelaide Oval for a crowd of almost 24,000 spectators. Involving performances of 14,000 children from the state's schools, it depicted the Yeomen of the Guard escorting an enthroned Britannia, and included tableaus of the empire's many colonies, from the Rajahs of India on elephant back, to boys dressed as Canadian 'Red Indians', to 'Wattle Blossom' girls performing a 'symbolic dance' of Australia. The pageant's combined tableaus offered a vision, as *The Mail* reported in its pictorial spread, 'in which Britannia gathered together all peoples of the British brotherhood of nations to pay homage to the flag'.[17] Also in November, two marble panels were modelled for the Centenary Memorial at Holdfast Bay, the site of the colony's Proclamation in 1836. One panel depicted Governor Hindmarsh reading the Proclamation, and the other told a story in marble of one hundred years of civilisation from the first overland journey of cattle to South Australia, to the building of the Overland Telegraph Line, to the moment of Federation.[18]

Centenary celebrations accelerated in December, in anticipation of Proclamation Day on 28 December. Throughout the month, local governments and schools across the state organised re-enactments of historic moments. These included the Glenelg Carnival's 'Proclamation Pageant', and a performance by the Marist Brothers College in Mount Gambier of the laying down of the Overland Telegraph Line.[19] The culmination of celebratory activities across South Australia was the Pageant of Progress, which coursed through Adelaide's main city streets for more than two miles and contained 236 floats. It was headed by an escort of Mounted Police dressed in uniforms of 1852, and led off with historic floats of Captain Flinders on the *Investigator* in 1802, Captain Sturt's journey of exploration along the Murray in 1831, and Governor Hindmarsh's landing in the HMS *Buffalo* at Holdfast Bay in 1836.[20]

In this celebration of European discoveries and arrivals, Aboriginal people appeared only fleetingly as the minor characters who prepared the historical stage for the main act. A 'Stone Age' float preceding Flinders on the *Investigator* captured this role, depicting twenty Aboriginal people in a wattle tree setting 'centuries in time removed from the white man'. In a nod to South Australia's pride in its humanitarian beginnings, Aboriginal people were also included in the float depicting Captain's Sturt's epic journey along the Murray. The float's image of Sturt and his men in their whaleboat while 'armed natives' menaced them with spears referenced Sturt's famed reputation as a conciliator in avoiding bloodshed in first encounters with Aboriginal parties and turning potential aggression to goodwill.[21] The last float to include Aboriginal figures depicted the arrival of Governor Hindmarsh on the HMS *Buffalo*, flanked by four Aborigines who added a picturesque touch 'as puzzled spectators of this historic event'.[22] Aboriginal people did not figure in the some 230 floats that followed in the Pageant of Progress; they had appeared to introduce the authenticity of nativeness to the story of white Australian arrival, and here their role ended. 'Nativeness' as a borrowed symbol of authentic Australianness appeared in other celebratory events, such as a Corroboree of 5000 Boys Scouts, which attracted visiting scouts from across the British Empire, and opened to the public with an admittance fee of 1/–.[23]

A special centenary issue of the *Advertiser* in September paid much attention to 'a century of progress', and devoted only one column to the subject of Aboriginal people as the 'vanishing race', 'an anachronism in a fast-moving world'. Having played their introductory role as shadowy extras to the main actors of history, they naturally exited the stage: 'These, then, were the people who flitted, like dusky shadows, across the background of a stage on which was enacted the drama of the settlement of the colony'.[24] In the Royal Geographical Society's *Centenary History of South Australia*, Aboriginal people appear again only as a kind of pre-historical sketch, an introduction to the more substantial story of settlement: 'Into the story, in a vague and shadowy way, came those pleasant, pathetic, nomadic people, the aborigines. As we occupied the stage they receded from it'.[25] Shadows without substance, who then depart in silence: this was to be their proper place on the stage of history.

In 1938, Australia celebrated its 150th anniversary of European settlement. The activities were focused mostly in Sydney, commencing on Australia Day, 26 January, and concluding on ANZAC Day, 25 April. The organising committee had Adelaide and Melbourne's recent centenaries in mind when planning its own re-enactments and parades.[26] Starting the celebrations was a re-enactment of Phillip's landing, held at Farm Cove rather than Sydney Cove to accommodate more spectators. As Phillip and his boatload of marines pulled ashore, they were met by two dozen Aboriginal people who had been shipped in specially from Western New South Wales to add colour to the re-enactment. Lieutenant Ball's misgivings at the appearance of these spear-waving 'Indians' were communicated to the spectators by loudspeaker, as were his instructions to disperse them. With the landing place secured, the Union Jack was raised and a *feu de joie* fired for King George III.[27] Like Adelaide's Pageant of Progress, Sydney also organised an elaborate procession of motorised floats, the 'March to Nationhood', featuring key moments of the young nation's history. Aboriginal people were again minor players, leading off the parade with a tableau depicting an Aboriginal family 'cooking possum outside their gunyah' as the 'before' preceding the inevitable 'after' of explorers, pioneers, arts and industry. If Aboriginal people were marginal, convicts, as a matter of policy, were entirely absent. Some protested at this omission but it was defended on the grounds that the aim was to reflect Australia's 'peaceful development and progress'. As Gavin Souter has put it, 'It was an early decision of the executive that there should be no representations of war scenes and ... it was equally undesirable to depict incidents of convict life in the colony'.[28]

As Aboriginal extras were being stripped down and painted up to take part in the re-enactment of Phillip's landing, Aboriginal leaders met to protest their treatment and demand their rights. For the Aborigines' Progressive Association, 26 January 1938 marked 'the 150th Anniversary of the Whiteman's seizure of our country' and they observed this 'Day of Mourning' with a meeting in Sydney's Australia Hall. The leading resolution protested 'against the callous treatment of our people by the whiteman during the last 150 years', and appealed for 'full citizen status and equality within the community'.[29] Speeches at the Day of Mourning urged equal citizen rights, ownership of land and the abolition of the Aborigines' Protection Board.[30]

'Honouring ... their obligations'

In retrospect, the Day of Mourning protest meeting in 1938 would come to be seen as the culmination of an inter-war campaign by Aboriginal people for civil and political rights. In New South Wales, William Ferguson and Jack Patten established the Aborigines Progressive Association and challenged the oppressive rule of the Aborigines Protection Board; in Victoria, William Cooper, Secretary of the Australian Aborigines' League, began circulating a petition calling for citizenship rights and a reserved seat for Aboriginal people in Federal parliament;[31] in South Australia, the Aborigines Progressive League, led by J.C. Genders, campaigned for a 'Model Aboriginal State'.[32] Aboriginal demands for citizen's rights were becoming increasingly voiced, from state to state and on a national stage. The commemorative events of the 1930s provided an opportunity for Aboriginal people and their supporters to challenge their marginalisation from a celebratory story of British settlement. David Unaipon, prominent Aboriginal activist and member of the Aborigines Progressive Association, marked South Australia's 1936 Centenary with a speech from the steps of Parliament House protesting against state surveillance and control over Aboriginal people.[33]

There was also a mood for change within the broader non-Aboriginal community. The anthropologist A.P. Elkin called for an end to the protectionist policies that had characterised the early years of the century and advocated what was regarded as a more positive policy of 'uplift'; but although

Elkin's influential book *The Australian Aborigines*, first published in 1938, paid honour in many ways to the richness of traditional Aboriginal culture, he regarded the only viable future for Aboriginal people as one of 'absorption'.[34] In 1937 the federal government called a meeting of State and Federal Aboriginal authorities in Canberra to discuss and co-ordinate Aboriginal policy. By the end of their deliberations they had agreed that the 'destiny of the natives of Aboriginal origin, but not of the full-blood, lies in their ultimate absorption by the people of the commonwealth'.[35] For William Cooper of the Australian Aborigines' League, absorption within the Commonwealth did not preclude the realisation of unfulfilled rights. Writing to the Minister for the Interior in October 1936, he emphasised that contemporary Aboriginal people were 'heirs with the white race of all the rights of British nationhood', but were also 'the descendants of the original owners of Australia,' and that title to their lands was not invalidated by conquest.[36]

While it seems inevitable that public celebrations happening around the country would have an air of settler triumphalism, the place of Aboriginal people in reflections on South Australia's history, while minor, was by no means invisible. A number of centennial publications brought Aboriginal people forth from the shadows, not in light of the contemporary rise of Aboriginal rights, but rather in order once again to remember the fraught frontier as an essential part of the pioneer legend. 'Story of the State: From Wilderness to Wealth in a Hundred Years' was published by the journalist Ernestine Hill in the *Centenary Chronicle*. Her piece reminded South Australian readers of many of the more dramatic episodes of violent conflict in the colony's early history – the murder of young Frank Hawson at Port Lincoln, the massacre of the *Maria* survivors on the Coorong and the 'troubles' on the Rufus River – as illustration of the hardships endured by pioneers in making 'the country safe for the settlers for all time', and their efforts in bringing South Australia to modern 'success and achievement.'[37] Ruth Hawker, the granddaughter of prominent pioneer George Hawker, published a centennial children's story in which a family of modern children journey back into the 'yesterday' of the early pioneers. Amongst the excitements they face is an Aboriginal attack on the homestead. This dramatic episode ends happily enough for them: while the girls and women remain stoic throughout, the men, aided by the modern-day boys, beat back the attacking 'savages' by shooting as many as they possibly can.[38] As centennial contributions to the pioneer legend, Hill's work harks back to John Bull's unapologetic tone of pioneer stoicism, while Hawker draws on the literary tradition of 'Girl's Own Annual'. In an age divided between increasing demands for Aboriginal rights on the one hand and the significant invisibility of Aboriginal people in commemorations of 'progress' on the other, these local commemorative stories served both to announce the violent history of the frontier and to disguise it within an orthodox story of the pioneer.

Yet if an orthodox pioneer legend provided one kind of framework for remembering Aboriginal people, the original intent embodied in South Australia's Proclamation provided another. A feature of the voices of disquiet that emerged in the 1920s and 1930s is that contemporary calls for Aboriginal rights were anchored in a sense of historical obligation and moral responsibility to fulfil the colony's original undertakings to protect Aboriginal rights. In 1921, for instance, Dr Herbert Basedow gave a talk in the Adelaide Town Hall in which he outlined his efforts to provide 'relief' to the 'natives of the interior,' and he reminded his audience of the colony's first Proclamation in which the Governor 'promised justice to the blacks and bespoke for them the kindly consideration of the white invaders'.[39] In 1929 a correspondent wrote to the *Advertiser* and protested South Australia's history of its treatment of Aboriginal people. Quoting extensively from the Proclamation, he emphasised particularly the pledge to punish with 'exemplary severity' any acts of injustice against them. 'Is it not an irony', he concluded, 'to speak of the rights of the natives being equal to those of the colonists, and can anyone point out how or where the privileges of British subjects have been allowed the blackfellow? It appears to me that the humane and generous intentions of Governor Hindmarsh have been studiously ignored, rather honored in the breach than the observance'.[40]

On the eve of South Australia's centennial year, prominent natural scientist John Burton Cleland addressed the Royal Society with the reminder that 'the proclamation read by Governor Hindmarsh at the establishment of the Province dealt with the rights and protection of the natives, and only one-third with the affairs of the white inhabitants. Governor Hindmarsh stated that the natives were to be considered as much under the safeguard of the law as the colonists themselves, and equally entitled to the privileges of British subjects.' He suggested that 'South Australians could not mark the centenary of their State in a better way than by honouring some of their obligations to the Aborigines'.[41] In a letter to the editor on the 'centenary effort', a correspondent argued that the current most important task was to enforce 'the proclamation of His Excellency Governor Hindmarsh' regarding justice to Aborigines.[42] Another noted Hindmarsh's promise to pursue 'every legal means to secure to the aborigines all the rights of British subjects', and asked whether the centennial celebrations would include 'anything worthy ... in living out those charges?'[43]

A similar sense of historical obligation drove the Aborigines' Protection League campaign in the late 1920s for the establishment of an Aboriginal State which would be governed by Aboriginal people themselves. The League attracted the support of campaigners such as Herbert Basedow and Dr Charles Duguid, as well as prominent Aboriginal activists including George Rankine, Mark Wilson and David Unaipon. J.C. Genders imagined that the experiment might be commenced in Arnhem Land and, if successful, be replicated in other parts of the country. A petition seeking the establishment of a model Aboriginal state, with 7,000 signatures, was put to the Australian government in 1927.[44] The plan was driven by a deep sense that an historical injustice had to be corrected. Aboriginal people, Genders wrote, were 'landless proletarians' whose lands had been over-run, and who 'wanted some of the land back which has been stolen'. For him, the recognition of land rights and self-government was not a radical innovation; it was the belated honouring of a 'time-honoured policy'. He reminded his readers that early Governors, like Gawler in South Australia, 'had definite instructions' that 'land was not to be taken' from Aboriginal people 'without their consent'. This was a 'sacred trust' that had 'been greatly neglected'.[45] Genders was an octogenarian at the time these proposals were made, a radical conservative who wanted imperial obligations honoured. As historian Andrew Markus has observed, some people humoured Genders for being 'ahead of his time', but Genders himself later reflected that 'in reality his ideas were 150 years out of date'.[46]

The Sturt re-enactment of 1951

The year 1951 offered a new opportunity for both national and state commemoration with the Jubilee of Federation. As they had done during the national and state commemorations of the 1930s, Aboriginal people used the occasion to promote their rights and culture. The Aboriginal production *An Aboriginal Moomba: Out of the Dark* was staged at Melbourne's Princess Theatre, sponsored at the urging of the Australian Aborigines' League by the Melbourne City Council, which feared the risk of another proposed Day of Mourning.[47] In an age of assimilationist policies, as Sylvia Kleinhert has argued, *An Aboriginal Moomba* served as an affirmation of unbroken Aboriginal cultural identity and ongoing political agency.[48] But across the nation, the event that most forcefully captured the public imagination was the re-enactment of Charles Sturt's epic voyage of exploration from

Sydney to the mouth of the River Murray. Sturt's original journey had been symbolically significant in unifying three states of the Federation, but it also held especial significance for South Australians, for his expeditions of 1830 and 1831 had been influential in the establishment of the South Australian colony.[49] The re-enactment of Sturt's journey would re-animate a foundational moment, one in which the complex history of British possession and Aboriginal dispossession would be channelled into the individual achievements of the explorer.[50] The expedition departed Sydney on New Year's Eve 1950, amidst 'a blaze of pageantry'. Crowds dressed in period costume sent off the expedition from Government House on what would be a six-week journey. Actors played Sturt and his second-in-command McLeay, while their crew was made up of members of the Australian Military Forces, and was supported by a convoy of army vehicles. The convoy travelled overland to Maude, on the Murrumbidgee River, where their whaleboat was launched into the river. The re-enactment would retrace each stage of Sturt's original journey based on the record of his journal.

The journey was followed avidly by the public. Each day the press reported on its progress, and each evening the Australian Broadcasting Commission put to air the 'Sturt Report,' which documented the expedition's progress, interviewed the crew about the events of the day, and spoke with local officials about their district. Anthony Sturt, the great grand-son of the explorer, was flown in from Britain to read for radio audiences daily accounts from Sturt's journal. The crew's arrival in Waikerie, in South Australia's riverland, is typical of the nightly broadcasts. It had been a day of wild winds; Grant Taylor, playing Sturt, had fallen into the river but had grabbed hold of a rope and was pulled out; another member of the crew had his nose broken, but they had battled through. The crew members marvelled at how much tougher it must have been when Sturt made the original voyage without the sort of back-up they enjoyed. An elderly pioneer was interviewed; she had arrived in the district in the 1890s, depression years. For seven years, she told the listeners, her family had lived in a house with hessian walls and an iron roof before they were able to move onto their 'block'. The achievements of the men, she said, had been marvellous.[51]

At each port of call locals would gather, many in period costume, to welcome the crew ashore. The crew, in turn, would present to the mayor a Memorial Scroll signed by the Governor-General, and local dignitaries would make speeches on the progress and industry of the district. Discussion of the 'explorers' would naturally flow into praise for the 'pioneers' and 'settlers': this was an assumed genealogy. The re-enactment, as one journalist put it, awakened appreciation of 'our heritage of resolution and resource'.[52] Such days would often end with a country dance in the local Institute Hall or packing shed. One can imagine the trails of dust rising on rough country roads as locals streamed into the town.

The story of encounters with Aboriginal people was not central to the unfolding re-enactment, but nor was it absent. On the North-West Bend Station the owner made mention that the homestead had been built on an old Aboriginal graveyard, and that Canoe Trees dotted the district. At Mannum, a local reported that all the Aborigines had disappeared from the district by the 1890s – the still pervasive view that only 'full-bloods' were 'real' Aborigines serving to make invisible the significant indigenous population of the Murray Lands. But most pertinently, the re-enactment provided South Australians with the opportunity to remember its foundational story of the enlightened treatment of Aboriginal people. While the official Centenary celebrations of 1936 had barely referenced Aboriginal people except as passing pre-historical witnesses to the moment of European arrival, the 1951 re-enactment of exploration provided space to highlight Sturt's historical reputation as conciliator and protector of Aboriginal people, and as the personification of South Australia's difference. This was distilled in a speech made by Governor Willoughby Norrie at Murray Bridge. In the course of his voyage, Norrie said, Sturt was met by some 6,000 'dark coloured natives', but not once did he order aggressive action; it was this quality of 'tact and forbearance' that made Sturt great.[53]

This theme of 'tact and forbearance' formed a kind of sub-narrative to the journey. Along the way, Aboriginal groups were brought forth from mission communities like Point McLeay (Raukkan) to welcome the passing party. Sturt's well-known encounter with a hostile Aboriginal party on the Murray River, whose aggressive approach he disarmed with friendliness, also received picturesque reference. At Gundagai and at Narrandera, painted Aboriginal people formed part of the costumed crowds who greeted the whaleboat crew.[54] Only one crude joke marred the preferred story of mutual goodwill. On 20 January at Red Cliffs, members of the local RSL sub-branch posing as 'hostile natives' 'attacked' the whaleboat with practice army hand grenades, blank-loaded rifles and sulphur dioxide stink bombs. When the 'explorers' stepped forth for their 'famed parley with the natives', the 'blacks' began 'a fiendish dance' and pelted the crew with tomatoes.[55] It is impossible to know whether Governor Norrie – an Englishman – knew anything of Australia's frontier history when he praised Sturt's 'tact and forbearance', but his was a resonant observation. Indeed, it echoed Governor Galway's earlier speech observations about Sturt in 1914. As the frontier expanded inland, and as subsequent generations wrote about the events that unfolded, the motif of settler 'tact and forbearance' became stubbornly persistent. Sometimes it was a sentiment that masked violence, but more often it attached itself to accounts of violence, as a justification of sorts and as a reinforcing reminder of pioneer stoicism.

For two months, Australians had sat in their living rooms and listened intently to this 'Australian story' designed to unify a nation. In late February, the crew of the expedition arrived in Adelaide – the prophetic terminus of Sturt's journey – where they were greeted by the thousands who took part in a welcoming street pageant, and feted at a civic reception. Those who missed the radio broadcasts could watch the re-enactment in Movietone News footage at their local cinema. As a Jubilee celebration, it had been an enormous success in 'arousing a sense of history, and in making that history live'.[56] The legacy of Captain Sturt had inspired thousands who followed the re-enactment in 1951, for as a foundational historical figure he was compelling. Not only did he represent a nostalgia for 'the heroic age of Australian exploration', but he conveniently reinforced South Australia's belief that in its dealings with Aboriginal people, its history represented one of humanitarian concern and forbearance.[57]

Bitter Springs

Just six months before the Sturt re-enactment, Australians had the rare privilege of witnessing their frontier history on the silver screen with the release of the film *Bitter Springs*.[58] Produced by Britain's Ealing Studios, it was one of three films they made at the time centring on frontier experiences in different parts of the old empire. The film starred Chips Rafferty as the pioneering settler Wally King, Bud Tingwell as his hot-headed son, the English Vaudevillian Tommy Trinder as the 'new chum', and Michael Pate as Mounted Policeman Ransom – the last an actor who, ironically, would spend much of the '50s typecast as a 'Red Indian' in Hollywood westerns. *Bitter Springs* was filmed in South Australia's Flinders Ranges, the South Australian government having won its bid against Queensland to secure the film. Its purpose was to tell a story of pioneering days, when a man 'would face the desolation of the desert and 600 miles of inland emptiness in the hope of building a life.' At the same time, as part of that story, it would tell of 'the encroachment by white pioneers on the aboriginal hunting ground'.[59] Despite the fact that it was a popular 'Australian Western', *Bitter Springs* also had a serious story to tell of frontier relations.

South Australians embraced the novelty of having a motion picture made on home ground. Local department store John Martin's took the opportunity in a full-page advertisement to salute 'a fine pioneer effort – the Australian-made film "Bitter Springs"' – and to advertise itself as 'a pioneer South Australian Institution'.[60] Stories of the film's progress filled the newspapers, but the good feeling was somewhat marred by news reports about the treatment of the Aboriginal extras who would act in the film. Though never named in the credits, 115 Aboriginal people had been brought from the West Coast by the Aborigines Department, under government directive, to play as extras. In the rail journey from the West Coast to the Flinders Ranges, they were accommodated in cattle trucks and a dog-box, without seating or sanitary facilities. When they eventually arrived at Quorn, where they were to join the film team, no accommodation had been arranged for them: 'off-loaded in the rain into open trucks and driven to the oval', they were obliged to shelter all night in a refreshment room until a tarpaulin was erected to house them.[61] When interviewed, the Railway spokesperson directed the responsibility for the travel arrangements to the State Aborigines Department, whose spokesperson stated that they had been satisfactory.[62]

When the film finally premiered a year later, the treatment of the Aboriginal actors was forgotten in the flush of pride in South Australia's achievement in holding the film's world premiere. The newspaper which had reported on the Aboriginal actors' transport to the set by cattle truck a year earlier now reported on the film's 'orchids-and-ermine premiere, with handsome furs and elaborate corsages dominating the women's dressing', and attended by the State's Premier and the nation's Prime Minister.[63] Soon after the film opened, a small article appeared reporting that 'Aborigines who played in the film "Bitter Springs"' were begging along the East-West railway line.[64]

If the treatment of the Aboriginal actors left much to be desired, how were their characters' rights portrayed in the film's saga of pioneer life? Set at an unspecified location in 1900, the story focuses on a pioneer family travelling north to establish their property. The film follows their hardships as they drive their sheep and battle with a wagon-load of all their earthly possessions through rough passes and seemingly interminable plains. When they finally reach Bitter Springs, they find no water. About to turn back, a Mounted Constable arrives at their camp, and pointing to a nearby creek bed tells them, 'if you dig down into the sand a couple of feet you'll get all the water you want'.[65] He also offers a caution and a prophecy: the Karagarni have lived on that land a thousand years, perhaps two; someone pays eighty quid at an office in Adelaide, and all of a sudden the Karagarni don't have a tribal land anymore; it's a sheep property, and the police are 'left to clean up the trouble'. 'The land', he adds, 'is sort of sacred to them, and they don't budge easy'. In response to the settler's claim that he's not going to let 'no stone-age blacks stand in my road,' the Trooper offers some advice: you can 'shove them off', you can 'ease them off', or you can 'find some way of taking them in with you'.

The film follows the settlers as they dig their wells, graze their sheep and build their homestead. Their relationship with the Aboriginal people is cautious at first, sometimes friendly – the New Chum's young son is seen throwing boomerangs with Aboriginal boys – but when the settlers interrupt a hunting party and shoot a kangaroo that the Karagarni had been patiently stalking, relations sour. The Aboriginal group spear a sheep and carry it off; the settlers pursue them to retrieve the animal. In the stand-off that ensues, the settler's son shoots and kills an Aboriginal man. The Karagarni respond by burning down the lovingly built homestead and abducting the New Chum's young son.[66] Bereft of supplies and cut off from their only source of water, Bitter Springs, the settlers' fate looks grim. In desperation, Wally King's son goes for water, but as he returns he is struck by a well-aimed spear. Meanwhile, the New Chum has inveigled his way into the Aboriginal camp and, with comic guile, rescues his son and sets off for the Trooper. Just as the settlers are preparing to fight their way out, the Trooper arrives with reinforcements and drives off the tribe.

The jubilant liberation of the homestead cuts away to a scene of Aboriginal people confined in a cart, ready to be 'eased off' the land. Wally King, as he attends to his injured son, observes that 'fighting don't get you nowhere', and asks the Trooper to remind him of the advice he had given earlier: you can 'shove them out', you can 'ease them out', or you can 'take them in with you'. World-weary after having tried and failed at the first two options, Wally opts for the third. The scene cuts away to a new scene of busy station life, Aboriginal men happily shearing alongside the settlers, before the screen fades to black.

The film's portrayal of violence between Aboriginal people and settlers on the frontier has some insightful moments. Not unrealistically, it portrays the origins of that violence as a contest over land and resources. The portrayal of the Aboriginal tribe, while often patronising, nonetheless presents their response to the settlers' incursion into their country as both considered and reasonable: deprived of water, and their food supply threatened, what options did they have but to attack the settlers' stock and, eventually, to meet violence with violence? Interestingly, given the historical role of Mounted

Police in protecting pastoral stations, the Trooper is the one character who displays some sympathy and understanding of the situation. He is the one who cautions Wally that he is moving onto Karagarni land, and he is the one who has to do the settler's dirty work by 'easing' the Karagarni out after the siege of the homestead. The director originally intended to end the film with a massacre of Aboriginal people, but was persuaded by the studio to end it on a lighter note.[67] Despite its rather idealised picture, the resolution of the film, which shows Aboriginal people working side by side with white pastoralists on the station, carries a degree of truth. Once the worst of the violence had passed, Aboriginal people in remote Australia did become the backbone of labour in the pastoral industry. At the time the film was made, they were the mainstay of the cattle industry.

The fictional Mounted Constable's dictum calls to mind an observation that the settler Robert Warburton made about the Central Australian frontier in 1890, although in this instance, he did not represent it as a set of alternatives as much as an inevitable sequence:

> Of course things are difficult and will be until the blacks knuckle under, but not before, when you have subdued them you can be as kind as you like to them, its only the same old story of pioneer settlement over and over again ever since Australia was first settled.[68]

'Ultimate absorption into the general community'

Whereas accounts of the violence that accompanied frontier life, however circumspect, figured fitfully in commemorative publications and works of popular culture, academic historians through the mid-twentieth century indicated little interest in this thread of the national history. Richard Broome has mapped how textbook histories and encyclopaedias of the mid-twentieth century had little to say about the place of Aboriginal people in the national story beyond a role as 'fleeting cardboard figures on the backdrop of European exploration'.[69] Gordon Greenwood's *Australia: A Social and Political History* of 1955 for instance, which was sponsored by the 1951 Jubilee Celebrations Committee, barely referenced Aborigines at all.[70] Other national histories produced between the 1930s and 1950s, such as Max Crawford's *Australia* (1952) and the multiple-authored, nine volume *Australian Encyclopaedia* (1958), did include significant reference to Aboriginal people, but primarily through the filter of an anthropological eye, and shaped by contemporary assimilationist values. If Aboriginal people were seen to have a future in these expositions on the past, it was one seen to be best served, as Norman Tindale put it in the *Australian Encyclopaedia*, 'by their ultimate absorption into the general community'.[71] Perhaps the most culturally enduring of historical works to be produced in this decade was Russel Ward's *The Australian Legend* (1958), which sought to trace a distinctive Australian character back to the 'nomad tribe' of white bush workers. Although it includes some references to Aboriginal people, it does so through a somewhat uncomfortable attempt to make white bushmen 'heirs to important parts of Aboriginal culture', in the sense that they too needed to develop an understanding of the land. Given that Ward's bushmen were often on the frontline of European expansion, the absence of comment on any further relationship between Aboriginal people and 'bushmen' seems a surprising omission. Indeed, Ward's claim in the book that bushmen 'rarely went armed' is astonishing.

A year before Ward's book was published, Douglas Pike published what remains the definitive account of South Australia's foundation and settlement, *A Paradise of Dissent*. The most extensive discussion of relations with Aboriginal people in Pike's book is his reference to the violence on the overland route from New South Wales in 1841. However, the reality of violence was not Pike's point in itself; his point was about the cut-backs and economies Grey was forced to introduce into the bankrupt colony, and his refusal to allow 'rumours of desperate villainy to interfere' with them.[72] Perhaps the most interesting omission in *Paradise of Dissent* is the absence of any reference to the often fraught and seemingly interminable discussions about the rights and protection of Aboriginal people that occurred on the eve of settlement. For most of 1835, the Colonial Office and the Colonisation Commissioners exchanged correspondence on the issue, and especially the question of Aboriginal rights to land. Pike glosses the issue in a few sentences.[73] Five years later, Pike would publish a broader national history, *Australia: The Quiet Continent* (1962). As in his history of South Australia, the history of Aboriginal dispossession barely rates a mention; indeed, Australia's history of 'peaceful isolation' is seen to be one undisturbed by 'battles or revolutions'.[74] In representing Australia's history as primarily peaceful and positive, Pike and his contemporaries were not writing bad history but simply writing history for their time. At the national level, mid-twentieth century Australia was the heyday of assimilation policies and the heartland of the 'great Australian silence'. Although attitudes would change dramatically in just a few short years, the fate of Aboriginal people was still thought to be absorption into the body of the Commonwealth. As such, their part in the story of South Australia's foundation and development was thought to have little or no contemporary valency.

Regional foundational histories

While in this period there was little engagement with the place of Aboriginal people in the national story or in state commemorative events that expressly articulated with the national story, regional histories of the mid twentieth century much more visibly engaged the stories of frontier encounter, just as memoirs and reminiscences of the nineteenth century had done. Aboriginal communities, of course, have always remembered this history,[75] but local histories produced by settler-descended communities also remember the struggles between settlers, Mounted Police and Aboriginal people on South Australia's early frontiers as a key part of the story of regional origins. These regional histories do not so much bring to the surface a set of colonial secrets that had been 'hidden' as keep in view a local knowledge about the violence of frontier encounters that has never disappeared from public circulation.

Many of these South Australian regional histories were published from the 1950s onwards, and were written to commemorate the jubilee or centennial years which marked the beginning of European settlement in the district. Often they have been prepared by descendants of early settler families, or by local council committees. Broadly, their aim is to describe the region's history of settlement and express a sense of regional identity, both past and present. In chronicling the times of early settlement, these histories often describe the state of relations between settlers and the local Aboriginal people. In doing so, what kinds of patterns do they illustrate?

Not surprisingly, these settler-descendent histories usually provide a general description of frontier life that reflects a pioneer perspective: according to its trajectory, European settlement was met with some degree of Aboriginal resistance; settlers and their property were attacked, and acts of retribution followed; eventually, mutual bloodshed resolved itself into some kind of settled peace. This repeated story of how settlement took place is in keeping with most nineteenth century accounts of the pastoral frontier, which commonly regard Aboriginal people as the aggressors, and settler and police acts of retribution as a regrettable but necessary response. But unlike most nineteenth century accounts, which commonly position Aboriginal resistance as unprovoked, most twentieth century local histories identify Aboriginal attacks on settlers and their property as motivated by invasion of country and increasing starvation, or as retaliation against settler crimes such as sexual exploitation of Aboriginal women. As one local history of the Yorke Peninsula puts it:

Whom shall we blame; The British Government who declared the whole colony to be 'Waste Lands of the Crown'; the sheep farmers who despoiled the hunting grounds and the waterholes; the overseer who was commended by the press for protecting his employer's interests, or the shepherds who ravaged the native women and disrupted the centuries-old social system?[76]

As pioneering memoirs had done in the late nineteenth century, local histories of the twentieth century tend most commonly to remember the key, well-known episodes of frontier conflict. In the south east, for instance, the *Maria* massacre stands out as the most memorable event. Much discussed at the time for its legal and ethical repercussions, this event has remained perpetually in public circulation ever since. Sometimes it appears in regional histories as an example of the tragedies that beset settlers in the early days of the colony, but it is also related as a reminder of the loss of life that took place on both sides of the frontier in the course of European settlement and Aboriginal dispossession.[77] An account from 1944 that is unusual for its time in raising an Aboriginal perspective is Gordon Hastings' sketch 'Tragedies of the Coorong'. Hastings relates the story as it was told to him by his Ngarrindjeri neighbour, Mr Cameron, whose grandparents had been members of the original party that had found the shipwreck survivors and assisted them in their initial journey along the coast. Their viewpoint structures the account from the start, and is unbroken over the span of a century with Hastings' assurance that Mr Cameron 'related the story to me as it was told to him by the old couple.'[78] In local histories of the upper Murray, the remembered key event is the Rufus River massacre of August 1841, which is recalled as 'that disastrous battle when the Rufus Creek ran red with the blood of the natives'.[79] On the west coast, where Aboriginal resistance to occupation was more concerted and targeted than anywhere else in the colony, the memory of the fraught frontier is also alive and well, recounted in stories of settlers attacked, stations abandoned, and reprisals against Aborigines that took place at the hands of the 96th military regiment sent in by Governor Grey in 1842, which 'indiscriminately' took Aboriginal lives.[80]

While such key moments and their aftermaths were sufficiently well-known to have kept a constant shape over a century of retelling, other less public frontier episodes have remained in circulation through an unbroken process of mythologisation. One of the most enduring yet malleable of these relates to the case of James Brown. As we know, there is little room for doubt that in 1849 James Brown murdered nine Aboriginal people on his Avenue Range sheep station, not far south of the Coorong where several years earlier the *Maria* massacre had taken place. An Aboriginal witness guided Protector of Aborigines Matthew Moorhouse in exhuming the remains of the Aboriginal bodies that had been burnt in an attempt to disguise the evidence, and he identified James Brown and his hutkeeper Eastwood as present at the scene of the crime. Eastwood fled the district and the colony, but the murder charge against Brown came before the Supreme Court in June 1849. Although the evidence against him was considered strong, the lack of willing witnesses to corroborate the Aboriginal witness' account meant that the case was unable to go to trial, and the charges were eventually dropped.

In most published local histories, James Brown remains a known name, and the murder charge against him is a remembered part of his historical reputation, but with two significant variations. One enduring thread of his story is that he was charged with poisoning an unspecified number of Aborigines, not shooting nine. The other more curious detail is that he is credited with a great feat of horsemanship: after laying the poison bait, he is said to have taken to his horse and ridden up the Coorong to Adelaide, thereby establishing a water-tight alibi. How might we account for these alterations, which enter the story like 'Chinese whispers' and replace the historical event? More importantly, what do these alterations tell us about the shape that the violence of the frontier takes in historical memory?

It is likely that in shifting from shooting to poisoning, the charge against James Brown became blurred in local memory with another case which occurred almost simultaneously elsewhere in the colony, that involving shepherd Patrick Dwyer who was strongly suspected in May 1849 of poisoning five Aboriginal people with arsenic-laced flour near the settlement of Port Lincoln. Like Brown's hutkeeper Eastwood, Dwyer fled the colony before he could be charged, and the case was dropped. Over time, the image of poisoned flour or poisoned waterholes became a familiar aspect of stories about violence perpetrated against Aboriginal people on the Australian frontier. While there are relatively few documented cases of poisoning in South Australia, rumours of the practice did circulate in the south east, and were recorded by the lay missionary Christina Smith.[81] Given that suggestions of such a practice existed already as a suspected part of the south east's frontier culture, and that the charge against Dwyer on the west coast had occurred within weeks of the charge against Brown, it is likely that these two events became conflated as one in public memory.

Brown's momentous horse ride to create an alibi could also readily have arisen from conflated sources. Brown's hutkeeper Eastwood did in fact flee the district to Encounter Bay before boarding a whaling vessel and leaving the colony. But the more enduring source is Simpson Newland's popular novel *Paving the Way*, the historical romance first published in 1893. In Newland's novel, which drew on the Avenue Range massacre, the parts of James Brown and his hutkeeper are played by the fictional characters of Roland Grantley and his mate 'Darkie'. Frustrated by lack of adequate police protection against 'marauding' Aboriginal sheep stealers, they take vengeance into their own hands, slaying a number of their Aboriginal enemies and burning the bodies. When authorities in Adelaide decide to 'make an example' of them, Grantley gives his worker his best horse, enabling Darkie, a potentially incriminating witness, to flee the district. *Paving the Way* was an influential historical novel of the late colonial period and it remained in print until the late twentieth century. While it is certainly possible that James Brown undertook a difficult horse ride worthy of memory – at the time of his murder charge, he was obliged to report to police in Adelaide, which was indeed a long ride from Avenue Range – it is probably Newland's fictionalised version of Darkie's wonderful ride to evade the law that has entered into twentieth century stories about James Brown, and remained there ever since. Just as Newland drew on the living memory of history to shape his fiction, so too has his fiction helped to shape the living memory of history.

Yet what is most striking about James Brown in local memory is not so much that the details of his story have changed over time, but that he is remembered largely for his gumption and skill in undertaking a great horse ride, more than for the crime that is known to have precipitated it. The story of Brown's magnificent horsemanship receives comment in almost every twentieth century local history which mentions him, and overtakes what one could otherwise expect as repulsion at the likely fact that he murdered an Aboriginal family group. What might have led to this change of emphasis, where disquiet about the murder of nine innocent people becomes all but erased by admiration of the pioneer's impressive horse skill? One likely influence in maintaining Brown's reputation as a memorable pioneer into the present day is Rodney Cockburn's sketch in the 1920s series 'Pastoral Pioneers of South Australia'. Cockburn's tribute to James Brown begins with an account of his status as a great benefactor to the colony in establishing, through a bequest in his name, the charitable institutions Kalyra hospital and Estcourt House. Cockburn remembers Brown as an 'eminently worthy' figure in the state's pioneer history. He also refers to the 'suffering' Brown received 'at the hands of untamed blacks', and the 'severe setback' Brown experienced when he became 'involved in a charge of poisoning a blackfellow'.[82] In Cockburn's account, Brown's 'involvement' is reduced from a charge of shooting nine Aboriginal people to poisoning one, and he absolves Brown from even this crime by adding the assurance that he 'emerged from the trial with a clean escutcheon, a jury of his fellow countrymen finding him not guilty'.[83] As we know, James Brown was never acquitted of the murder charge, because willing witnesses could not be found to enable the trial to proceed.

Cockburn's 'Pastoral Pioneers' was published when the pioneer legend was still in the making. Yet it has continued to be influential as a source for local histories published in subsequent decades. Tom McCourt and Hans Mincham's 1987 local history of the Coorong and lower Murray draws extensively from Cockburn's sketches in its chapter on 'Pastoral Pioneers'. In their account of James Brown, Cockburn's account is repeated without editorial change, including the assertion that a jury found Brown innocent.[84] Interestingly, their account also includes reference to Brown's skill as a horseman, yet here it stands alone as a feature of his memorable reputation, now completely disassociated from his crime of murder: 'He was a great man in the saddle, and is credited with having ridden a horse from Naracoorte to Adelaide in a little over a day'.[85] The enduring story of James Brown's fabulous horse ride is an instance of the way that a mythologising process works to create a narrative of frontier life that is on the one hand specifically local, and on the other emblematic of the Australian pioneer experience.

A similar process can be seen in accounts of the otherwise unmemorable death of John Hamp, the shepherd killed by Aboriginal people on Eyre Peninsula in June 1848.[86] John Hamp's body was found a distance from his hut with a number of spear wounds and a deep laceration on the side of his head, probably made with the cross-cut saw he was carrying. Government Resident Charles Driver reported to the Colonial Secretary that the murder was particularly violent, the dead man's head having been 'sawn nearly half round with a hand-saw'.[87] In local accounts of the twentieth century, the death of John Hamp has become tied to the gruesome detail that his head had been cut off and placed in a camp oven, where it was found by his son John Chipp Hamp.[88] Possibly this particularly gothic detail originates with John Chipp Hamp himself, at least as told by locals who had known him. Over the twentieth century this detail became a regular feature of published reminiscences within the region up to the 1970s, its authenticity either asserted or questioned but cemented in local knowledge.[89] Just as James Brown's crime has probably become conflated with Patrick Dwyer's, the 'head in the camp oven' story drifts from the Eyre to the Yorke Peninsula, appearing in relation to the death of the shepherd William Bagnall, who was killed by Aborigines in May 1851 on Milner Stephen's run, three years after the killing of John Hamp. Bagnall was apparently resented by the local Aborigines, both for sexually exploiting Aboriginal women and for training his dog 'to bite the natives whenever he saw one'.[90] When found, his body was mutilated, and police considered that 'his own indiscretions' had led to his death.[91] In a local history published in 1972, the detail relating to Hamp's death has transferred to Bagnall's with the discovery of 'his head placed in a camp oven', locating the source of this story with 'Local tradition'.[92]

It is hardly surprising to see separate events from the frontier compressed or crossed with others, since twentieth century accounts frequently draw on the same set of nineteenth century accounts which also reference one another. Books like John Wranthall Bull's *Early Experiences of Colonial Life in South Australia*, Alexander Tolmer's *Reminiscences of an Adventurous and Chequered Career at Home and at the Antipodes*, James Hawker's *Early Experiences in South Australia*, and Simpson Newland's *Paving the Way*, among others, became key sources of South Australian historical memory; well-thumbed copies could probably have been found in most local libraries. While they draw upon the memoirs and memories of contemporaries, they in turn are often drawn upon as sources for twentieth century regional histories.

Whether or not such details as the head in the camp oven or the unforgettable horse ride are assumed to be authentic, their existence serves to enrich a localised sense of history by keeping alive the hardships experienced or the achievements earned by the early pioneers of the district. The key difference between these two particularly enduring stories, of course, is that John Hamp's murder by Aborigines is remembered for its brutality, whereas James Brown's murder of Aborigines is deferred to the memory of a spectacular horse ride. It is surely not surprising that such dramatic, if apocryphal, features might attach to remembrances of the frontier era. Each detail adds local specificity to the region's frontier history, and at the same time gives the frontier a generalised character with the pioneer experience at its heart.

Yet many regional histories of the twentieth century also acknowledge that settlers often operated beyond the reach of the law. Sometimes European violence is excused as desperation brought on by Aboriginal stock theft and by an absence of sufficient police support, and at other times it is sheeted home to the less reputable characters who inhabited the isolated reaches of the early colony: shepherds who were of a rough and unsympathetic nature, or ex-convicts from other colonies.[93] Yet the names of respected pastoralists, such as Yorke Peninsula settler George Penton, also recur as examples of a legal double standard whereby Aboriginal lives could be taken without charge or conviction. Penton and his neighbours were known to have organised punitive actions against local Aborigines, to have shot at least three, 'and not one conviction recorded'.[94] Such individuals serve as a reminder of how white men took 'the law into their own hands and ministered summary justice'.[95]

Beyond the question of how 'blame' is apportioned for the violence of the frontier, what can we take from the fact that, from the late nineteenth century and throughout the twentieth century, violent clashes on the frontiers of settlement continued to be recorded and re-recorded as a key aspect of regional origins? To a significant degree, the continuing visibility of these stories indicates that local historical knowledge has never been subject to the same kind of silence on the history of the frontier that pertained for so long at the national level. Well known events from particular regions have never disappeared from public circulation. The loss of life is remembered on both sides. On the one hand, cases of settler fatalities at Aboriginal hands remain firmly remembered as a sign of the tragedies of remote settler life.[96] On the other hand, settler violence emerges as something discomforting, something that draws forth a side of pioneering life that 'we would like to forget', but is nonetheless remembered.[97]

Chapter 10

PLACING THE PAST IN THE PRESENT

The 1967 Referendum and the politics of change

While through much of the twentieth century white Australia had largely ignored, or only partially remembered, the terms of Aboriginal dispossession and the continuing neglect of Aboriginal rights, Aboriginal people knew their history only too well, and by the 1960s white Australians were beginning to hear their calls for reform. The 1967 Referendum marked the culmination of a generation-long civil rights campaign by Aboriginal people. While technically the Referendum changed very little – amending two discriminatory clauses in the constitution – its symbolic importance was much more far-reaching. Supporters of change campaigned on the basis that it would extend 'citizen's rights' or 'equal rights' to Aboriginal people. The more than 90% of the Australian population who voted 'yes' were voting to the redress of injustices of the past and for the acceptance of Aboriginal people, without discrimination, into the broader Australian community. At the time, it was regarded as the day Aboriginal people 'got the vote', or became citizens, and many people still think of it in those terms today. As a number of scholars have recently pointed out, this is both a misrepresentation and a mis-remembrance of the Referendum. Aboriginal people had always been citizens, albeit citizens systematically denied many of the rights and privileges enjoyed by non-Aboriginal people. Furthermore, many of those rights and privileges had already been won by 1967. The right to vote, for instance, was extended to Aboriginal people at the Commonwealth level in 1964 and individual states were already over-turning discriminatory legislation. However, the Referendum galvanised the emerging mood for change and gave the Commonwealth a clear mandate to take a lead in Aboriginal affairs.

In particular the Referendum also marked a turn toward the recognition of Aboriginal rights achieved on the basis of cultural difference rather than cultural surrender. During the campaign the anthropologist W.E.H. Stanner was interviewed on national television and firmly rejected the idea that Aboriginal people were a 'stone-age people, a primitive people'; he wanted to 'kill the notion stone dead'.[1] For generations assimilationist presumptions had constructed Aboriginal culture according to a deficiency model; it was something that had to be reformed. A new respect for Aboriginal culture emerged as something 'different' rather than 'inferior'.

South Australia was at the forefront of this shift toward cultural pluralism. In 1962 the government introduced a new Act that removed many of the restrictive and segregationist provisions of the *Aborigines Act 1934–39*. Although assimilation was still embedded in government policy, attitudes were beginning to change. In 1964 the anthropologist Ted Strehlow said of assimilation that it was 'only a new name given to old and discredited methods of forced cultural change which have been employed in Australia for the last century and a half'.[2] Don Dunstan, who as Minster for Aboriginal Affairs and later as Premier was a strong advocate for change, called for a new policy of 'integration'. The Aboriginal Affairs Board explained the new policy in 1964:

> 'Assimilation' itself has some implications that are not particularly clear and have aroused disquiet especially at the thought that Aborigines may lose their cultural identity as a people and become simply members of the community, distinguished only by their colour. The alternative is integration which suggests that Aborigines might join the white community on equal terms and yet retain the right to maintain both their physical and cultural identity so far as the latter does not conflict with the law of the land.[3]

The reforms of the Walsh and Dunstan Labour governments were extensive. In 1965 the *Aboriginal and Historic Relics Preservation Act* was introduced with the intention of protecting Aboriginal Heritage. In 1966 Dunstan introduced *The Prohibition of Discrimination Act* which had the effect, among other things, of making illegal what had been socially enforced 'colour-bars' within the community. In 1967 further amendments were introduced to the *Aborigines Affairs Act* which provided additional powers for Aboriginal people to administer their own reserves, because it was 'considered desirable that the Aboriginal people should be encouraged to run their own affairs'.[4]

One of the most significant reforms of this era was the passage of the *Aboriginal Lands Trust Act* in 1966, which gave control of Aboriginal reserve lands to a board made up entirely of Aboriginal people. It is generally regarded as the 'first legislative acknowledgement of Indigenous rights to land in Australian history'.⁵ Significantly, when Dunstan introduced the Bill to parliament he reached back into history to give legal authority and moral legitimacy to these changes. This Bill, he said, was a significant step in the treatment of Aboriginal people not only in this State but in Australia. 'The Aboriginal people of this country are the only comparable indigenous people who have been given no specific rights in their own land.' 'It is not surprising', he went on, 'that Aborigines everywhere in this country have been bitter that they have had their country taken from them, and been given no compensatory rights to land in any area.'⁶

Like Cleland in the 1930s, he made clear in his speech that the nature of the State's very foundational ideals gave South Australia a moral obligation to address this issue. 'I intend to trace the history of Aboriginal land rights in South Australia', he continued, 'because on examination it is clear that Aborigines were wrongfully deprived of their just dues. We must as far as we can, right the wrongs done by our forefathers'. He then quoted in detail the passage from the Letters Patent which acknowledged Aboriginal prior title to the land. He outlined the principles that were to guide the Commissioners in their negotiations for Aboriginal land, and he pointed out that it was the duty of the Protector 'not only to see that such bargains or treaties were faithfully executed ... but also ... to protect the natives in the undisturbed enjoyment of their lands of which they should not be disposed to make voluntary transfer'.⁷ He cited the instructions given to the Resident Commissioner regarding the proper process of negotiation, before noting that, with the exception of a few small areas, Aboriginal rights to land were not protected. The least that could now be done was to ensure that Aboriginal rights to the little land they had been granted were recognised in law and given over to their control.⁸ 'These were matters', he concluded, that went to 'the moral stature of the Australian people as a whole'.⁹

In his later memoir, Dunstan reflected on his battles in the 1960s to reform Aboriginal policy and to further the case for Aboriginal land rights, actions clearly informed by a consciousness of the State's foundational undertakings: 'The Letters Patent to the Governor of the time of the founding of the colony', he wrote, somewhat conflating the Letters Patent with the Proclamation, 'had required protection of the rights of the indigenous inhabitants.'¹⁰ There is no small irony in the fact that South Australia's story of its honourable and benevolent intentions toward Aboriginal people was largely a myth, yet over time, the myth itself was employed to provide the moral legitimacy for genuine reform.

Like the changes that the Referendum have been credited with, but did not initiate, the writing of Aboriginal people back into the nation's history was a process already underway, but in fits and starts. It would be a mistake to think that the floodgates opened. A year before the Referendum the Library's Board of South Australia published Kathleen Hassell's *Relations between Settlers and Aborigines in South Australia, 1836–1860*. There was a clear sense that this was now a story that needed telling, but the irony is that the work itself was an Honours thesis written in 1921. Nationally, the breakthrough publication was C.D. Rowley's *The Destruction of Aboriginal Society*, published in 1970. It was the first of three volumes describing the history and contemporary circumstances of Australian Aboriginal people, produced under the auspices of the Social Sciences Research Council of the Australian National University.

Australia's premier historical journal *Australian Historical Studies* began life in 1940 as *Historical Studies: Australia and New Zealand*, but it would not be until the late 1950s that it published its first article on Aboriginal history, something that remained an unusual subject for some time to come. Henry Reynolds' landmark book *The Other Side of the Frontier* was published in 1981. It endeavoured, for the first time, to explore frontier conflict from an Aboriginal perspective, but the work might have been difficult to locate under the subject of 'history'; works about Aboriginal people were not uncommonly shelved under 'anthropology' in the nation's bookstores. While scholars may have been writing Aboriginal people back into the nation's history, in the popular imagination they were still regarded as the province of anthropology, still not sufficiently within time to be within history. It was not until the mid-to-late 1980s that articles on Aboriginal history began to appear on a regular basis in the pages of *Australian Historical Studies* and other Australian historical journals, while a steady stream of books, mostly regional studies, began to appear in print.

The Bicentenary of 1988 was an important marker of the movement of Aboriginal history into the mainstream of Australian history. The publication that most tellingly marks the Bicentenary was a ten volume set entitled *The Australians: An Historical Library*. Written by many of the country's leading scholars, the principal volumes were designed as time-slice 'snapshots' of Australia at fifty-year intervals. Not only was the first volume devoted to Aboriginal Australia prior to 1788, but authors were assiduous in their efforts to incorporate Aboriginal people into the story. At the state level, South Australia's sesquicentenary in 1986 was marked by the publication of the *Flinders History of South Australia,* which included a chapter on 'prehistory', another on traditional Aboriginal culture and two describing the experiences of Aboriginal people in nineteenth and twentieth century South Australia. More significantly, the government funded an Aboriginal History of the state entitled *Survival in our own land: 'Aboriginal' Experiences in 'South Australia' since 1836*. Co-edited by Anglo-Australian writer Christobel Mattingley and Aboriginal writer Ken Hampton, the author line on the title page reads 'told by Nungas and others'. The quotation marks around 'Aboriginal' and 'South Australia' and the reference to 'Nungas' – the collective term for South Australian indigenous people – makes the ownership of the volume unambiguous.

The 'Great Australian Silence' was shattering, and the voices that emerged in that space – their tenor, tone and volume – unsettled those generations of settler Australians who had grown up so secure with their given script of regional, provincial and national origin. For some, the response was to reject the challenge and adhere to the script; for others the challenge was to reconcile these seemingly irreconcilable histories and develop a new story.

Memorialising the Frontier

Just three years after the Referendum the debate over the 'Elliston Massacre' resurfaced, initiated by Aboriginal people and their supporters. The Federal Council for the Advancement of Aborigines and Torres Strait Islanders and the Aborigines Progress Association put forward a plan to erect a cairn on the Elliston cliffs, a memorial to 'commemorate a massacre of 250 aborigines by white settlers', as 'part of a national mourning campaign by Aborigines'.[11] John Moriarty, who had been a prominent campaigner during the Referendum, argued in the press that the massacre was 'part of the history of the West Coast Aboriginal population' despite attempts by the European population to discredit what was a 'well-known fact'.[12] The chairman of the local district council, J.B. Cameron, claimed that 'the council will agree to the cairn if it could be proved that the massacre took place', adding more generally that a memorial to Aboriginal people who lost their lives in the development of the region would also be considered.[13]

Moriarty's article raised responses and counter-responses. One correspondent, Norman Ford, claimed to know Archie Beviss who 'invented the Waterloo Bay massacre story'.[14] This in turn provoked Laurie Bryan, a member of the Federal Council for the Advancement of Aborigines and Torres Strait Islanders, to respond. He began by deploring what he described as the 'racist tone' of Ford's letter and asserting that Ford's dismissal of the Elliston massacre as a myth was 'directly contrary to the opinions of the aboriginal people of the West Coast'. He finished with a reference to the Referendum:

Australians voted ten to one in favour of Aboriginal equality at the Aboriginal Rights Referendum. Our proposal is that those who voted for equality be invited to share in bringing it about.[15]

No memorial of the sort called for has ever been erected. Yet stories of a massacre on the Elliston cliffs have endured, a symptom of unreconciled tensions in the region's past. In 2002 members of the Elliston community initiated a community arts project, Sculpture on the Cliffs, as part of the state-wide 'Encounter 2002' commemoration, a bicentennial celebration of the meeting of Matthew Flinders' and Nicholas Baudin's navigating vessels on the South Australian coastline in 1802. Sculpture on the Cliffs aroused so much public interest in 2002, it has since become a biennial event. One of the project's first art installations in its Bicentennial Encounters year was 'The Sea Wailing', by local artists Cameron Robbins and John Turpie. A sound work installed on the cliffs which draws on the ocean's movement to play 'a moaning lament', 'The Sea Wailing' was designed, according to the artists, to respond 'the stigma of the "Elliston Incident" and ... try to redress some of the bad feeling.'[16] The power of the Sculpture on the Cliffs project to express a local need for reconciliation has remained strong. When the leader of the South Australian branch of the Australian Democrats, the Honourable Sandra Kanck, opened the 2006 exhibition of Sculpture on the Cliffs, she addressed it directly as an opportunity to break silence on the nature of Aboriginal dispossession:

> Today I am going to say the 'M' word, – massacre, murder, mayhem – because this art event is inspired by that history. We all know about the power of words, but sometimes words can be powerful when they are not said. When we avoid saying some words, the words have power over us. We must recognise what happened here and embrace it. Only then will we have the power to deal with it, perhaps even with the prospect of reconciliation.[17]

The kinds of questions that have defined local discussion of 'the Elliston incident' for generations – did it happen? how can that be proved? – have perhaps become, with Sculpture on the Cliffs, less significant than the desire for reconciliation, which takes 'the Elliston incident' as a marker and a reminder of the violences committed in the area against Aboriginal people in the name of European settlement.

Yet despite community projects like Elliston's Sculpture on the Cliffs, it is still unusual to see memorials in the Australian landscape to the land wars fought on colonial frontiers.[18] Two examples notable for their exceptionality are those to the 1838 Myall Creek massacre in New South Wales (now on the National Heritage list) and to the 1928 Coniston Massacre in the Northern Territory, both of which were only erected in 2001. When the new National Museum of Australia opened in 2001, its exhibit 'Contested Frontiers' sparked an extended controversy about historical authenticity in representing frontier violence.[19] Yet if the stories of that history still circulate in regional historical memory, might not regional museums, memorials and other local history projects also challenge the concept of a 'great Australian silence' on frontier conflict and Aboriginal dispossession? It has become commonplace to regard the contemporary museum and memorial site as opportunities for public debate rather than as repositories for the celebrated past, and much has been written about their role in fostering a sense of conversation with more than one understanding of history.[20] This trend is visible right across contemporary heritage practices more widely. James Young, for instance, describes the ways in which contemporary heritage sites have deliberately become locations 'of contested and competing meanings' rather than demonstrations, as once was true, 'of shared national values and ideals'.[21] If this is the case, one might expect contemporary heritage sites to be designed for the confrontation and debate of contested issues in the public domain.[22] To what degree is this true in acknowledging the history of South Australia's land wars?

Not far from Elliston, where the Sculpture on the Cliffs installations create an intriguing outlook to the Indian Ocean, lies the much larger regional centre of Port Lincoln. Port Lincoln was a site of significant frontier conflict in the early 1840s, to a degree that justified Governor Grey sending a military detachment to curb Battara attacks on settlers. How does this early history exist in memorial form in the town today?[23] Port Lincoln's attachment to an earlier pioneer history is commemorated in two plaques, one paying tribute to the navigator Matthew Flinders and the other to the explorer John McDouall Stuart, situated side by side on the main street under the 'Flinders Archway'. A nearby street sign carries the name of the explorer Edward Eyre who also had a local presence for a brief period in the early 1840s. These references to a story of discovery and exploration are, of course, an orthodox part of twentieth century public consciousness about national beginnings, and are familiar throughout Australia. Port Lincoln's pioneer origins are also remembered in other sites. A settler museum is housed in the historic Mill Cottage, built by a foundational pastoral family in 1866, and recreating for the visitor the atmosphere of settler life. Nearby are the nineteen-acre 'Pioneer Memorial Park' and the Centenary Oval, which was laid down in the centenary year to honour the arrival of the first settlers.[24]

Yet over the last decades of the twentieth century, other kinds of memorial and memorial restoration projects have served to recall Port Lincoln's more fraught past. In 1978, the Port Lincoln Caledonian Society undertook the restoration of pioneer grave sites. The restoration project included the Hawson plot, which contains the graves of the early pastoralist Henry Hawson, the former Government Resident (and Henry's son-in-law) Charles Driver, and Henry's older son Thomas, who after Charles Dutton's death married his widow. The cemetery's restoration was described in the press by Caledonian Society representative Perc Baillie as an opportunity to remember 'the pioneers who laid the foundation of Eyre Peninsula's prosperity'. But as the *Port Lincoln Times* put it, it also provided an opportunity to remember 'the serious problem of conflict' between early settlers and traditional owners in the region.[25]

The site that most clearly condenses Port Lincoln's early history of frontier conflict is the Hawson Memorial. Unveiled on 30 March 1911 at Kirton Point on the coastal fringe of Port Lincoln, it is a tribute to the 12 year-old boy Frank Hawson, Henry Hawson's son, whose death marked the beginning of almost a decade of conflict in the region. The Memorial was funded by public donation, and the remains of the boy were exhumed from their original burial place to be re-buried beneath the monument. Its inscription reads, in part: 'Although only a lad, he died a hero'. Over the twentieth century, the site fell into disrepair and became overgrown by surrounding scrub, with many locals apparently never knowing what it was, let alone its history.[26] In 1999, the local Kirton Ward Progress Association, in consultation with the Port Lincoln Pioneers and Descendants' Club, restored the memorial site and erected a plaque at the original grave site. The restoration project became the occasion for focusing local attention on the history in a new way. A feature article in the *Port Lincoln Times* not only focused on the death of the young Hawson boy, but also opened a perspective on the history of Aboriginal resistance to dispossession that had been missing from the memorial itself. The journalist made note of the fact that unfortunately, 'history has rarely recorded acts of violence or murder against local Aborigines by the settlers', and suggested that here is a 'rich history' from which lessons might be learned in the present.[27]

The history encapsulated by these pioneer memorials at Port Lincoln has moved in and out of focus over the decades, as the physical memorials themselves have deteriorated or become invisible to public view. But although their restoration might have been more motivated by a wish to remember early pioneers rather than to reflect on Aboriginal dispossession, this second effect has in fact become a consequence of the first. These projects have brought together two kinds of remembrance to resonate in public consciousness: one of pioneer origins and the other, necessarily entailed in this, the more discomforting realities of Aboriginal dispossession.

The frontier in the contemporary museum

If the realities of the frontier have been revived as a by-product of pioneer restoration projects at Port Lincoln, they are more deliberately foregrounded elsewhere in some regional museums where the first frontiers of settlement were most contested. In the south east, the Lady Nelson Discovery Centre, established in 1996, is a local museum that devotes a permanent exhibition to representing Aboriginal-settler relations on the frontier. The days of early settlement are revitalised into living history through the figure of Christina Smith: the first white woman in the district, lay missionary, and author of *The Booandik Tribe of Aborigines*. In the Discovery Centre's 'living' exhibition, an auditorium is fronted by a theatre set modelled as a settler's hut, and features a framed photograph of Christina Smith with several of her Aboriginal 'converts'. The idea of 'lived history' is imparted through the ghostly figure of Christina Smith herself, who is made oddly material when, at a trigger, she steps forth from the photograph as a glowing hologram and moves around the auditorium, telling the audience in her own 'voice' about her experiences and impressions of those past times. Her account includes the devastating effects of European occupation on the local Buandig people, her views on their pre-contact cultural life, and her own efforts to convert them to Christianity.

Around this installation are written panels conjoining Aboriginal prehistory and European history in a timeline of the region's past. Sociologist Jane Haggis has analysed the Centre's spatial organisation in terms of its conscious effort to depict Aboriginal and European civilisations and their technologies in terms of equivalence.[28] A panel of text entitled 'Aboriginal People Survive' emphasises the continuity of Aboriginal cultural life within and alongside the evolution of the region's post-settlement identity. The concept of overlapping cultures is also emphasised through use of Christina Smith herself, as an historical figure who demonstrates that on the colonial frontier, Aboriginal-settler relations were not entirely defined in terms of antagonism but allowed for other forms of negotiated relationships.

But how much does the museum achieve its aim to view 'two sides' of the story, as one of written panels puts it? In many ways, Christina Smith comes to 'stand in' for Aboriginal people's points of view: it is through her recollections that the colonial frontier is revived, and it is her late colonial work of missionary ethnography that is called upon to describe Aboriginal culture. As Haggis puts it, it is more Christina Smith than the Buandig people she 'speaks for' who has locally enduring visibility, and her authority as historical eyewitness is cemented by her perceived role as the exemplary benevolent civiliser.[29] The Discovery Centre does remember the violence of the frontier, but primarily to the degree to which it was defined by 'roughnecks' rather than being something more systematic. Undoubtedly 'roughnecks' committed various violent deeds on the south-eastern frontier, but what of reputable settlers, like James Brown, whose names survive as part of the making of South Australian prosperity? Although the Christina Smith installation brings into view the region's history of Aboriginal dispossession, it does so through a conventional filter of the 'good' pioneer, whose nostalgic regret for the 'dying race' forms an integral part of her benign intentions.

Just as the colony's early pastoral frontiers were settling down in the south east and across the gulf on the west coast, they were only just opening up further north, in the southern Flinders Ranges. How is the social memory of cultural contact and conflict visible in the local museums of that region? Port Augusta was established in 1854 as a harbour settlement that provided a departure point for pastoral expansion both to the western Eyre Peninsula and to the northern Flinders Ranges. As a natural crossroads, it was also a culturally significant trading point for various Aboriginal groups from the broader region, including the Nukunu people around the gulf, the 'Parnkhalla' (Banggarla) people to the west, and the Adnyamathanha and Ngadjuri peoples to the north and north-east. As we know, European occupation did not go uncontested by these Aboriginal groups, and within a few years, conflict between Aboriginal people and settlers in the north was exacerbated by the great drought of the 1860s. From as early as the 1850s Mounted Police were stationed at Port Augusta and nearby at Melrose in the southern Flinders Ranges. When the paramilitary Native Police corps was established under Mounted Constable Willshire in 1884 to subjugate Aboriginal attacks on pastoral properties in the Centre, Port Augusta was the divisional headquarters.

In all these respects, Port Augusta has a significant place in the history of colonial contact and frontier policing. Today, the Wadlata Outback Centre is one of the state's most visited attractions: it averages 100,000 visitors a year and is a four-times Regional Attraction winner. It was first opened in the Bicentennial year of 1988, funded in part by sponsorship by the Australian Bi-Centennial Authority. Its Establishment Committee at that time included representation from the Bi-Centennial Authority, the Department of Tourism and the History Trust of South Australia, as well as from the local Aboriginal and business communities. It was recently closed for a one million dollar upgrade, and re-opened in mid-2008. It is, by its own measure, a key entry point to the history of the wider 'outback' for visitors: the sign at its front door invites visitors to come in and 'Get the Whole Story' and it is named after the Banggarla word 'to teach' or 'to communicate'.

In its intention to tell 'the whole story', the Centre is clearly structured around highlighting both an Aboriginal and a European history of the broader region. Organised as a 'tunnel through time', the visitor sets off on a journey to be experienced through Aboriginal and European eyes – or 'two views', as one of the text panels puts it. Yet in its organisation, this journey does not dwell on colonial contact; it is rather a walking tour of 'progress' through time. Aboriginal history and Aboriginal perspectives are associated with the 'ancient time' of an 'ancient land'. Adnyamathanha dreaming stories are available to be read as an alternative to a scientific narrative of the land's geological formation from millions of years past, but the Centre's attention to Aboriginal history ends at this point: thereafter, the visitor moves through various rooms that illustrate the evolution of European settlement in chronological order, from the trials of early European explorers, to the hardships of early pastoral settlers, to the coming of civilisation and prosperity with the railway, the overland telegraph, and the mining industry.

The concept of contact between Aboriginal people and European settlement is almost entirely absent in the Centre's organisation of regional history, except in one illustrated text panel, 'And Then Came the Europeans', which marks the visitor's departure from rooms about Aboriginal Dreaming to rooms about European settlement. In this illustration, traditional Aboriginal figures and European pioneers are imagined as co-existing, for a brief moment, in the same time and space. With one group occupying the left of the frame while the other approaches from the right, they appear together yet remain separate. Their configuration side by side suggests either a peaceful relationship, or no relationship at all. This illustration is the only instance within the museum where Aboriginal and European groups appear side by side, and it is emblematic of the way that the museum as a whole offers these 'two views' of the land's history without depicting that there was any relationship between them.

To a large extent, the Wadlata Outback Centre represents a model of historical consciousness that Tony Bennett regarded as characteristic of Australia's museum sector twenty years ago. Writing in 1988, the year of Australia's Bicentenary, he argued that the Australian public historical sphere was expanding dramatically to become more regionally localised in its focus, and also more inclusive, especially in acknowledging Aboriginal history. But, he argued, this re-imagining of the national past to include Aboriginal history was limited by the degree to which heritage policy was becoming 'centrally linked to the promotion of tourism'.[30] With the modern museum's eye to the touristic gaze, he argued then, Aboriginal history might be becoming more visible in museums, but was becoming visible in a way that did not challenge an orthodox national story of settlement. Rather, the trend was to absorb Aboriginal history into the national story, giving it the role of the ancient tradition that lends the country a longer and richer history than European settlement alone allows.[31]

In fact, the Wadlata Outback Centre was first opened in the bicentennial year when Bennett made this observation. But given its status as a primary point of access to the region's history, its recent overhaul and re-opening might have suggested an opportunity to revise an orthodox presentation of history. Instead it presents an example of the way that the stories around Aboriginal and European history in Australia still remain locked into two, apparently unconnected roles: the one bound to ancient time, the other bound to the pioneer legend.

A more deliberate effort to directly engage the history of early contact between Europeans and Aboriginal people is evident at the Melrose Police Station Museum, a National Trust site in the southern reaches of the Flinders Ranges. Until 1856, Melrose was the most northerly post in South Australia for the mounted troopers who patrolled the frontier and protected settlers' stock and properties, and it later became the headquarters of the far-northern police division. Established in 1848 and rebuilt in 1862, the Melrose police building is the oldest historic site representing colonial settlement in the northern region, and in terms of the state-sanctioned subjugation of Aboriginal people, it is the most significant.

Fully restored and opened in 1998, the Melrose Police Station Museum is structured around an aim to portray a glimpse into the different nineteenth century communities that occupied the region in uneasy proximity. One aspect of this, of course, is the institutional history of the Mounted Police force. Some of the museum's exhibits point to the daily routines of police station life, while others, such as an exhibit of leg irons and a photograph of chained Aboriginal prisoners, imply the nature of the troopers' real business on the pastoral frontier. One panel shows a studio photograph of Mounted Constable William Willshire and his Native Police Constables, although the accompanying text does not suggest anything of the historical notoriety they earned for their violence in subduing Aboriginal 'cattle killers' in central Australia. A second section of the museum represents the life of early pioneers through displays that depict settlers' daily lives. A third section is dedicated to Aboriginal 'stories of heritage and identity', which traces the social and ceremonial significance of the land around what is now Melrose and Mount Remarkable, and describes the 'profound disruption' to the cultural life of the local Nukunu people that followed in the wake of European settlement. Through the exhibit, visitors are invited to bear witness 'to the survival and evolution of Nukunu people and their culture and … their continuing connection to the Mount Remarkable area'. Each of these perspectives on this pastoral frontier – that of the pioneers, of the Nukunu, and of the Mounted Police who secured contested lands for pastoral occupation – are recognised in plaques mounted on the front face of the main police station building. One is a National Trust plaque identifying the building as the 1862 police headquarters; one is a Centenary of Federation plaque, 'dedicated to the memory of the pioneers of this district'; and one is a plaque in the form of the indigenous flag, acknowledging 'the traditional custodians of this land'. These three plaques frame the museum's entrance, and are echoed by three flags – the British flag, the Australian flag and the Aboriginal flag – which fly side by side inside the front gate.

The Melrose Police Station Museum's explicit engagement of these different historical perspectives is a sign of how contemporary museum culture is changing in acknowledging the displacement and survival of Aboriginal culture alongside the story of European settlement. At the same time, a structural separation remains in the museum's representation of these perspectives: the policing, pioneer and Nukunu 'stories' are each contained in their own section; and although the role of the police in facilitating 'punishment' of Aboriginal resistance to European occupation is in some ways implicit, this location itself as a key regional site from the 1850s through to the 1880s of a concerted colonial project to dismantle Aboriginal sovereignty in order to secure colonial settlement is nowhere specifically addressed.

Jane Lydon has recently argued that historic sites structured to acknowledge the Aboriginal experience demonstrate a 'shift from settler assertions of the possession of landscape and history' and open 'new spaces for reconciliation'.[32] In their own ways, each of these regional museums and memorial projects offer examples of how historical memory within settler-descended communities has attempted to acknowledge Aboriginal experience within the settler story. But although it is increasingly common in museum practice to represent both pioneer and Aboriginal perspectives in order to throw different lights on the broader historical story of the colonial past, it is not common to emphasise the discomforting ways in which these histories are essentially linked: that is, that settlers, police and colonial governments actively dispossessed Aboriginal peoples of their lands, and did so through a practiced culture of surveillance, intimidation and often violence. This is an aspect of Australia's history that has always been subject to a partial knowledge and a partial forgetting – a pattern of conceiving of the past in the half-light of the 'twilight of knowing and not knowing'.[33]

CONCLUSION

Reconciling history and memory

Despite the fact that South Australia was founded with an explicit principle to protect Aboriginal peoples as British subjects in line with Colonial Office concerns in the 1830s, their actual treatment under the law proved to be little different to that which prevailed in Australia's earlier settled colonies.[1] The realities of the ever-expanding settler frontier simply did not match the legal code which was intended to apply to it. Over the decades of evolving British settlement this truth was cyclically demonstrated, not only through settler behaviour that was elusive to the eyes of the authorities, but also through the actions of the state itself in not protecting but rather punishing Aboriginal peoples 'with exemplary severity'. That it was able to do so was a symptom, somewhat perversely, of the putative status of Aboriginal people as British subjects, for their actions against settlers could be treated as criminality to be policed, rather than understood as the resistance of sovereign peoples to occupation of their lands. Ultimately, as David Neal puts it, 'the rule of law proved an effective instrument for groups and individuals within white society, [but] for the Aborigines the protections it promised came to little'.[2]

For almost two centuries, the violence of Aboriginal dispossession has shifted in and out of visibility, depending on the forums in which the colony's foundation has been commemorated as well as on changing political needs. The foundational principle that South Australia protected Aboriginal peoples as British subjects has conventionally been enlisted as demonstrating the state's humanitarian 'difference' at the level of state commemorations like Proclamation Day, though perhaps there appeared to be less need to assert this perceived 'difference' at times when the history of contact with Aboriginal people – or indeed the concept that they would play any role in the future Australia – had little national purchase. On the whole, until very recently, South Australia's official commemorations of foundational moments have largely served to tell a story that closely accords with the national tradition of a 'great Australian silence' on frontier violence, one of British settlement that was benign and progressive, and in which the history of the former colony was conceived as feeding seamlessly into the future of the Australian nation. Yet if state-sanctioned commemorations of foundation have largely channelled a story of origins that gave little voice to the history of Aboriginal subjugation and dispossession, at a more localised level this pattern of silence has never held in the same way. Just as Aboriginal people themselves have long engaged in the production of a counter-history to Australia's orthodox narrative of settlement, stories of foundation generated by settler-descended communities – from first-generation pioneering reminiscences in the late nineteenth century to local commemorative histories in the late twentieth century – have remembered and retold the often violent history of European settlement and Aboriginal dispossession in the process of chronicling a land hard won. Sometimes this history has inspired expressions of regret and at other times served to justify the colonial endeavour, but even in the heyday of the 'great Australian silence', stories of the contested frontier have remained persistently present.

Many of these forms of settler remembrance may perhaps inevitably be conservative, but other forms of historical consciousness might find voice in local and personal connections. Mike Brown is a South Australian author and activist, brother of the former state Premier Dean Brown. In 2002, the same year that saw the publication of Keith Windschuttle's *The Fabrication of Aboriginal History*, Brown published a work directed towards reconciliation, *No Longer Down Under: Australians Creating Change*. In this book he describes leafing through a local history of the Flinders Ranges and discovering a personal link to the region's frontier past. The Brown family's ancestors were pioneer settlers who had arrived in the colony in 1841. Over the years the family prospered, and the descendents of those pioneers are known in farming, business and politics. As it transpired, Mike's great-great uncle, James Brown, was the 17 year-old youth who had been killed by Aboriginal people on his brothers' sheep station near Mount Arden in the spring of 1852. Mike Brown spoke with local historians who gave him more details about the event and pointed out that there were Aboriginal graves in the area associated with an act of retribution that had taken place for James' death. 'No-one', he would later write, 'would recognise it as a war cemetery. Yet that's what it was.'[3] Researching the family records, Mike Brown uncovered the memoir of James' older brother Thomas Brown, which recorded the events of the day in 1852 on which he and a party of two dozen settlers, accompanied by a mounted constable, took the law into their own hands in retaliation for James' death. 'What the finish was' on that day, he wrote, 'needs no telling'; 'I can only say that in this case we carried out God's decree', and that following their 'severe but necessary lesson' of that day, 'there was no more trouble with the blacks'. He also wrote that with the presence of the mounted constable, 'in all we did there was no concealment or action outside the law'.[4]

If Thomas Brown's memoir reveals something of the lived culture of the violent frontier, Mike Brown's efforts to uncover it foregrounds some of the unresolved questions that face the descendents of pioneers.[5] As Deborah Bird Rose points out, there is 'no shortage of triumphal narratives of nation-building', but the task facing non-Aboriginal Australian communities is to 'seek out spaces where we reveal glimpses of the knowledge of how we are implicated in the disasters of our histories, our homes and our own lives'.[6]

Proclamation Day in the present

An event officially commemorating the European settlement of South Australia was held for the first time on 28 December 1857 at the coastal suburb of Glenelg where, just 21 years earlier, Governor John Hindmarsh had read the Proclamation that symbolically marked Britain's claim to the new colony. The commemorative event, attended by Governor MacDonnell in the year that South Australia achieved Responsible Government, featured a reading of the Proclamation. Most of the document dealt with the question of Aboriginal people as subjects of the Crown protected from 'acts of violence and injustice', yet when this first Proclamation ceremony was instituted in 1857, 'acts of violence and injustice' were daily being played out on the western and northern frontiers of the colony. Over time 'Proclamation Day', as it came to be known, became the formal commemoration of South Australia's foundation, and by the turn of the century it had become a major celebratory event.

The commemoration of Proclamation Day endures today. On 28 December 2007, we attended the annual Proclamation Day ceremony at Glenelg. It was a warm morning, but there was plenty of shade from the many gum trees which had been ceremonially planted over the decades. An honour-guard of men dressed in the uniforms of colonial police, all armed with muskets, took their place near the official podium beneath the gum tree as the official guests arrived. As the crowd awaited the Governor, a pair of modern-day mounted police rode forward to shield a small group of Aboriginal protesters who waited on the footpath opposite the entrance gate. Once all the dignitaries had taken their places, the event began, as it had begun for generations, with the reading of the Proclamation.

As the Chief Executive Officer of the Holdfast Council read the passage of the Proclamation which promised 'to punish with exemplary severity all acts of violence and injustice ... against the natives', an Aboriginal protester called out: 'what justice?' The protesters carried placards calling for a treaty, and stood before a banner that read: 'Aborigines were wrongfully deprived of their just dues. We must, as far as we can, right those wrongs.' These were the very words spoken by Don Dunstan in parliament in 1966 to underscore what he believed was the State's moral responsibility to address the issue of Aboriginal land rights. Forty one years later they were the words protesters chose to employ to press home their calls for Native title and reconciliation. As Premier, Don Dunstan appointed Sir Doug Nicholls as 28th Governor of South Australia, the first, and up to this point the only Aboriginal person to be appointed as a state Governor. One can only wonder what Governor Nicholls thought when he attended the Proclamation Day ceremony in 1976 and heard the 1836 promises of justice to Aboriginal people read aloud.

The following year we attended the Proclamation Day ceremony again. Unlike the previous year, it was an unseasonably cool summer's day. The weather was not the only thing that had changed. In the intervening twelve months, the Kaurna Heritage Committee and the Holdfast Bay City Council had negotiated to develop an inclusive ceremony. An Aboriginal 'welcome to country' performance began the formalities. When the Governor arrived, the official Aboriginal delegation presented him with a bunch of seven emu feathers, representing the seven 'Rs' of reconciliation: Recognition, Respect, Rights, Reform, Reciprocity, Responsibility and Reparations. Much of the ceremony that followed accorded with past formalities, but the atmosphere had changed from the previous year. Where the reading of the Proclamation promising justice to Aboriginal people had been redolent with irony, there was now a different air in its sentiments. Each non-Aboriginal speaker responded to the welcome to country with an acknowledgement of Kaurna land and culture. The formal ceremony closed with two Kaurna elders who rose and spoke of the ongoing importance of reconciliation. The last speaker referred to the Kaurna as the 'original Stolen Generation', and called for a Bill of Rights and a commemoration of the Letters Patent. As a gesture of reconciliation, the Governor, Rear Admiral Kevin Scarce, agreed to host such an event. On 19 February 2009, a ceremony to commemorate the 173rd anniversary of the Letters Patent, as a gesture of 'reconciliation and healing', was held in the grounds of Government House. At the event, various speakers addressed the State's foundational undertakings to recognise Aboriginal legal rights and rights to land. The Governor spoke admiringly of the colony's founding documents, and the 'good intentions' contained in them which, unfortunately, had not been fulfilled. 'Accordingly', he went on, 'it is necessary for us now to renew the spirit of those good intentions, and define our resolve'.[7]

The changing nature of Proclamation Day as an annual commemoration of foundation is an indication of how such occasions for public remembering can shift over time from affirming 'shared values and meanings' to become opportunities to explore complex histories in a changing political climate.[8] It is still largely to be seen how such changes will translate into a broad transformation of public historical consciousness amongst settler-descended Australians about the terms on which colonial authority on Australia's frontiers was secured, or the terms on which the pioneer legend was built. In anticipation of the next Proclamation Day ceremony, a local Aboriginal advocacy group sent out an advance call for protesters to attend, and to hold banners calling for a Treaty. These calls serve as a reminder of Janna Thompson's point in *Taking Responsibility for the Past* that historical injustices 'cast a long shadow,' one that is not necessarily diminished by the passage of time.[9] History, perhaps, is the present in constant and ongoing negotiation with the past.

NOTES

Introduction

1. Paul McHugh, *Aboriginal Societies and the Common Law: A History of Sovereignty, Status, and Self-Determination*, Oxford University Press, Oxford, 2004, p. 121–123.
2. House of Commons, Sessional Papers, 1837, 7, no. 425. Report of the Select Committee on Aborigines (British Settlements), p. 77.
3. Ibid., p. 5.
4. Ibid., p. 82.
5. Elizabeth Elbourne, ' "The Sin of the Settler" The 1835–36 Select Committee on Aborigines and Debates over Virtue and Conquest in the Early nineteenth Century British White Settler Empire', *Journal of Colonialism and Colonial History*, 4, no. 3 (2004).
6. *South Australian Gazette and Colonial Register* (hereafter *Register*), 3 June 1837.
7. Bruce Kercher, *An Unruly Child: A History of Law in Australia*, Allen & Unwin, Sydney, 1995, pp. 5–10; Alex C. Castles, *An Australian Legal History,* Law Book Co., Sydney, 1982, pp. 151–519.
8. Castles, pp. 520–1.
9. Kercher, p. 5.
10. Ibid.
11. Cited in Castles, p. 524.
12. John Connor, *The Australian Frontier Wars 1788–1838*, University of New South Wales Press, Sydney, 2002, pp. 56–58.
13. Connor, pp. 93–94.
14. Tim Castle, 'Watching them Hang: Capital Punishment and Public Support in Colonial NSW 1826–1836', *History Australia*, 5, no. 2 (2008): pp. 43.3–43.8.
15. Kercher, p. 10; Castles, p. 527.
16. Kercher, p. 7.
17. Castles, pp. 521–522.
18. Susanne Davies, 'Aborigines, Murder and the Criminal Law in Early Port Phillip 1841–1851', *Historical Studies*, 22, no. 88 (1987): pp. 316–20.
19. Ibid.

20 Richard Broome, 'The Statistics of Frontier Conflict,' in *Frontier Conflict: The Australian Experience*, ed. Bain Attwood and S.G. Foster, National Museum of Australia, Canberra, 2003, p. 95.
21 John MacGuire, 'Judicial Violence and the "Civilizing Process": Race and the Transition from Public to Private Executions in Colonial Australia', *Australian Historical Studies*, 29, no. 111 (1998): pp. 196–7.
22 Cited in Jonathan Richards, *The Secret War: A True History of Queensland's Native Police*, University of Queensland Press, St Lucia, 2008, p. 51.
23 Kercher, p. 5.
24 Proclamation of Lieutenant-Governor Stirling, 18 June 1839, in J.M. Bennett and Alex C. Castles, *A Sourcebook of Australian Legal History*, Law Book Co, Sydney, 1979, p. 257.
25 Ann Hunter, 'The Boundaries of Colonial Criminal Law in Relation to Inter-Aboriginal Conflict in Western Australia in the 1830s-1840s', *Australian Journal of Legal History*, 8 (2004): pp. 221–222.
26 Chris Owen, '"The Police Appear to be a Useless Lot up There": Law and Order in the East Kimberley 1884–1905', *Aboriginal History*, 27 (2003): pp. 109–127.
27 Kercher, p. 62.
28 Kercher, pp. 60–62.
29 The only monograph-length survey of frontier conflict in South Australia is Alan Pope's *Resistance and Retaliation*, but this was published over twenty years ago and examines only the first decade of settlement. Alan Pope, *Resistance and Retaliation*, Heritage Action, Adelaide, 1989.
30 See for instance David Neal, *The Rule of Law in a Penal Colony*, Cambridge University Press, Melbourne, 1991; Mark Finnane, *Police and Government: Histories of Policing in Australia*, Oxford University Press, Melbourne, 1994; Chris Cunneen, *Conflict, Politics and Crime*, Allen & Unwin, Kensington, 2001.
31 GRG 5/2/1863/306 encl. 1262, State Records of South Australia (hereafter SRSA).
32 Amanda Nettelbeck and Robert Foster, *In the Name of the Law: William Willshire and the Policing of the Australian Frontier*, Wakefield Press, Adelaide, 2007.
33 Henry Reynolds, 'Reviving Indigenous Sovereignty', *Macquarie Law Journal* (2006) 2. Reynolds cites M.F. Lindey's *The Acquisition and Government of Backward Territory in International Law* (1928) that 'the broad rule is that the possession of a power extends as far as, and no further, than its administrative machinery is in efficient exercise'.
34 Julie Evans, 'Colonialism and the Rule of Law: the case of South Australia' in Barry S. Godfrey and Graeme Dunstall, eds., *Crime and Empire 1840–1940: Criminal Justice in Local and Global Context*, Willan Publishing, Cullompton, 2005, p. 59.
35 Tom Griffiths, 'The Language of Conflict' in B. Attwood and S. Foster, eds, *Frontier Conflict: The Australian Experience*, National Museum of Australia, Canberra, 2003, p. 139.

36 See for instance Tony Roberts, *Frontier Justice: A History of the Gulf Country to 1900*, University of Queensland Press, 2005.
37 W.E.H. Stanner, *After the Dreaming*, ABC Book, Crows Nest, 1991 (first published in 1968), pp. 22–25.
38 Tom Griffiths, 'Past Silences: Aborigines and convicts in our history', in Penny Russell and Richard White, eds, *Pastiche I: Reflections on nineteenth-century Australia*, Allen and Unwin, Sydney, 1994, pp. 7–26.
39 Robert Foster, '"Don't mention the war": Frontier violence and the language of concealment', *History Australia*, 6, no. 3 (2009), pp. 68.5–68.7.
40 Griffiths, 1994, p. 8.
41 Derek Whitelock, *Adelaide 1835–1976: A History of Difference*, University of Queensland Press, St Lucia, 1977, p. 4.
42 Douglas Pike, *Paradise of Dissent: South Australia 1829–1857*, Melbourne University Press, Melbourne, 1957,pp. 3–28.
43 Janna Thompson, *Taking Responsibility for the Past: Reparation and Historical Justice*, Polity Press, Cambridge, 2002, p. xviii.

Chapter 1 • Foundations

1 Charles Sturt, *Two Expeditions into the Interior of Southern Australia*, Smith, Elder and Co, London, 1833, vol. II, p. 111.
2 Sturt, p. 126.
3 Sturt, p. 105–108.
4 Sturt, p. 163.
5 Sturt, p. 166.
6 Sturt, p. 167.
7 Sturt, p. 124.
8 Sturt, p. 126.
9 Sturt, p. 246.
10 J.M. Main, 'The Foundation of South Australia' in Dean Jaensch, ed., *The Flinders History of South Australia: Political History*, Wakefield Press, Adelaide, 1986, pp. 1–12.
11 Douglas Pike, *Paradise of Dissent*, Melbourne University Press, Melbourne, 1967, p. 55.
12 Main, pp. 6–9.
13 Ibid.
14 Cited in Main, p. 9.
15 Henry Reynolds, *The Law of the Land*, Penguin, Ringwood, 1992, pp. 97–103.
16 George Arthur to Spring Rice, CO 280/55 27 January 1835, SRSA.
17 Ibid.
18 CO 13/3, SRSA.
19 CO 13/3, SRSA.
20 CO 13/4, SRSA.

21 John Brown, unpublished diary, 17 December 1835, Nos. 36–27, SRSA, p. 75.
22 CO 13/4/21, SRSA.
23 House of Commons, Sessional Papers, 1837, 7, no. 425. Report of the Select Committee on Aborigines (British Settlements), p. 77.
24 R.H.W. Reece, *Aborigines and Colonists: Aborigines and Colonial Society in New South Wales in the 1830s and 1840s*, Sydney University Press, Sydney, 1974, p. 104.
25 Ibid.
26 Neal, p. 17.
27 Reece, p. 107–108.
28 Ibid.
29 Connor, pp. 56–58; 93–94.
30 Reece, p. 22.
31 Report of the Select Committee on Aborigines (British Settlements), p. 83.
32 Report of the Select Committee on Aborigines (British Settlements), p. 84.
33 Minute by James Stephen, 22 July 1839, CO 201/286, cited in A.G.L. Shaw, 'British Policy towards the Australian Aborigines, 1830–1850', *Australian Historical Studies*, 25, no. 99 (1992): p. 279.
34 House of Commons, Sessional Papers, 1836, 39, no. 426. First Annual Report of the Colonization Commissioners for South Australia, pp. 9–10.

Chapter 2 • British subjects or enemy aliens?

1 *Register*, 3 June 1837.
2 Ibid.
3 Ibid.
4 Lauren Benton, *Law and Colonial Cultures: Legal Regimes in World History 1400–1900*, Cambridge University Press, Cambridge, 2002.
5 Elbourne.
6 See for instance Frances Thiele, 'Superintendent La Trobe and the Amenability of Aboriginal People to British Law', *Provenance* 8 (2009) and Damen Ward, 'Constructing British Authority in Australasia: Charles Cooper and the Legal Status of Aborigines in the South Australian Supreme Court, c. 1840–60', *Journal of Imperial and Commonwealth History*, 34., no. 4 (2006).
7 Brian Dickey and David Howell, eds., *South Australia's Foundation Documents*, Wakefield Press, Adelaide, 1986, p. 75.
8 First Annual Report of the Colonization Commissioners, p. 8.
9 CO 13/7, SRSA.
10 *South Australian Government Gazette*, 11 July 1839.
11 *Southern Australian*, 5 June 1839.
12 GRG 24/6/1838/103, SRSA.
13 An Act to Amend an Act of the Fourth and Fifth Years of His Majesty, empowering His Majesty to erect South Australia into a British Province or Provinces, 31 July 1838 (1 & 2 Vic., c. 60).

14 Colonization Commissioner's Instructions to Resident Commissioner, GRG 48/1/1/1838, SRSA.
15 *Southern Australian*, 28 July 1840.
16 Ibid.
17 Ibid.
18 *Register*, 1 August 1840.
19 G. Jenkin, *Conquest of the Ngarrindjeri*, Raukkan Publishers, Adelaide, 1979, pp. 56–57.
20 *Register*, 15 August 1840.
21 *Register*, 19 September 1840.
22 Ibid.
23 Ibid.
24 *Register*, 27 April 1839.
25 Clyne, *Colonial Blue: A History of the South Australian Police Force 1836–1916*, Wakefield Press, Adelaide, 1987, p. 45.
26 Clyne, pp. 30–31.
27 Clyne, p. 32.
28 Robert Clyne, 'War with the Natives: From the Coorong to the Rufus, 1841', *Journal of the Historical Society of SA*, 9 (1981): p. 92.
29 Clyne, *Colonial Blue*, p. 41.
30 Ibid.
31 Clyne, *Colonial Blue*, p. 51.
32 Clyne, *Colonial Blue*, p. 15.
33 *Register*, 19 September 1840.
34 Ibid.
35 Ibid.
36 *Register*, 3 October 1840.
37 Ibid.
38 Ibid.
39 *Southern Australian* 6 November 1840; *The Register* 7 November 1840.
40 *Southern Australian*, 4 December 1840.
41 *Southern Australian*, 6 October 1840.
42 *Southern Australian*, 2 October 1840.
43 *Southern Australian*, 8 December 1840.
44 *Southern Australian*, 29 September 1840.
45 *Register*, 26 September 1840.
46 *Register*, 12 September 1840.
47 *Courier*, cited in the *Adelaide Chronicle*, 4 July 1841.
48 *Register*, 19 September 1840.
49 *Register*, 12 September 1840.
50 Ibid.

51. *Register*, 16 September 1840.
52. *Register*, 23 September 1840.
53. *Register*, 12 September 1840.
54. 'A Briton', letter to the *Register*, 26 September 1840.
55. *Register*, 24 October, 1840.
56. *Register*, 14 November, 1840.
57. *The Diary and Letters of Mary Thomas 1836–1866: Being a Record of the early Days of South Australia*, ed. Evan Kyffin Thomas, W.K. Thomas & Co., Adelaide, 1915, p. 169.
58. GRG 2/1/2/1842.
59. *Register*, 4 December 1844.
60. Geoffrey Dutton, *The Hero as Murderer: The Life of Edward John Eyre*, F.W. Cheshire, Melbourne, 1967, pp. 34–51.
61. J. Crawford, 'Diary of J. Crawford: extracts on Aborigines and Adelaide 1839–1841', *South Australiana*, 4, no. 1 (1965), pp. 34.
62. *Register,* 3 October 1840.
63. A. Buchanan, 'Diary of a journey overland from Sydney to Adelaide', *Royal Geographical Society of Australasia, South Australian Branch, Proceedings,* 15 (1922–23): p. 72.
64. Buchanan, p. 75.
65. Ibid.
66. *Register*, 16 November 1839.
67. *Register* 18 January 1840.
68. Deposition of Henry Inman, *Papers Relative to South Australia* (hereafter PRSA) No. 87/Encl. 1.
69. Diary of Thomas O'Halloran, 27 April 1841, GRG 5/81, SRSA.
70. Diary of James Hawker, 13 May 1841, PRG 201/1, SRSA.
71. John Morphett, et al., to Grey, PRSA No. 87/ Encl. 5. This petition and Alfred Langhorne's letter of appeal were published alongside Grey's response in the *Register*, 29 May 1841.
72. PRSA No. 87/Encl. 6, published in the *Register*, 29 May 1841.
73. GRG 5/83, SRSA and PRSA No. 87/Encl. 8.
74. Moorhouse's report of Charles Langhorne's verbal account to the police party states that five Aboriginal men were shot dead by the overlanders (Moorhouse's PRSA No. 92/Encl. 2); news of these deaths does not appear in Langhorne's official report to Major O'Halloran (22 June 1841, PRSA No. 92/Encl. 3) or in O'Halloran's report to Grey (27 June 1841, GRG 5/82, SRSA).
75. Diary of Major T.S. O'Halloran, 22–23 June 1841, GRG 5/81, SRSA.
76. PRSA No. 94/Encl.2.
77. Grey's PRSA No. 94/Encl. 1.
78. PRSA No. 94/Encl. 7.
79. First report from Moorhouse to Grey, 4 September 1841, PRSA No. 97, Encl. 1.

80 James Hawker, *Early Experiences in South Australia,* E.S. Wigg & Son, Adelaide, 1899, p. 79.
81 Proceedings of the Meeting of the Bench of Magistrates, 20–22 September 1841, PRSA No.98/Encl.
82 GRG 2/5/52/1841.
83 Ibid.
84 Grey to Undersecretary Stephens, 23 December 1840, *Historical Records Of Australia* (hereafter HRA), Series 1: Governors' Despatches to and from England, Library Committee of the Commonwealth Parliament, Sydney, 1914–1925, vol. XXI, p. 140.
85 Gipps to Grey, 14 June 1841, HRA, vol. XXI, pp. 408–10.
86 Grey to Gipps, 12 July 1841, HRA Vol. XXI, p. 465.
87 Colonial Secretary to Captain Butler, 22 October 1841, GRG 24/4, vol 4, p. 137.
88 Eyre to Colonial Secretary, 10 January 1842, PRSA, p. 308.
89 Henry Dudley Melville, 'Reminiscences', undated, unpublished in 5 volumes, D6976 (L), State Library of South Australia.

Chapter 3 • 'Our declared enemies'

1 P.J. Baillie, *Port Lincoln and District: A Pictorial History*, Lynton Publications, Blackwood, 1978, p. 19.
2 Cited in Margaret Davies, 'Settlers and Aborigines at Port Lincoln 1840–45', *South Australiana*, 18, no. 1 (1979), p. 25.
3 E.J. Eyre, *Journals of Expeditions of Discovery into Central Australia and Overland to King George's Sound in the years 1840–1841*, T. & W. Boone, London, 1845, vol. 1, pp. 163–65.
4 Eyre, pp. 167–69.
5 Eyre, pp. 169–70.
6 Eyre, p. 175.
7 GRG 5/2/1854/247, SRSA.
8 GRG 24/4/1841/308, SRSA.
9 Davies, 'Settlers and Aborigines at Port Lincoln 1840–45', pp. 29–31.
10 C. Schurmann, Correspondence file, 22 March 1842, S138, Lutheran Archives.
11 *Register*, 2 April 1842.
12 Cited in Davies, 'Settlers and Aborigines at Port Lincoln 1840–45', p. 33.
13 GRG 24/6/1842/100, SRSA.
14 Ibid.
15 GRG 24/6/1842/125, SRSA.
16 GRG 24/6/1842/1514, SRSA.
17 C. Schurmann, Correspondence Files, S144, Lutheran Archives.
18 GRG 24/6/1842/151, SRSA.
19 Edwin Schurmann, *I'd Rather Dig Potatoes: Clamor Schurmann and the Aborigines of South Australia 1838–1853*, Lutheran Publishing House, Adelaide, 1987, p. 149.

20 GRG 24/6/1842/152, SRSA.
21 GRG 24/4 Vol. 4, pp. 601–602.
22 Colonial Secretary to Lieut Hugonin, 14 April 1842, GRG 24/4 Vol. 4, pp. 609–11.
23 C. Schurmann to Protector Moorhouse, Correspondence file, 18 May 1842, Lutheran Archives.
24 Schurmann, *I'd Rather Dig Potatoes*, p. 151.
25 C. Schurmann to Protector Moorhouse, Correspondence file, 18 May 1842, Lutheran Archives.
26 Schurmann, *I'd Rather Dig Potatoes*, pp. 151–152.
27 GRG 24/6/1842/354, SRSA.
28 Schurmann to Moorhouse, Correspondence file, 18 May 1842, Lutheran Archives.
29 GRG 24/6/1842/354.
30 Schurmann, *I'd Rather Dig Potatoes*, p. 152.
31 Schurmann to Protector Moorhouse, Correspondence file, 18 May 1842, Lutheran Archives.
32 GRG 24/6/1842/354, SRSA.
33 Ibid.
34 Schurmann, *I'd Rather Dig Potatoes*, p. 154.
35 GRG 24/6/1842/399, SRSA.
36 Hawker, *Early Experiences*, 1899, p. 5.
37 GRG 24/6/1842/236, SRSA.
38 *Register*, 25 January 1840.
39 GRG 24/6/1842/526, SRSA.
40 *Register* 17 July 1878.
41 John Wrathall Bull, *Early Experiences of Colonial Life in South Australia*, E.S. Wigg & Son, Adelaide, 1878, pp. 303–4.
42 Bull, p. 307.
43 Ibid.
44 GRG 24/6/1842/757, SRSA.
45 GRG 24/6/1842/757, SRSA.
46 Bull, p. 299.
47 *Register*, 15 October 1842.
48 GRG 24/4 Vol. 4, p. 209.
49 Schurmann correspondence, 3 July 1843, S164–165, Lutheran Archives.
50 *Register*, 25 March 1843 and 29 March 1843.
51 GRG 24/6/1843/504, SRSA.
52 Schurmann correspondence, 3 July 1843, p. S168–69, Lutheran Archives.
53 *Register*, 22 July 1843.
54 Schurmann correspondence, 27 November 1843, Lutheran Archives.
55 Protector's Letterbook, 27 July 1843, GRG 52/7, SRSA.
56 Schurmann, *I'd Rather Dig Potatoes*, p. 164.

57 GRG 24/6/1844/1288, SRSA.
58 GRG 24/6/1846/411, SRSA.
59 Ibid.
60 Ibid.
61 GRG 24/6/1846/741, SRSA.
62 GRG 24/6/1846/276, SRSA.
63 Bull, p. 309.
64 B. Morris, 'Frontier Colonialism as a Culture of Terror', in B. Attwood and J. Arnold, eds., *Power, Knowledge and Aborigines*, La Trobe University Press, Melbourne, 1992, p. 86.

Chapter 4 • Trials of the criminal justice system

1 George Grey, 'Suggestions with reference to the practicability of improving the moral and social condition of the Aboriginal Inhabitants of Australia', *Register*, 18 April 1840.
2 Ibid.
3 *Register*, 19 September 1840.
4 *Register*, 12 November 1842.
5 *Register*, 19 July 1845.
6 Ibid.
7 Attorney General's Office, Letters received, GRG 1/2, 10 October 1846, SRSA.
8 Ibid.
9 GRG 24/1/1847/383.5, SRSA.
10 Ibid.
11 Martin Krygier, 'The Rule of Law' in Neil J. Smelser & Paul B. Baltes, eds., *International Encyclopedia of the Social and Behavioural Sciences*, Elsevier Science, Oxford, 2000, p. 13403.
12 Alan Pope, 'Aborigines and the Criminal Law in South Australia: The First Twenty Five Years', PhD Dissertation, Deakin University, 1998, p. 69.
13 Pope, 'Aborigines and the Criminal Law', p. 70.
14 GRG 24/6/1843/170, SRSA.
15 Ibid.
16 Cited in Castles, p. 533.
17 Castles, pp. 533–34.
18 Mark Finnane and Jonathon Richards, '"You'll Get Nothing Out of It": The Inquest, Police and Aboriginal Deaths in Colonial Queensland', *Australian Historical Studies*, 35. no. 123 (2004), p. 90.
19 An Act to authorise the legislatures of certain of her Majesty's colonies to pass laws for the admission in certain cases of unsworn testimony in civil and criminal proceedings, 1843 (6 and 7, Vic. c. 22), cited in John McCorquodale, *Aborigines and the Law: A Digest*, Aboriginal Studies Press, Canberra, 1987, p. 3.
20 *Register*, 18 September 1847 and 1 December 1847.

21 Aborigines Witnesses Act 1848 (11 and 12, Vic. No. 3), sections 2,7, & 10. Further amendments of the Evidence Act were made in 1849, removing some of the previous ambiguities.
22 Aborigines Evidence Act 1844 (7 and 8 Vic. No. 8).
23 Pope, 'Aborigines and the Criminal Law', pp. 93–94.
24 Cited in Pope, 'Aborigines and the Criminal Law', p. 120.
25 *Register,* 12 September 1849.
26 Skye Krichauff, The Narungga and Europeans: Cross Cultural Relations on Yorke Peninsula in the nineteenth century, Masters Thesis, University of Adelaide, 2008, p. 102.
27 GRG 24/6/1849/1908, SRSA.
28 Protector's Letterbook, GRG 52/1, 8 October 1849, SRSA.
29 Pope, 'Aborigines and the Criminal Law', chapter 11.
30 MacGuire, 187.
31 Barry Patton, 'Unequal Justice: Colonial Law and the Shooting of Jim Crow', *Provenance* no. 5 (September 2006), http://www.prov.vic.gov.au/provenance/no5/UnequalJustice6.asp.
32 Ordinance to Facilitate the Performance of the Duties of Justices of the Peace, 1849, No 15. Magistrates could act singly, while Justices of the Peace held the same powers if two were present. Act to confirm the Appointment and Jurisdiction of Special Magistrates, 1865, No 6.
33 Ibid.
34 GRG 5/2/1854/125, SRSA.
35 Ordinance to regulate the Office of Coroner of South Australia, 1850, No 7.
36 GRG 24/6/1846/100, SRSA.
37 Pope, p. 236.
38 GRG 24/6/1851/1559, SRSA.
39 Ibid.
40 GRG 24/6/1843/764, SRSA.
41 GRG 24/6/1843/804, SRSA.
42 GRG 24/6/1844/721, SRSA.
43 GRG 24/6/1843/769, SRSA.
44 GRG 24/6/1852/773, SRSA.
45 During the 1850s and 1860s, the Police Commissioner complained that settlers needed to be more active in defending themselves and their property. In 1863, he observed that 'we have few instances in which a moderately resolute and well-armed man could not protect both his own life and his employer's property'. *Register*, 23 October 1863.
46 GRG 2/1/1842/15, SRSA.
47 Ibid.
48 *Examiner*, 23 March 1843.
49 GRG 24/6/1847/24, SRSA.

50 Ibid.
51 Ibid.
52 GRG 24/6/1852/3249, SRSA.
53 GRG 24/6/1847/1077 and 1261, SRSA.
54 GRG 24/6/1847/1462, SRSA.
55 Mark Finnane and Jonathan Richards, '"You'll Get Nothing Out of It": The Inquest, Police and Aboriginal Deaths in Colonial Queensland', *Australian Historical Studies*, 35. No. 123 (2004): p. 87.
56 GRG 5/2/1854/395, SRSA.
57 GRG 24/6/1843/804, SRSA.
58 GRG 24/6/1847/24, SRSA.
59 GRG 5/1511847/1, SRSA.
60 GRG 24/6/1847/1131, 1137 and 1462, SRSA.
61 *Register,* 7 January 1864.
62 *Register,* 10 December 1863; 7 January 1864.
63 GRG 5/2/1863/306, SRSA; *Register,* 24 February 1864.
64 *Register,* 4 May 1864.
65 *Register,* 6 May 1864.
66 Finnane and Richards, p. 105; pp. 101–105.
67 Pope, p. 103.
68 Pope, p. 103–4.
69 Robert Foster, Rick Hosking & Amanda Nettelbeck, *Fatal Collisions*, p. 215.
70 *Register,* 13 June 1849.
71 GRG 24/6/1388/1849, SRSA.
72 Aborigines Testimony Amendment Act, 1849 (12 and 13 Vic. No 4).
73 James Levison, 'The Trial of Thomas Donnelly', *Journal of the Anthropological Society of South Australia*, 30, no. 2 (1993): pp. 55–56.
74 GRG 24/6/1847/382, SRSA.
75 Levison, p. 60.
76 *Register,* 8 September 1849.
77 *Register,* 9 June 1849.
78 GRG 24/6/1846/721, SRSA.
79 GRG 24/6/1851/1744, SRSA.
80 Kercher, 7.
81 Castle, 43.2; Davies, 316–20.
82 MacGuire, table opp. 187.
83 GRG 2/1/1842/15, SRSA.
84 GRG 24/6/1847/220, SRSA.
85 For instance Castles, p. 527; Hunter, p. 216; Thiele (2009); Ward (2006).
86 *Register,* 28 November 1846.
87 *Register,* 25 November 1846.

88 *Register*, 17 March 1847; Pope, p. 72.
89 This was the case of Nam Moing Yu, or Jemmy, charged with assault with intent to murder. He was found guilty and sentenced to one year's hard labour in December 1849. See *Adelaide Observer*, 8 December 1849.
90 *Register*, 16 May 1851.
91 Ibid.
92 Ibid.
93 *Adelaide Observer*, 24 May 1851.
94 *Register*, 7 June 1851.
95 GRG 24/1/383.5/1847, SRSA.
96 Pope, p. 148.
97 Hunter, 215–216.

Chapter 5 • The culture of the settler frontier

1 Leith MacGillivray, '"We have found our paradise": The South-East Squattocracy, 1840–1870', *Journal of the Historical Society of South Australia*, no. 17 (1989): p. 26.
2 GRG 24/6/1844/1527, SRSA.
3 Ordinance to regulate the Office of Coroner of South Australia, 1850, No 7.
4 Ibid.
5 GRG 24/6/1844/961, SRSA.
6 GRG 24/6/1844/1527, SRSA.
7 GRG 24/6/1845/26, SRSA.
8 GRG 24/6/1846/1096, SRSA.
9 GRG 24/6/1845/589, SRSA.
10 Ibid.
11 GRG 24/6/1845/1526, SRSA.
12 GRG 24/6/1849/2001, SRSA.
13 MacGillivray, p. 27.
14 GRG 24/6/1846/1096, SRSA.
15 Ibid.
16 Edward Arthur, 'Journal of Events from Melbourne, Port Phillip, to Mount Shanck, in the District of Adelaide, New Holland'. 1844; rpt. Libraries Board of South Australia, Adelaide, 1975, p. 45.
17 GRG 24/6/1844/1120, SRSA.
18 GRG 24/6/1844/1293, SRSA.
19 GRG 24/6/1844/1120, SRSA.
20 GRG 24/6/1844/1135, SRSA.
21 Ibid.
22 GRG 24/6/1844/1446, SRSA.
23 Ibid.

24 GRG 24/6/1844/1248, SRSA.
25 Ibid.
26 GRG 24/6/1844/1293, SRSA.
27 GRG 24/6/1844/1528, SRSA.
28 GRG 24/6/1845/143, SRSA.
29 Pope, 235.
30 GRG 24/6/1849/2001, SRSA.
31 GRG 24/6/1848/1127, SRSA.
32 GRG 24/6/1848/151, SRSA and *Register* 17 March 1849.
33 Ibid.
34 Foster, Hosking and Nettelbeck, p. 47.
35 Foster, Hosking and Nettelbeck, p. 48.
36 *Register*, 9 June 1849.
37 GRG 24/6/1849/1404, SRSA.
38 *Register* 9 June 1849.
39 GRG 24/6/1849/947, SRSA.
40 Ibid.
41 *Register*, 21 July 1849.

Chapter 6 • Administrative responses to frontier violence

1 GRG 24/6/1851/1577 and 1744, SRSA.
2 *Observer*, 3 May 1851.
3 GRG 24/6/1851/1559, SRSA.
4 Ibid.
5 GRG 24/6/1849/2001, SRSA.
6 GRG 24/6/1851/1758, SRSA.
7 GRG 24/6/1851/1577, SRSA.
8 GRG 24/6/1851/1581, SRSA.
9 GRG 24/6/1851/1733, SRSA.
10 Ibid.
11 GRG 24/6/1851/1758, SRSA.
12 *South Australian Government Gazette*, 11 July 1839.
13 Robert Foster, 'Feasts of the full-moon: the distribution of rations to Aborigines in South Australia 1836–1861', *Aboriginal History*, 13, no. 1 (1989): p. 69.
14 GRG 24/6/1847/286, SRSA.
15 Foster, 'Feasts of the full-moon', p. 69.
16 Protector's Letterbook, 1 November 1852, p. 321, GRG 52/7, SRSA.
17 *South Australian Government Gazette*, 2 June 1853.
18 Robert Foster, 'Rations, Co-existence and the colonisation of Aboriginal Labour in South Australia, 1860–1911', *Aboriginal History*, 24 (2000): p. 11.

19 Robert Foster, 'Coexistence and Colonization on Pastoral Leaseholds in South Australia 1851–99' in J. McLaren, A.R. Buck & Nancy E. Wright (eds.) *Despotic Dominions: Property Rights in British Settler Societies*, University of British Columbia Press, Vancouver, 2005, p. 253–55.
20 Ibid.
21 Moorhouse to Commissioner of Police, 6 April 1850, GRG 24/7, SRSA.
22 GRG 5/2/1854/541, SRSA.
23 Clyne, *Colonial Blue*, p. 120.
24 GRG 5/2/1853/18, SRSA.
25 GRG 5/2/1854/210, SRSA.
26 GRG 5/2/1856/235, SRSA.
27 GRG 5/2/1856/186, SRSA.
28 Nettelbeck and Foster, *In the Name of the Law*, 2007.
29 Robert Foster, 'The Origin of the Protection of Aboriginal Rights in South Australian Pastoral Leases', *Land, Rights, Laws: Issues in Native Title, Issue Paper No. 24*, 1998.
30 Ibid.
31 GRG 24/6/1850/2726, SRSA.
32 GRG 2/6/6/1851/23, SRSA.
33 Ibid.
34 *South Australian Government Gazette*, 30 January 1851.
35 Foster, 'The Origin of the Protection of Aboriginal Rights'.
36 Ibid.
37 *South Australian Government Gazette*, 23 December 1852.
38 GRG 24/6/1852/773, SRSA.
39 Ibid.
40 *Adelaide Observer*, 14 February 1852.
41 *South Australian Government Gazette*, 24 August 1854.

Chapter 7 • The Mounted Police and the tyranny of distance

1 D.W. Meinig, *On the Margins of the Good Earth*, SA Government Printer, Adelaide, 1988, p. 45.
2 Thomas Brown, 'Concerning the Murder and the Following of the Blacks and Sheep. Account prepared by Thomas Brown about 1901', Family papers of Mike Brown, Adelaide.
3 Ibid.
4 *South Australian Government Gazette*, 31 January 1856.
5 *South Australian Government Gazette*, 2 August 1855.
6 GRG 5/2/1856/239, SRSA.
7 Ibid.
8 *Register* 23 November 1857.

9   *Register* 26 November 1857.
10 GRG 5/2/1858/662, SRSA.
11 GRG 5/2/1858/749, SRSA.
12 GRG 5/2/1855/431 25 June 1855, SRSA.
13 GRG 5/2/1855/431 1 July 1855, SRSA.
14 GRG 5/2/1855/431 25 June 1855, SRSA.
15 GRG 5/2/1855/431 1 July 1855, SRSA.
16 GRG 5/2/1855/431 1 August 1855, SRSA.
17 GRG 5/2/1855/431 n.d, SRSA.
18 GRG 5/2/1855/455, SRSA.
19 GRG 5/2/1857/748, SRSA.
20 GRG 5/2/1867/1817, SRSA.
21 Ibid.
22 Ibid.
23 GRG 5/2/1860/940, SRSA.
24 GRG 5/2/1861/361.5, SRSA.
25 GRG 5/2/1855/725, SRSA.
26 GRG 5/2/1858/585, SRSA.
27 GRG 5/2/1858/842, SRSA.
28 Copies of General Orders, No. 23 of 1853, GRG 5/28, SRSA.
29 GRG 5/2/1869/792, SRSA.
30 Frederick Hayward, 'Reminiscences of Johnson Frederick Hayward', *Proceedings of the Royal Geographical Society of Australasia, South Australian Branch,* 29 (1929): p. 131.
31 Samuel Stuckey, 'Reminiscences', undated, A 1083 A, SRSA.
32 GRG 5/2/1861/980, SRSA.
33 *Register,* 16 August 1864.
34 'Report of the Select Committee on Aborigines (British Settlements)', pp. 85–86.
35 GRG 5/2/1857/195.5, SRSA.
36 Report of the Select Committee of the Legislative Council upon the Aborigines, 3, no. 165 (1860), p. 4.
37 GRG 5/2/1863/306, SRSA.
38 GRG 5/2/1863/197, SRSA.
39 GRG 5/2/1863/306 encl. 1167, SRSA.
40 Ibid.
41 Ibid.
42 GRG 5/2/1863/306 encl. 1262, SRSA.
43 GRG 5/2/1870/331, SRSA.
44 GRG 5/2/1858/109, SRSA.
45 GRG 5/2/1863/306 encl. 1590, SRSA.
46 Ibid.

47 GRG 291/1/1864/2, SRSA.
48 Ibid.
49 *Register*, 19 May 1865; GRG 5/2/1865/714, SRSA.
50 GRG 5/2/1865/714 and 1549, SRSA.
51 *Register*, 13 October 1865.
52 *Register* 23 November 1865.
53 *Register* 13 December 1865.
54 *Register* 9 December 1865.
55 *Register* 13 December 1865.
56 Rodney Cockburn, *Pastoral Pioneers of South Australia, Adelaide Stock and Station Journal* (1923–1925), ed. Dorothy Adlersey, South Australian State Library, Adelaide, Vol. 2, p. 175.
57 Ibid.
58 Ibid.
59 GRG 5/2/1866/56 and GRG 5/2/1868/1338, SRSA.
60 GRG 5/2/1866/56, SRSA.
61 Ibid.
62 Cockburn, Vol. 2, p. 175.
63 Ibid.
64 GRG 5/2/1863/197, SRSA.
65 GRG 5/2/1863/1866, SRSA.
66 *Register*, 10 June 1882.
67 Philip Jones, *Ochre and Rust: Artefacts and Encounters on Australian Frontiers*, Wakefield Press, Adelaide, 2007, p. 367–68.
68 Ibid.
69 Christine Stevens, *White Man's Dreaming: Killalpaninna Mission 1866–1915*, Oxford University Press, Melbourne, 1994, p. 45.
70 Stevens, p. 48–9.
71 Stevens, p. 50.
72 Stevens, p. 54–55.
73 GRG 5/2/1873/753, SRSA.
74 Cited in Stevens, p. 55.
75 GRG 5/2/1867/633, SRSA.
76 GRG 5/2/1870/319, SRSA.
77 GRG 5/2/1871/468, SRSA.
78 GRG 5/2/1871/537, SRSA.
79 GRG 5/2/1869/1491, SRSA.
80 GRG 5/2/1873/1103, SRSA.
81 GRG 5/2/1873/753, SRSA.
82 GRG 5/2/1866/56, SRSA.
83 *Register*, 30 December 1865.

84 *Register*, 5 September 1866.
85 *Register*, 5 September 1866.
86 Gordon Reid, *A Picnic with the Natives: Aboriginal-European Relations in the Northern Territory to 1910*, Melbourne University Press, Melbourne, 1990, pp. 62–66.
87 GRG 5/2/1874/261, SRSA.
88 William Willshire, *The Aborigines of Central Australia*, C E Bristow, Adelaide, 1891, p. 33.
89 Amanda Nettelbeck and Robert Foster, *In the Name of the Law: William Willshire and Policing of the Australian Frontier*, Wakefield Press, Adelaide, 2007.
90 *Advertiser*, 20 February 1878.
91 Ibid.
92 John Brown, *Diary*, 16 December 1835 – 12 January 1836, SLSA PRG 1002/2.
93 *Advertiser*, 29 December 1871.

Chapter 8 • Paving the way back

1 Stephen Turner, 'Settlement as Forgetting' in Klaus Neumann, Nicholas Thomas and Hilary Ericksen, eds., *Quicksands: Foundational Histories in Australia and Aotearoa New Zealand*, University of New South Wales Press, Sydney, 1999, p. 23–26; Deborah Bird Rose, 'Hard Times: An Australian Study' in Neumann, Thomas and Ericksen, eds., p. 11.
2 See for instance Chris Healy, *In the Ruins of Colonialism: History as Social Memory*, Cambridge University Press, 1997; Bain Attwood, *Telling the Truth about Aboriginal History*, Allen & Unwin, Sydney, 2005; Foster, Hosking and Nettelbeck, 2001.
3 J.C.R. Camm & J. McQuilton, eds., *Australians: An Historical Atlas*, Fairfax, Syme & Weldon, Sydney, 1987, p. 146.
4 J.B. Hirst, *The Sentimental Nation: The Making of the Australian Commonwealth*, Oxford University Press, Melbourne, 2000, pp. 36–44.
5 C.M.H. Clark, *A History of Australia*, Vol 5: *The People Make Laws*, Melbourne University Press, Melbourne, 1987, pp. 129–131.
6 Russell McGregor, *Imagined Destinies: Aboriginal Australians and the Doomed Race Theory 1880–1939*, Melbourne University Press, Melbourne, 1997.
7 E. Stirling, 'Ethnology in Australia', *Adelaide Observer*, 29 December 1894.
8 For instance, *Adelaide Observer*, 17 September, 1 October 1898, 5 November 1898, 8 September & 13 October 1900.
9 Minutes of Evidence on the Aborigines Bill, *South Australian Parliamentary Papers*, 1899, 2, 77, p. 99–101.
10 *Adelaide Observer*, 24 July 1886.
11 Sianan Healy, 'Years ago some lived here: Aboriginal Australians and the Production of Popular Culture, History and Identity in 1930s Victoria'. *Australian Historical Studies* 37, no. 128 (2006), p. 21.

12 *Register*, 30 May 1885.
13 *Adelaide Observer*, 6 June 1885; *South Australian Register*, 30 May 1885 & 14 January 1887.
14 Nettelbeck and Foster, *In the Name of the Law*.
15 *Advertiser*, 29 December 1891; 29 December 1899; 29 December 1903.
16 *Advertiser*, 30 December 1890.
17 *Advertiser*, 29 December 1891.
18 *Advertiser*, 29 December 1893.
19 *Advertiser*, 29 December 1914.
20 *Advertiser*, 28 December 1909.
21 *Advertiser*, 28 December 1914.
22 *Advertiser*, 28 December 1920.
23 *Advertiser*, 28 December 1914.
24 *Advertiser*, 30 December 1890.
25 *Advertiser*, 29 December 1914.
26 For instance, J.F. Conigrave, *South Australia: A Sketch of its History and Resources*, London, 1886; W.F. Morrison, *The Aldine History of South Australia*, Sydney & Adelaide, 1890; E. Hodder, *The History of South Australia from its Foundation to the Years of its Jubilee*, London, 1893.
27 W. Harcus, *South Australia: Its History, Resources and Productions*, Sampson Low, Marston, Searle & Rivington, London, 1976, p. 2.
28 Foster, Hosking and Nettelbeck, *Fatal Collisions*, pp. 20–24.
29 J.B. Hirst, 'The Pioneer Legend', pp. 114–115.
30 Bain Attwood, *Telling the Truth About Aboriginal History*, pp. 14–16.
31 Bull, p. 130.
32 Bull, pp. 131–141.
33 See for instance 'A Native Massacre' by 'A South Australian', from the *Adelaide Observer*, republished by the *Register* 7 September 1868, pp. 3–4.
34 Robert Dixon, *Writing the Colonial Adventure*, Cambridge University Press, Melbourne, 1996; Melissa Bellanta, 'Fabulating the Australian Desert: Australia's Lost Race Romances 1890–1908', *Philament* December 2007.
35 Foster, Hosking and Nettelbeck, p. 51.
36 GRG 24/6/1849/1404, SRSA.
37 Foster, Hosking and Nettelbeck, p. 53.
38 Simpson Newland, *Paving the Way: A Romance of the Australian Bush,* Gay & Bird, London, 1893, p. 70.
39 Hayward, 'Reminiscences', pp. 137–40.
40 GRG 52/1/1885/150, SRSA.
41 William Benstead, 'Short Stories of my Life and Travels', typescript, n.d., private collection, p. 11.

42 Alexander Buchanan, 'Diary of a Journey Overland from Sydney to Adelaide with Sheep, July-December 1939', *Proceedings of the Royal Geographical Society of Australasia, South Australian Branch*, 23 (1924): pp. 51–76.

Chapter 9 • The great Australian whispering

1 *Observer*, 6 February 1909.
2 Derek Whitelock with Tony Baker, *Adelaide: A Sense of Difference*, Wakefield Press, Adelaide, 1985; rpt. Australian Scholarly Publishing, Melbourne, 2000.
3 *Adelaide Observer*, 6 February 1909.
4 Protector's Report for the Year ending 30 June 1908 (transcription), South Australian Museum, p. 3.
5 Protector's Report for the Year ending, 30 June 1909 (transcription), South Australian Museum, p. 3.
6 Regulations under the Aborigines Act 1911, para 1–5, gazetted on 10 May 1917.
7 John Chesterman and Brian Galligan, *Citizens Without Rights: Aborigines and Australian Citizenship*, Cambridge University Press, Melbourne, 1997.
8 Reverend John Blacket, *History of South Australia: A Romantic and Successful Experiment in Colonization*. 2nd Edition. Hussey and Gillingham, Adelaide, 1911, pp. 159–160.
9 Blacket, pp. 163–165.
10 Alan Powell, *Far Country: A Short History of the Northern Territory*, Melbourne University Press, Melbourne, 1982, pp. 179–180.
11 *Adelaide Observer*, 6 February 1909.
12 Cockburn's entry on Alexander Buchanan is typical in this respect: Cockburn, vol. 1, p. 188.
13 Julian Thomas, 'A History of Beginnings' in Klaus Neumann, Nicholas Thomas and Hilary Ericksen, eds., p. 118.
14 Thomas, 'A History of Beginnings', pp. 120–23.
15 Julian Thomas, '1938: Past and Present in an Elaborate Anniversary', *Australian Historical Studies*, 23, no. 91 (1988).
16 Nicholas Thomas, 'The Uses of Captain Cook: Early Exploration in the Public History of Aotearoa New Zealand' in Annie Coombes, ed., *Rethinking settler colonialism: history and memory in Australia, Canada, Aotearoa New Zealand and South Africa*, Manchester University Press, Manchester, 2006, p. 149.
17 *Mail*, 28 November 1936.
18 *Mail*, 7 November 1936.
19 *Adelaide Chronicle*, 17 December 1936.
20 *Adelaide Chronicle*, 17 December 1936.
21 Charles Sturt, *Two expeditions into the interior of Southern Australia*, London, 1833, vol. II: 105–108.
22 *Advertiser*, 23 December 1936; *Mail*, 19 December 1936.
23 *Advertiser*, 26 December 1936.

24 'Wanderers of the Wasteland', *Advertiser*, Special Centenary issue, 1 September 1936.
25 *The Centenary History of South Australia*, Royal Geographical Society: South Australian Branch, Adelaide, 1936, p. 22.
26 Gavin Souter, 'Skeleton at the Feast', in Australians 1938, Fairfax, Syme & Weldon, Broadway, NSW, 1987, p. 14.
27 Ibid., pp. 14–18.
28 Ibid., p. 18.
29 Attwood and Marcus, *Struggle for Aboriginal Rights*, illustration 11.
30 Jack Horner and Marcia Langton, 'The Day of Mourning', in B. Gammage and P. Spearitt, eds, *Australians 1938*, Fairfax, Syme and Weldon, Sydney, 1987, p. 34.
31 Attwood and Marcus, *Struggle for Aboriginal Rights*, pp. 58–64; 118–122.
32 Michael Roe, 'A Model Aboriginal State, *Aboriginal History*, 10, no. 1 (1986), pp. 40–44.
33 Christobel Mattingley and Ken Hampton, eds. *Survival in Our Own Land: 'Aboriginal' Experiences in 'South Australia' since 1836, told by Nungas and Others*, Hodder and Stoughton, Sydney, 1992, p. 57.
34 Richard Broome, 'Aboriginal Histories, Australian Histories, and the Law' in Bain Attwood, ed., *In the Age of Mabo: History, Aborigines and Australia*, Allen and Unwin, Sydney, 1996,p. 62.
35 Commonwealth of Australia, *Initial Conference of Commonwealth and State Aboriginal Authorities, April 1937,* Commonwealth Government Printer: Canberra, 1937, p. 2.
36 William Cooper, Secretary of the Australian Aborigines' League, to the Minister for the Interior, 31 October 1936 in Bain Attwood and Andrew Marcus, *Thinking Black: William Cooper and the Australian Aborigines' League*, Aboriginal Studies Press, Canberra, 2004, p. 55.
37 Ernestine Hill, 'Story of the State: From Wilderness to Wealth in a Hundred Years', *The Centenary Chronicle*, 5 October 1936.
38 Ruth Hawker, *Yesterday*, F.W. Preece and Son, Adelaide, 1936.
39 *Advertiser*, 19 August 1921, p. 6.
40 *Advertiser*, 31 December 1929, p. 10.
41 *Advertiser*, 15 November 1935, p. 16.
42 *Advertiser*, 26 November 1935, p. 22.
43 *Advertiser*, 5 February 1936, p. 22.
44 A. Markus, *Governing Savages*, Allen & Unwin, Sydney, 1990, p. 168.
45 J.C. Genders, *Australian Aboriginals, A Statement by the Aborigines' Protection League explaining its basic principles and proposals*, Adelaide, 1929, p. 2.
46 Markus, p. 172.
47 Sylvia Kleinhert, 'An Aboriginal Moomba: Remaking History', *Continuum* 13. 3 (1999), p. 348.
48 Kleinhert, p. 349.

49 Sturt, p. 246.
50 On the privileging on individual experience in historical re-enactment see for instance Vanessa Agnew, 'What is Re-enactment?', *Criticism* 46, no. 3 (2004).
51 The Sturt Report: Audio Recording of the ABC Historical Re-enactment of the Sturt Expedition, RADA Acc. No. 2122, no. 28, 2 Feb 1951.
52 *Advertiser*, 10 February 1951.
53 The Sturt Report: Audio Recording of the ABC Historical Re-enactment of the Sturt Expedition, RADA Acc. No. 2122, no. 33, 8 Feb 1951.
54 *Advertiser*, 1–2 January 1951.
55 *Advertiser*, 21 January 1951.
56 *Advertiser*, 12 February 1951.
57 *Advertiser*, 10 February 1951.
58 *Bitter Springs*, Ealing Studios, (Director: Ralph Smart), 1950.
59 *Advertiser*, 23 June 1950.
60 Ibid.
61 *Advertiser*, 19 May, 23 May and 25 May 1949.
62 *Advertiser*, 25 May 1949.
63 *Advertiser*, 24 June and 26 June 1950.
64 Ibid.
65 *Bitter Springs*, 22m 14s.
66 *Bitter Springs*, 54m 21s.
67 http://aso.gov.au/titles/features/bitter-springs/notes/
68 GRG 1/1/1890/395, SRSA.
69 Broome, p. 56.
70 Broome, p. 64.
71 Broome, pp. 61–65.
72 Pike, *Paradise of Dissent*, p. 290–91.
73 Pike, *Paradise of Dissent*, p. 140.
74 Douglas Pike, *Australia: The Quiet Continent*, Cambridge University Press, Cambridge, 1962, p. 223.
75 For instance, Christobel Mattingley and Ken Hampton, eds., *Survival in our own land: 'Aboriginal' experiences in 'South Australia' since 1836, told by Nungas and others*, Hodder and Stoughton, Sydney,1992.
76 Ern Carmichael, *The Ill-Shaped Leg: A Story of the Development of Yorke Peninsula*, published by the author, Adelaide, 1973.
77 See for instance Graham Jenkins, *Conquest of the Ngarrindjeri*, Rigby, Adelaide, 1974 and Foster, et al, pp. 18–28.
78 Tom McCourt and Hans Mincham, *The Coorong and Lakes of the Lower Murray*, Beachport Branch of the National Trust, Adelaide, 1987, p. 84.
79 L.M. Andison, *Berri: Hub of the Upper Murray*, SA Country Women's Association, Berri, 1953, p. 1. See also for instance R.M. Younger, *Australia's Great River*, Horizon, Swan River, 1976, p. 41.

80 Doreen Puckridge, *They Came with the Buffalo: A Saga of Port Lincoln*, Pioneer Books, Warradale, 1980, p. 63.
81 Christina Smith, *The Booandik Tribe of Aborigines*, E. Spiller, Adelaide, 1880.
82 Cockburn, vol 2, p. 140–141.
83 Ibid.
84 McCourt and Mincham, pp. 58–61.
85 McCourt and Mincham, p. 60.
86 John Hamp was one of three isolated Europeans whose lives were taken by Aborigines in that region over several months. Pastoral settler Captain James Beevor was speared on 3 May 1849, and Annie Easton, was killed at her hut four days later. Their deaths are set against other episodes of settler actions against Aborigines. In August 1848, the overseer of local pastoralist William Pinkerton shot and killed at least one Aboriginal man at Lake Newland, and in May 1849 five Aboriginal people were poisoned, probably by shepherd Patrick Dwyer, on William Mortlock's station. No charges were taken against Pinkerton's overseer, George Stewart, and as we know, Dwyer escaped charges by fleeing the colony.
87 GRG 24/6/1848/1127, SRSA.
88 See Foster, Hosking and Nettelbeck, pp. 46–58.
89 Max Fatchen, 'Massacre of the Aborigines', *Advertiser*, 11 April 1970; Elliston Centenary Committee, *Across the Bar to Waterloo Bay: Elliston 1978–1978*, Elliston Centenary Committee, Adelaide, 1978, p. 7.
90 Carmichael, p. 29.
91 Ibid.
92 Rhoda Heinrich, *Governor Fergusson's Legacy*, Adelaide, Maitland-Kilkerran Centenary Committee, 1972, p. 42.
93 Heather Carthew, *Rivoli Bay: A Story of Early Settlement at Rivoli Bay in the South East of South Australia 1845–1855*, published by the author, Adelaide, 1974. See also Rhoda Heinrich, *Wide Sails and Wheat Stacks: A History of Port Victoria and the Hundred of Wauraltee*, Port Victoria Centenary Committee, 1976.
94 Carmichael, p. 28.
95 Minlaton Branch of the National Trust, *Minlaton: A Skeletal History*, Minlaton Branch of the National Trust, Minlaton Branch of the National Trust, Adelaide, 1970; Diana Cook, *The Striding Years: A History of the Minlaton District Council Area*, Adelaide, 1975, p. 8.
96 The Book Centenary Committee, *Quorn and District Centenary 1878–1978*, Lynton Publications, Adelaide, 1978, p. 33.
97 Geoffrey Aslin, *Kongorong from Land to Sea: An Early History*, published by the author, Adelaide, 1991.

Chapter 10 • Placing the past in the present

1 Television Interview in *Aborigine: A Collision of Conscience*, Timewatch Documentary, BBC TV, 1996, 2m 44s.

2   Cited in J. Summers, 'Colonial race relations' in E. Richards, ed., *Flinders History of South Australia, Social History,* Wakefield Press, Adelaide, 1986, p. 497.
3   Ibid.
4   Summers, p. 499.
5   Paul Havemenn, 'The Rule of Law, betrayal and reparation' in Shaun Berg (ed.), *Coming to Terms: Aboriginal Title in South Australia*, Wakefield Press, Kent Town, 2010, p. 141.
6   *South Australian Parliamentary Debates*, 13 July 1966, p. 473.
7   Ibid.
8   Ibid., p. 475.
9   Ibid., p. 479.
10 Don Dunstan, *Felicia: the political memoirs of Don Dunstan*, MacMillan, South Melbourne, 1981, p. 110.
11 Foster, Hosking and Nettelbeck, p. 69.
12 Ibid.
13 Foster, Hosking and Nettelbeck, pp. 69–70.
14 Ibid.
15 Ibid.
16 Australian Sound Design Project. www.sounddesign.unimelb.edu.au
17 Honourable Sandra Kanck, Sculpture on the Cliffs 2006 opening, sa.democrats.org.au
18 Ken Inglis, *Sacred Places: War Memorials in the Australian Landscape*, Melbourne University Press, Melbourne, 1998.
19 Fiona Cameron, 'Transcending Fear. Engaging Emotions and Opinions: A Case for Museums in the 21st Century,' *New Museum Developments and the Culture Wars*, named issue of *Open Museum Journal*, 6 (2003). http://archive.amol.org.au/omj/volume6/volume6_index.asp
20 Mathew Trinca, 'Museums and the History Wars', *History Australia*, 1, 1 (2003), p. 88.
21 James E Young, *At Memory's Edge: After-Images of the Holocaust in Contemporary Art and Architecture*, Yale University Press, London and New Haven, 2000, pp. 96; 120.
22 Caroline Turner, 'Tomorrow's Museums', *Museums of the Future, The Future of Museums*, named issue of *Humanities Research*, 8. 1 (2001), p. 1; Fiona Cameron, 'Beyond Surface Representations: Museums, "Edgy" Topics, Civic Responsibilities and Modes of Engagement', *Contest and Contemporary Society: Redefining Museums in the 21st Century*, named issue of *Open Museum Journal*, 8 (2006). http://archive.amol.org.au/omj/volume8/volume8_index.asp
23 From an Aboriginal perspective, various educational resources are available. The Aboriginal Education Reference Library offers an Eyre Peninsula Aboriginal History activity, developed in consultation with the Port Lincoln Aboriginal Community Centre and other Aboriginal community members. The Port Lincoln Aboriginal Community Council is located in the town centre and offers

educational resources on the region's Aboriginal history, as well as functioning as an agency for community programs and services.
24 'An Oval to Honor First Settlers', *The News*, 26 November 1952.
25 'Historic Graves are Restored', *Port Lincoln Times*, 4 July 1978.
26 Nat Traeger, 'Memorial Marks Brutal History', *Port Lincoln Times*, 3 August 1999.
27 Ibid.
28 Jane Haggis, 'Placing the Post in the Landscape of Memory: Revisiting the Colonial Frontier,' paper for the Cultural Landscapes Symposium, 2005. http// ehlt.flinders.edu.au/humanities/exchange/asri/project_cl.html
29 Ibid.
30 Tony Bennett, 'Out of Which Past?: Critical reflections on Australian Museum and Heritage Policy', Cultural Policy Studies: Occasional Paper No 3, Institute for Cultural Policy Studies, Griffith University, 1988, p. 24.
31 Bennett, p. 14.
32 Jane Lydon, 'Driving By: Visiting Australian Colonial Monuments,' *Journal of Social Archaeology*, 5. No. 1 (2005).
33 Anna Haebich, citing Gitta Sereny, 'Lest We Forget: Activists, Human Rights and the Stolen Generations', paper presented to the Social Memory and Historical Justice symposium, Swinburne University, 13–15 March 2008.

Conclusion
1 Kercher, p. 6.
2 Neal, p. 18.
3 Mike Brown, *No Longer Down Under: Australians Creating Change*, Grosvenor Books, Toorak, 2002, p. 240.
4 Thomas Brown, 'Concerning the murder and the following of the blacks and sheep: account prepared by Thomas Brown about 1901', family papers of Mike Brown.
5 Brown, *No Longer Down Under*, p. 243.
6 Deborah Bird Rose, 'New world poetics of place: along the Oregon Trail and in the National Museum of Australia' in Coombes, p. 228.
7 Journey of Healing SA & ANTaR SA, *Wodlianni. Stolen Generations Coming Home Reconciliation and Healing Event. 173rd Anniversary of the Letters Patent*, Commemorative Booklet, 2009.
8 Leonard Bell, 'Auckland's centrepiece: unsettled identities, unstable monuments' in Coombes, ed., p. 116.
9 Janna Thompson, p. vvii.

BIBLIOGRAPHY

ABBREVIATIONS

GRG Government Record Group
CO Colonial Office
CSO Chief (Colonial) Secretary's Office
SLSA State Library of South Australia
SRSA State Records Office of South Australia
SAM South Australian Museum
PRG Private Record Group
BRG Business Records Group

OFFICIAL PRINTED SOURCES

Great Britain
British Parliamentary Debates.
House of Commons, Sessional Papers:
- 1836, 39, no. 426. First Annual Report of the South Australian Colonization Commissioners.
- 1837, 7, no. 425. Report from the Select Committee on Aborigines (British Settlements).
- 1841, 4, nos. 119 & 394. Select Committee on South Australia.
- 1843, 32, no. 505. Papers Relative to the Affairs of South Australia.

Commonwealth
Initial Conference of Commonwealth and State Aboriginal Authorities, April 1937, Commonwealth Government Printer, Canberra,1937.

South Australia
South Australian Acts.
South Australian Government Gazette.
South Australian Parliamentary Debates.
South Australian Parliamentary Papers.

1860, 3, no. 165, Report of the Select Committee of the Legislative Council upon the Aborigines.

1899, 2, no. 77a, Report of the Select Committee on the Aborigines Bill.

1899, 2, no. 77, Minutes of Evidence on the Aborigines Bill.

OFFICIAL MANUSCRIPT SOURCES

Great Britain

Australian Joint Copying Project: Colonial Office Records.
    South Australia, 1835, Despatches, Offices and Individuals, CO 13/3.
    South Australia, 1836, Despatches, CO 13/4.
    South Australia, 1836, Offices and Individuals, CO 13/5.
    South Australia, 1837, Despatches, CO 13/6.
    South Australia, 1837, Despatches, CO 13/7.
    Tasmania, 1835, Despatches, CO 280/55.

South Australia

State Records of South Australia

Aborigines Department
    Correspondence received, GRG 52/1.
    Protector of Aborigines, Letterbook, GRG 52/7.

Attorney General's Department
    Letters received, 1840–56, GRG 1/1.
    Letters received, 1856–1976, GRG 1/2.
    Letters sent. 1840–1975, GRG 1/6.

Colonization Commission for South Australia
    Instructions to Resident Commissioner, GRG 48/1.

Colonial Secretary's Office
    In letters, GRG 24/1 & 24/6.
    Out letters, GRG 24/4.
    In letters, GRG 24/90.

Department of Correctional Services
    Control register of prisoners, GRG 54/90.

Country and Suburban Courts Department
    Moorundie, records of proceedings of the Resident Magistrate's Court presided over by Edward John Eyre, 19 Jan. 1842 – 20 May 1844, GRG 4, Series 133.

Crown Lands and Immigration Office
    Inward correspondence, GRG 35/1.

Governor's Office
    Despatches from the Colonial Office to the Governor, GRG 2/1.
    Despatches, GRG 2/5/52.
Police Department
    Police Commissioner's Office, correspondence files, 1844–1979, GRG 5/2.
    Police Commissioner's Office, outletter books, 1839–53, 1857–63, 1881–1914, GRG 5/9.
    Copies of General Orders, No. 23 of 1853, GRG 5/28.
    Robe Police Station, copies of general orders, 1849–56, GRG 5/162/1.
    Mount Gambier, Station Journals, 1846–1902, GRG 5/151/1.
    Guichen Bay, Station Journal, 1851–57, 1861–63, GRG 5/159/2.
    Penola, Station Journal, 1853–1891, GRG 5/152/2.
Supreme Court of South Australia
    Criminal files (selected), 1863–87, GRG 36/26.
    Court files. 1841–79, GRG 36/35.
Supreme Court of South Australia Library
    Judges' notebooks, 1839 – 1911.
    Unclassified letterbooks, 1837–1961.
    Court of Oyer and Terminer, 1st Gaol Delivery, May 1837- Mar 1840.
    Supreme Court Letterbooks, 1879–80.

NEWSPAPERS

Adelaide Chronicle
Adelaide Examiner
Adelaide Observer
Advertiser
South Australian Gazette and Colonial Register
Southern Australian
Mail

PRIVATE RECORDS

Benstead, William. Short Stories of my Life and Travels, typescript, n.d. Private Papers.
Bonney, C. Autobiographical notes, vol. 2, SLSA A3305.
Brock, D. Journal of an expedition with Sturt, June 1844, SLSA D. 4745.
Brown, J. Papers of John Brown, 1837–49, SLSA Item nos. 36–37.
Brown, Thomas. 'Concerning the Murder and the Following of the Blacks and Sheep. Account prepared by Thomas Brown about 1901'. Family papers of Mike Brown, Adelaide.

Bull, J.B. Diary of John Bower Bull kept while exploring for pasture country north of Streaky Bay, 1864, SLSA PRG 507/1.
Bull, J.W. Reminiscences: 'Life of John Bull. The Australian Bushman and Explorer', SLSA PRG 507/3.
Butler, Capt. G.V. Letters written by Capt. Butler, Guichen Bay, to Capt. Bagot, SLSA 3746/1–3 (L).
Dean, William, Papers. 1864, BRG 291/1/3. SLSA.
Flett family. Letters concerning pastoral properties in northern South Australia, 1864–1886, SLSA D. 6390 (L).
Hale, Matthew. Papers, SLSA PRG 275.
Hawker, G.C. Diaries kept by George Charles Hawker, 1840, 1842–43, SLSA PRG 847/1–2.
Hawker, G.C. Reminiscences of life on Bungaree station, SLSA 1384/52a, Pt. 1.
Herbert, S.W. Reminiscences of life in the Northern Territory during the construction of the Overland Telegraph, 1870–1872, SLSA D. 6995 (L).
Holroyd, H. Reminiscences, 1829–1906, SLSA D. 4108/1–7 (L).
Hunter, J.A.C. Diaries, 1872–74, SLSA D. 3077/1–12 (L).
Hutchinson, J.R. Reminiscences of J.R., 1840–90, SLSA D. 4837 (L).
Jones, J.W. Lecture on the Aborigines, 1887, State Records GRG 53/266/14.
Leake, R.R. Letters of Robert Rowland Leake, 1811–60, 'Glencoe', Mount Gambier, SLSA PRG 183.
Lutz, E.E. Memoirs of 68 years spent on the West Coast of South Australia, 1893–1961, SLSA D. 4895 (L).
McLaren, David. Journal kept by David McLaren during his voyage in the South Australian from England to South Australia, November 26, 1836 – April 2, 1837, together with a conversation with the Aborigines. SLSA 790/2.
Melville, Henry Dudley. 'Reminiscences' in 5 Volumes. SLSA D6976.
Mudge, John, Letters written by John Mudge … whilst a trooper at Pt. Lincoln and Mt. Wedge, 1857–60, SLSA 1518.
Schurmann, C. Diary, 1830s – 1840s, Typescript of copy originally held by the Aboriginal Heritage Branch, South Australian Department of Environment and Planning.
Smith family. Papers of the Smith Family of Rivoli Bay and Mount Gambier, c. 1838–1950, SLSA PRG 144.
Stewart, D. Notebook, 1853, SLSA D. 2609 (L).
Samuel Stuckey, 'Reminiscences', undated, A 1083 A, SLSA.
Sturt, E.P.S. Copies of Letters by E.P.S. Sturt to John Robertson, Wando Vale, Victoria, 1846–1851, SLSA D. 6315 (L).
Warburton, M.E. Diary, 1868–70, SLSA D. 4804 (L).
Wells, William. Diary, SLSA D. 6735 (L).

AUDIO AND VIDEO SOURCES

Aborigine: A Collision of Conscience, Timewatch Documentary, BBC TV, 1996.
Bitter Springs, dir. Ralph Smart, Ealing Studios, 1950.
The Sturt Report: Audio Recording of the ABC Historical Re-enactment of the Sturt Expedition, RADA Acc. No. 2122, no. 28, 2 Feb 1951.

BOOKS AND ARTICLES

Aslin, Geoffrey. *Kongorong from Land to Sea: An Early History,* published by the author, Adelaide, 1991.
Atkinson, Alan. *The Europeans in Australia: A History, Volume II: Democracy,* Oxford University Press, Melbourne, 2004.
Attwood, Bain. *Telling the Truth about Aboriginal History,* Allen & Unwin, Sydney, 2005.
Attwood, Bain and Andrew Markus, *Thinking Black: William Cooper and the Australian Aborigines' League,* Aboriginal Studies Press, Canberra, 2004.
Attwood, Bain and S. Foster, *Frontier Conflict: The Australian Experience,* National Museum of Australia, Canberra, 2003.
Attwood, Bain and Andrew Markus, *The Struggle for Aboriginal Rights: A Documentary History,* Allen and Unwin, Sydney, 1999.
Attwood, Bain, ed. *In the Age of Mabo: History, Aborigines and Australia,* Allen and Unwin, Sydney, 1996.
Attwood, Bain and J. Arnold, eds. *Power, Knowledge and Aborigines,* La Trobe University Press, Melbourne, 1992.
Arthur, E.A. 'Journal of Events from Melbourne, Port Phillip, to Mount Shanck, in the District of Adelaide, New Holland'. 1844; rpt. Libraries Board of South Australia, Adelaide, 1975.
Baillie, P.J. *Port Lincoln and District: A Pictorial History,* Lynton Publications, Blackwood, 1978.
Bell, Leonard. 'Aukland's centrepiece: unsettled identities, unstable monuments' in Annie Coombes, ed. *Rethinking Settler Colonialism: History and Memory in Australia, Canada, Aotearoa New Zealand and South Africa,* Manchester University Press, Manchester and New York, 2006.
Bellanta, Melissa. 'Fabulating the Australian Desert: Australia's Lost Race Romances 1890–1908', *Philament* (December 2007).
Bennett, J.M. and Alex C. Castles, *A Sourcebook of Australian Legal History,* Law Book Co, Sydney, 1979.
Bennett, Tony. 'Out of Which Past?: Critical reflections on Australian Museum and Heritage Policy', *Cultural Policy Studies: Occasional Paper No 3,* Institute for Cultural Policy Studies, Griffith University, 1988.
Benton, Lauren. *Law and Colonial Cultures: Legal Regimes in World History 1400–1900,* Cambridge University Press, Cambridge, 2002.

Berg, Sean, ed. *Coming to Terms: Aboriginal Title in South Australia*, Wakefield Press, Adelaide, 2010.

Blacket, J. *A History of South Australia*, Hussey and Gillingham, Adelaide, 1911.

Broome, Richard. 'The Statistics of Frontier Conflict,' in *Frontier Conflict: The Australian Experience*, Bain Attwood and S.G. Foster, eds, National Museum of Australia, Canberra, 2003.

Broome, Richard. 'Historians, Aborigines and Australia: Writing the National Past' in Bain Attwood, ed. *In the Age of Mabo: History, Aborigines and Australia*, Allen and Unwin, Sydney, 1996.

Brown, Mike. *No Longer Down Under: Australians Creating Change*, Grosvenor Books, Toorak, Vic., 2002.

Buchanan, A. 'Diary of a journey overland from Sydney to Adelaide', *Royal Geographical Society of Australasia, South Australian Branch, Proceedings,* vol. 15. 1922–23.

Bull, J.W. *Early Experiences of Life in South Australia,* E.S. Wigg & Son, Adelaide, 1884.

Burgess, H.T. *The Cyclopedia of South Australia: An Historical and Commercial Review: Descriptive and Biographical, Facts, Figures and Illustrations: An Epitome of Progress*, Cyclopedia Co., Adelaide, 1907–1909.

Camm, J.C.R. & J. McQuilton, eds. *Australians: An Historical Atlas*, Fairfax, Syme & Weldon, Sydney, 1987.

Cameron, Fiona. 'Transcending Fear. Engaging Emotions and Opinions: A Case for Museums in the 21st Century,' *New Museum Developments and the Culture Wars*, named issue of *Open Museum Journal*, 6 (2003). http://archive.amol.org.au/omj/volume6/volume6_index.asp

Carmichael, Ern. *The Ill-Shaped Leg: A Story of the Development of Yorke Peninsula*, published by the author, 1973.

Carroll, J, ed. *Intruders in the Bush, the Australian Quest for Identity,* Oxford University Press, Melbourne, 1986.

Carthew, Heather. *Rivoli Bay: A story of early settlement at Rivoli Bay in the South East of South Australia 1845–1855*, published by the author, Adelaide 1974.

Castle, Tim. 'Watching them Hang: Capital Punishment and Public Support in Colonial New South Wales 1826–1836', *History Australia*, 5, no. 2 (2008).

Castles, A.C. *An Australian Legal History,* Law Book Co., Sydney, 1982.

Castles, A.C. & Michael C. Harris, *Lawmakers and Wayward Whigs; Government and Law in South Australia, 1836–1986*, Wakefield Press, Adelaide, 1987.

Chesterman, John & Brian Galligan. *Citizens Without Rights: Aborigines and Australian Citizenship*, Cambridge University Press, Melbourne, 1997.

Clark, C.M.H. *A History of Australia, Vol. V: The People Make Laws 1888–1915, Melbourne University Press*, Melbourne, 1978.

Clyne, Robert. *Colonial Blue: A History of the South Australian Police Force 1836–1916*, Wakefield Press, Adelaide, 1987.

Clyne, Robert. 'War with the Natives: From the Coorong to the Rufus, 1841', *Journal of the Historical Society of SA,* 9 (1981).

Cockburn, R. *Pastoral Pioneers of South Australia,* vols. I & II., Publishers Limited, Adelaide, 1925.

Cook, Diana. *The Striding Years: A History of the Minlaton District Council Area*, District Council of Minlaton, 1975.

Conigrave, J.F. *South Australia: A Sketch of its History and Resources*, Adelaide, 1886.

Connor, John. *The Australian Frontier Wars 1788–1838*, University of New South Wales Press, Sydney, 2002.

Coombes, Annie, ed. *Rethinking Settler Colonialism.* Manchester University Press, Manchester, 2006.

Cramm, J.C.R. & J. McQuilton, eds. *Australians: An Historical Atlas,* Fairfax, Syme & Weldon Associates, Sydney, 1987.

Crawford, J. 'Diary of J. Crawford: extracts on Aborigines and Adelaide 1839–1841', *South Australiana,* 4, no. 1 (1965).

Cunneen, Chris. *Conflict, Politics and Crime*, Allen & Unwin, Kensington, 2001.

Davenport, S. 'Letters of Samuel Davenport, chiefly to his father George Davenport, 1842–49'. Part II – Part VII, B.S. Baldwin (ed), *South Australiana,* vol. VI, no. 2, 1967 – vol. X, no. 2, 1971.

Davies, Margaret. 'Settlers and Aborigines at Port Lincoln 1840–45', *South Australiana*, 18, no. 1 (March 1979).

Davies, Susanne. 'Aborigines, Murder and the Criminal Law in Early Port Phillip 1841–1851', *Historical Studies*, 22, no. 88 (1987).

Davison, Graeme. 'Museums and the culture wars: in defence of civic pluralism' in *Contest and contemporary society: redefining museums in the 21st century*, special issue of *Open museum journal*, 8 (2006).

Dickey, B. & Peter Howell. *South Australia's Foundation: Select Documents*, Wakefield Press, Adelaide, 1986.

Dixon, Robert. *Writing the Colonial Adventure*, Melbourne, Cambridge University Press, 1996.

Dutton, Geoffrey. *The Hero as Murderer: The Life of Edward John Eyre*, F.W. Cheshire, Melbourne, 1967.

Elbourne, Elizabeth. ' "The Sin of the Settler" The 1835–36 Select Committee on Aborigines and Debates over Virtue and Conquest in the Early nineteenth Century British White Settler Empire', *Journal of Colonialism and Colonial History*, 4, no. 3 (2004).

Elliston Centenary Committee, *Across the Bar to Waterloo Bay: Elliston 1978–1978*, Elliston Centenary Committee, Elliston, 1978.

Evans, Julie. 'Colonialism and the Rule of Law: the case of South Australia', Barry S. Godfrey and Graeme Dunstall, *Crime and Empire 1840–1940: Criminal Justice in Local and Global Context* (2005).

Eyre, E.J. *Journals of Expeditions of Discovery into Central Australia, and Overland from Adelaide to King George's Sound in the years 1840–41,* 2 vols, T & W. Boone, London, 1845.

Finnane, Mark. *Police and Government: Histories of Policing in Australia*, Oxford University Press, Melbourne, 1994.

Finnane, Mark and Jonathan Richards. '"You'll Get Nothing Out of It": The Inquest, Police and Aboriginal Deaths in Colonial Queensland', *Australian Historical Studies*, 35. no. 123 (2004).

Forster, A. *South Australia: Its Progress and Prosperity,* Samson Low, Son, and Marston, London, 1866.

Foster, R.K.G. 'Co-existence and Colonization on Pastoral Lands in South Australia, 1851–1899', in *Despotic Dominion: Property Rights in British Settler Societies*, University of British Columbia Press, Vancouver, 2005.

Foster, R.K.G. 'Rations, Co-existence and the colonisation of Aboriginal Labour in South Australia, 1860–1911', *Aboriginal History*, 24 (2000).

Foster, R.K.G. 'The Origin of the Protection of Aboriginal Rights in South Australian Pastoral Leases', *Land, Rights, Laws: Issues in Native Title*, Issue Paper No. 24, 1998.

Foster, R.K.G. 'Feasts of the full-moon: the distribution of rations to Aborigines in South Australia 1836–1861', *Aboriginal History,* 13, no.1 (1989).

Foster, Robert, Rick Hosking & Amanda Nettelbeck, *Fatal Collisions: the South Australian frontier and the violence of memory*, Wakefield Press, 2001.

Frost, A. 'New South Wales as *terra nullius*: the British denial of Aboriginal land rights.' *Historical Studies,* 11, no. 77 (1981).

Furniss, Elizabeth. 'Challenging the myth of indigenous peoples' "last stand" in Canada and Australia: public discourse and the conditions of silence,' in Annie Coombes, ed., *Rethinking settler colonialism: history and memory in Australia, Canada, Aotearoa New Zealand and South Africa*, Manchester University Press, Manchester, 2006.

Gason, S. *The Dieyerie Tribe of Australian Aborigines; their Manners and Customs,* W.C. Cox, Government Printer, Adelaide, 1874.

Gibbs, R. 'Relations between Aboriginal inhabitants and the first South Australian colonists', *Royal Geographical Society of South Australia, South Australian Branch,* 61 (1959–60).

Godfrey, Barry S. and Graeme Dunstall, eds. *Crime and Empire 1840–1940: Criminal Justice in Local and Global Context*, Willan Publishing, Cullompton, 2005.

Grenfell Price, A. The Foundation and Settlement of South Australia 1829–1845, F.W. Preece, Adelaide, 1924,

Grey, G. *Journals of Two Expeditions of Discovery in north-west and Western Australia during the years 1837, 38, 39 under the authority of Her Majesty's Government,* 2 vols, T. & W. Boone, London, 1841.

Griffiths, Tom. 'Past Silences: Aborigines and convicts in our history', in Penny Russell and Richard White, eds. *Pastiche I: Reflections on Nineteenth-Century Australia*, Allen and Unwin, Sydney, 1997.

Griffiths, Tom. 'The Language of Conflict' in B. Attwood and S. Foster, eds. *Frontier Conflict: The Australian Experience*, National Museum of Australia, Canberra, 2003.

Haebich, Anna. 'Lest We Forget: Activists, Human Rights and the Stolen Generations', Social Memory and Historical Justice symposium, Swinburne University, 13–15 March 2008.

Haggis, Jane. 'Placing the Post in the Landscape of Memory: Revisiting the Colonial Frontier,' paper for the Cultural Landscapes Symposium, 2005. http//ehlt.flinders.edu.au/humanities/exchange/asri/project_cl.html

Hamilton, Paula. 'Memory Studies and Cultural History' in Hsu-Ming Teo and Richard White, eds. *Cultural History in Australia*, University of New South Wales Press, Sydney, 2003.

Hamilton, Paula. 'The Knife-edge: Debates about Memory and History' in Kate Darian-Smith and Paula Hamilton, eds. *Memory and History in Twentieth Century Australia,* Oxford University Press, Melbourne, 1994.

Harcus, W. *South Australia: Its History, Resources and Productions,* Sampson Low, Marston, Searle & Rivington, London, 1876.

Hassell, K. *The Relations between Settlers and Aborigines in South Australia 1836–1860,* Libraries Board of South Australia, Adelaide, 1966.

Havemann, Paul. 'The Rule of Law, Betrayal and Reparation' in Shaun Berg, ed., *Coming to Terms: Aboriginal Title in South Australia*, Wakefield Press, Adelaide, 2010.

Hawker, J.C. *Early Experiences in South Australia,* E.S. Wigg & Son, Adelaide, 1899.

Hawker, Ruth. *Yesterday*, F.W. Preece and Son, Adelaide, 1936.

Hayward, J.F. 'Reminiscences of Johnson Frederick Hayward', *Proceedings of the Royal Geographical Society of Australasia, South Australian Branch,* 29 (1929).

Healy, Chris. *In the Ruins of Colonialism: History as Social Memory*, Cambridge University Press, Melbourne, 1997.

Healy, Chris. *Forgetting Aborigines*, University of New South Wales Press, Sydney, 2008.

Healy, Sianan. 'Years Ago Some Lived Here: Aboriginal Australians and the Production of Popular Culture, History and Identity in 1930s Victoria', *Australian Historical Studies* 37, no. 128 (2006).

Heinrich, Rhoda. *Wide Sails and Wheat Stacks: A History of Port Victoria and the Hundred of Wauraltee*, Port Victoria Centenary Committee, 1976.

Heinrich, Rhoda. *Governor Fergusson's Legacy*, Maitland-Kilkerran Centenary Committee, Adelaide, 1972.

Hirst, J.B. 'The Pioneer Legend', in J. Carroll, ed., *Intruders in the Bush*, Melbourne University Press, Melbourne, 1986.

Hirst, JB. *The Sentimental Nation: The Making of the Australian Commonwealth*, Oxford University Press, Melbourne, 2000.

Hitchcock, W. *South Australia: Its History, Its Climate, and a Few Particulars of its Products and Capabilities*, E.S. Wigg & Son, Adelaide, 1900.

Hodder, E. *The History of South Australia from Its Foundation to the Year of Its Jubilee*, Sampson Low, Marston, London, 1893.

Hosking, Rick. '"A Projection Part of the Main": An Elliston Palimpsest," Understanding Cultural Landscapes Symposium, 11–15 July Flinders University. www.dspace.flinders.edu.au.

Horner, Jack and Marcia Langton, 'The Day of Mourning' in B. Gammage and P. Spearitt, eds. *Australians 1938*, Fairfax, Syme & Weldon, Sydney, 1987.

Howitt, W. *Colonization and Christianity: a Popular History of the Treatment of the Natives by the Europeans in all their Colonies,* Longman, Orme, Brown, Green & Longmans, London, 1838.

Hunter, Ann. 'The Boundaries of Colonial Criminal Law in Relation to Inter-Aboriginal Conflict in Western Australia in the 1830s-1840s', *Australian Journal of Legal History*, 8 (2004).

Hunter, Rosemary. 'Aboriginal Histories, Australian Histories and the Law' in Bain Attwood, ed., *In the Age of Mabo: History, Aborigines and Australia*, Allen and Unwin, Sydney, 1996.

Inglis, Ken. *Sacred Places: War Memorials in the Australian Landscape*, Melbourne University Press, Melbourne, 1998.

Janson, Susuan and Stuart MacIntyre, eds. 'Making the bicentenary'. Special issue of *Australian Historical Studies* 23, no 91 (1988).

Jenkin, G. *Conquest of the Ngarrindjeri: The Story of the Lower Murray Lakes Tribes,* Rigby, Adelaide, 1979.

Jones, Philip. *Ochre and Rust: Artefacts and Encounters on Australian Frontiers*, Wakefield Press, Adelaide, 2007.

Kercher, Bruce. *An Unruly Child: A History of Law in Australia*, Allen & Unwin, Sydney, 1995.

Kanck, Sandra. Sculpture on the Cliffs 2006 opening, sa.democrats.org.au

Kimber, Richard. 'Genocide or Not? The Situation in Central Australia 1860–1895' in Colin Tatz, ed. *Genocide Perspectives I: Essays in Comparative Genocide*, Centre for Comparative Genocide Studies, Sydney, 1997.

Kleinhert, Sylvia. 'An Aboriginal Moomba: Remaking History', *Continuum* 13, no 3 (1999).

Krichauff, Skye. *The Narungga and Europeans: Cross-Cultural Relations on Yorke Peninsula in the Nineteenth Century*, MA Thesis, University of Adelaide.

Krygier, Martin. 'The Rule of Law' in Neil J. Smelser & Paul B. Baltes, eds, *International Encyclopedia of the Social and Behavioural Sciences*, Elsevier Science, Oxford, 2001, p. 13403.

Levison, James. 'The Trial of Thomas Donnelly', *Journal of the Anthropological Society of South Australia*, 31. 2 (1993).

Liston, Ellen. *Pioneers: Stories by Ellen Liston,* Hassell Press, Adelaide, 1936.

Lydon, Jane. 'Driving By: Visiting Australian Colonial Monuments,' *Journal of Social Archaeology*, 5, no. 1 (2005).

MacGillivray, Leith. '"We have found our paradise": The South-East Squattocracy, 1840–1870', *Journal of the Historical Society of South Australia*, 17 (1989).

MacIntyre, Stuart and Anna Clark. *The History Wars*, Melbourne University Press, Melbourne, 2003.

McCorquodale, J. *Aborigines and the Law: a Digest,* Aboriginal Studies Press, Canberra, 1987.

McCourt, T. & Minchin, H. *The Coorong and Lakes of the Lower Murray*, Beachport Branch of the National Trust, Adelaide, 1987.

McGregor, Russell. *Imagined Destinies: Aboriginal Australians and the Doomed Race Theory 1880–1939*, Melbourne University Press, Melbourne, 1997.

MacGuire, John. 'Judicial Violence and the "Civilizing Process": Race and the Transition from Public to Private Executions in Colonial Australia', *Australian Historical Studies*, 29, no. 111 (1998).

McHugh, P.G. *Aboriginal Societies and the Common Law: A History of Sovereignty, Status, and Self-Determination*, Oxford University Press, Oxford, 2004.

McLean, J. 'Police Experiences with the Natives. Reminiscences of the Early Days of the Colony', *Royal Geographical Society of Australasia, South Australian Branch*, 6 (1902–03).

Main, J.M. 'The Foundation of South Australia', in Dean Jaensch, ed., *The Flinders History of South Australia: Political History*, Wakefield Press, Adelaide, 1986.

Mattingley, Christobel and Ken Hampton, eds. *Survival in our own Land: 'Aboriginal' Experiences in 'South Australia' since 1836, told by Nungas and others*, Hodder and Stoughton, Sydney, 1992.

Meinig, D.W. *On the Margins of the Good Earth*, SA Government Printer, Adelaide, 1988.

Minlaton: A Skeletal History, Minlaton Branch of the National Trust, 1970.

Morris, B. 'Frontier Colonialism as a Culture of Terror', in B. Attwood and J. Arnold, eds, *Power, Knowledge and Aborigines*, La Trobe University Press, Melbourne, 1992.

Morton-Robinson, Aileen. 'Unmasking Whiteness: A Goori Jondal's Look at Some Duggai Business' in Belinda McKay, ed. *Unmasking Whiteness: Race Relations and Reconciliation*, Griffith University, Brisbane, 1999.

Nance, Beverly. 'The Level of Violence: Europeans and Aborigines in Port Phillip 1835–1850', *Historical Studies*, 19, no. 77 (1981).

Neal, David. *The Rule of Law in a Penal Colony*, Cambridge University Press, Melbourne, 1991.

Nettelbeck, Amanda and Robert Foster. *In the Name of the Law: William Willshire and the Policing of the Australian Frontier*, Wakefield Press, Adelaide, 2007.

Nettelbeck, Amanda and Robert Foster. 'Reading the Elusive Letter of the Law: Policing the Australian Frontier', *Australian Historical Studies*, 38, no. 130 (2007).

Neumann, Klauss, Nicholas Thomas and Hilary Ericksen, eds. *Quicksands: Foundational Histories in Australia and Aotearoa New Zealand*, University of New South Wales Press, 1999.

Newland, S. *Paving the Way. A Romance of the Australian Bush,* Gay and Bird, London, 1893.

Owen, Chris. '"The Police Appear to be a Useless Lot up There": Law and Order in the East Kimberley 1884–1905', *Aboriginal History*, 27 (2003).

Pascoe, J.J, ed. *History of Adelaide and Vicinity With a General Sketch of the Province of South Australia and Biographies of Representative Men*, Hussey & Gillingham, Adelaide, 1901.

Patton, Barry. 'Unequal Justice: Colonial Law and the Shooting of Jim Crow', *Provenance,* no. 5 (September 2006).

Pike, D. *Paradise of Dissent,* Melbourne University Press, Melbourne, 1957.

Pike, D. *Australia: The Quiet Continent*, Cambridge University Press, Cambridge, 1962.

Pope, Alan. Aborigines and the Criminal Law in South Australia: The First Twenty Five Years, PhD thesis, Deakin University, 1998.

Pope, Alan. *Resistance and Retaliation: Aboriginal-European Relations in Early Colonial South Australia* Heritage Action, Adelaide, 1989.

Powell, Alan. *Far Country: A Short History of the Northern Territory*, Melbourne University Press, Melbourne, 1982.

Reece, R.H.W. *Aborigines and colonists: Aborigines and Colonial Society in New South Wales in the 1830s and 1840s,* University of Sydney Press, Sydney, 1974.

Reid, Gordon. *A Picnic with the Natives: Aboriginal-European Relations in the Northern Territory to 1910*, Melbourne University Press, Melbourne, 1990.

Reynolds, H. *Frontier: Aborigines, Settlers and Land,* Allen and Unwin, Sydney, 1987.

Reynolds, H. *The Law of the Land,* Penguin, Melbourne, 1987.

Reynolds, H. 'Reviving Indigenous Sovereignty', *Macquarie Law Journal*, 2 (2006).

Richards, E, ed. *The Flinders History of South Australia. Social History*, Wakefield Press, Adelaide, 1986.

Richards, Jonathan. *The Secret War: A True History of Queensland's Native Police*, University of Queensland Press, St Lucia, 2008.

Richardson, N. *The Pioneers of the North-West of South Australia 1856–1914*, W.K. Thomas, Adelaide, 1925.

Riggs, Damien. 'Idealising Place: Art, Appropriation and the "Pre-colonial Landscape"' in Susanne Scheck and Ben Wadham, eds, *Placing Race and Localising Whiteness*, Flinders Press, Adelaide, 2004.

Roberts, Tony. *Frontier Justice: A History of the Gulf Country to 1900*, University of Queensland Press, 2005.

Roe, Michael. 'A Model Aboriginal State, *Aboriginal History*, 10, no. 1 (1986).

Rose, Deborah Bird. 'Hard Times: An Australian Study' in Klaus Neumann, Nicholas Thomas and Hilary Ericksen, eds, *Quicksands: Foundational Histories in Australia and Aotearoa New Zealand*, University of New South Wales Press, 1999.

Rose, Deborah Bird. 'New world poetics of place: along the Oregon Trail and in the National Museum of Australia' in Annie Coombes, ed. *Rethinking Settler Colonialism: History and Memory in Australia, Canada, Aotearoa New Zealand and South Africa*, Manchester University Press, Manchester and New York, 2006.

Schurmann, C.W. *The Aboriginal Tribes of Port Lincoln*, Adelaide, 1846.

Schurmann, E. *I'd Rather Dig Potatoes: Clamor Schurmann and the Aborigines of South Australia 1838–1853*, Lutheran Publishing House, Adelaide, 1987.

Scott, H.J. *South Australia: A Handbook for the Adelaide Jubilee International Exhibition* (1887); rpt. Bibliolife, 2009.

Shaw, A.G.L. 'British Policy towards the Australian Aborigines, 1830–1850', *Australian Historical Studies*, 25, no. 99, October 1992.

Smith, Christina. *The Booandik Tribe of South Australian Aborigines*, E. Spiller, Adelaide, 1880.

South Australia, Crown Lands and Immigration Commissioner. *South Australia: A Brief Account of Its Progress and Resources*, Adelaide, 1881 & 1882.

South Australian Register. South Australia: An Account of Its History, Progress, Resources and Present Position, Adelaide, 1879. Written for the Sydney Exhibition and revised for the Adelaide Exhibition of 1881.

Souter, Gavin. 'Skeleton at the Feast' in B. Gammage and P. Spearritt, eds, *Australians 1938*, Fairfax, Syme & Weldon, Broadway NSW, 1987.

Spencer, B. & F.J. Gillen. *The Native Tribes of Central Australia*, Macmillan, London, 1899.

Standfield, Rachel. '"A Remarkably Tolerant Nation"? Contradictions of Benign Whiteness in Australian Political Discourse', *borderlands ejournal,* vol 3, no 2, 2004, http//www.borderlandsejournal/issues/vol3no2.html.

Stanner, W.E.H. *After the Dreaming*, Boyer Lecture Series, ABC, 1968.

Stevens, Christine. White *Man's Dreaming: Killalpaninna Mission 1866–1915*, Oxford University Press, Melbourne, 1994.

Stow, J.P. *South Australia: Its History, Productions and Natural Resources*, Adelaide, 1883. Written for the Calcutta Exhibition.

Sturt, C. *Two Expeditions into the Interior of Southern Australia,* 2 vols, Smith, Elder, London, 1833.

Summers, J. 'Colonial race relations', in E. Richards, ed., *Flinders History of South Australia, Social History,* Wakefield Press, Adelaide, 1986.

Taplin, G, ed. *The Folklore, Manners, and Customs of the South Australian Aborigines,* Government Printer, Adelaide, 1879.

Thiele, Frances. 'Superintendent La Trobe and the Amenability of Aboriginal People to British Law', *Provenance,* 8 (2009).

Thomas, Julian. 'A History of Beginnings' in Klaus Neumann, Nicholas Thomas and Hilary Ericksen, eds, *Quicksands: Foundational Histories in Australia and Aotearoa New Zealand*, University of New South Wales Press, 1999.

Thomas, Julian. '1938: Past and Present in an Elaborate Anniversary', *Australian Historical Studies,* 23, no. 91 (1988).

Thomas, Nicholas. 'The Uses of Captain Cook: Early Exploration in the Public History of Aotearoa New Zealand' in Annie Coombes, ed., *Rethinking settler colonialism: history and memory in Australia, Canada, Aotearoa New Zealand and South Africa*, Manchester University Press, Manchester, 2006.

Tolmer, A. *Reminiscences of an Adventurous and Chequered Career at Home and at the Antipodes,* 2 vols, Sampson, Low, Marston, Serle & Rivington, London, 1882.

Trinca, Mathew. 'Museums and the History Wars', *History Australia*, 1, no. 1 (2003).

Thompson, Janna. *Taking Responsibility for the Past: Reparation and Historical Justice*, Polity, Cambridge, 2002.

Turner, Caroline. 'Tomorrow's Museums', *Museums of the Future, The Future of Museums*, special issue of *Humanities Research*, 8, no. 1 (2001).

Turner, Stephen. 'Settlement as Forgetting' in Klaus Neumann, Nicholas Thomas and Hilary Ericksen, eds. *Quicksands: Foundational Histories in Australia and Aotearoa New Zealand*, University of New South Wales Press, Sydney, 1999.

Ward, R. *The Australian Legend,* Melbourne University Press, Melbourne, 1958.

Ward, Damen. 'Constructing British Authority in Australasia: Charles Cooper and the Legal Status of Aborigines in the South Australian Supreme Court, c. 1840–60', *Journal of Imperial and Commonwealth History*, 34, no. 4 (2006).

Whitelock, Derek with Tony Baker, *Adelaide: A Sense of Difference*, Australian Scholarly Publishing, Melbourne, 2000.

Willshire, W.H.A. *The Aborigines of Central Australia. With a Vocabulary of the Dialect of the Alice Springs Natives,* C.E. Bristow, Government Printer, Port Augusta, 1888.

Willshire, W.H.A. *The Aborigines of Central Australia,* C.E. Bristow, Government Printer, Adelaide, 1891.

Woods, J.D, ed. *The Native Tribes of South Australia,* E.S. Wigg and Son, Adelaide, 1879.

Woods, J.D. *The Province of South Australia*, Government Printer, Adelaide, 1894.

Young, James E. *At Memory's Edge: After-Images of the Holocaust in Contemporary Art and Architecture*, Yale University Press, London & New Haven, 2000.

INDEX

A

Aboriginal and Historic Relics Preservation Act, 1965, 168
Aboriginal evidence, 4, 58, 59, 60, 61, 62, 69, 70, 72, 84
Aboriginal interpreters, 58, 60, 125
Aboriginal labour, 76, 97, 98, 143, 144
Aboriginal Lands Trust Act, 1966, 168
Aboriginal legal status, 2, 3, 17, 18, 19, 26, 35, 57, 59, 99, 102, 103, 121, 124, 143
Aboriginal prisoners, 52, 83, 107, 108, 109, 179
Aboriginal trackers, 44, 93, 94, 102, 107
Aboriginal traditional law, 56, 77, 110, 111, 121
Aboriginal witnesses, 59, 60, 61, 62, 70, 108, 109
Aboriginal Witnesses Act, 1848, 60, 70
Aborigines Act 1934–39, 168
Aborigines Affairs Act, 1967, 168
Aborigines Evidence Act, 1844, 59
Aborigines Progress Association, 171
Aborigines Progressive Association, 149
Aborigines Progressive League, 149
Aborigines Protection Board, 149
Aborigines Protection Society, 32, 59
Aborigines' Protection League, 152
Adelaide, 25, 26, 27, 28, 32, 33, 34, 35, 36, 37, 42, 44, 49, 68, 70, 81, 82, 84, 90, 101, 109, 115, 118, 119, 125, 132, 140, 145, 146, 147, 148, 155, 156, 162, 163, 164
Adelaide Gaol, 52, 109
Adnyamathanha, 176, 177
Advocate General, 31, 60, 64, 65, 66, 70, 82, 83
Alice Springs, 124
Angipena, 104, 112
Anthropology, 132
Arkaroola Creek, 105
Arthur, Edward, 81
Arthur, Governor George, 3, 15, 16
Atkins, Judge Advocate Richard, 3, 18
Attorney General, 104, 105

Australia Day, 148
Australian Aborigines' League, 149, 150, 152
Australian Broadcasting Commission, 153
Australian Natives Association, 131
Avenue Range, 138, 163

B

Bagnall, William, 164, 165
Baillie, Perc, 174
Baker, John, 66
Banggarla, 176, 177
Barossa Valley, 118
Barrow Creek telegraph station, 124
Barton, Russell, 110
Basedow, Dr Herbert, 151, 152
Battara, 42, 43, 46, 47, 48, 53, 173
Beard, Henry, 95
Beevor, James, 62, 84, 85, 86, 137
Beltana, 104, 118
Benstead, William, 140
Beviss, Archie, 171
Bicentenary, 170, 178
Bi-Centennial Authority, 177
Biddle, James Rolles, 44, 45, 46, 49, 51, 52, 53
Big Murray tribe, 30
Bishop of Adelaide, 104
Bitter Springs, 155, 156, 157
Black Line, 3
Blacket, John, 144, 145
Blanchewater, 114, 118
Blinman, 104, 108, 118, 120
Blue Mountains, 3
Bonney, Crown Lands Commissioner Charles, 96
Borthwick, William, 104
Brachina Gorge, 117
Brisbane, Governor Thomas, 3
Bromley, Walter, 23
Brooks, Fred, 145
Broome, Richard, 4
Brown, Government Resident John, 86

227

Brown, James, 70, 101, 102, 138, 145, 161, 162, 163, 164, 165, 176, 182
Brown, John, 43, 101, 125, 126
Brown, Mike, 182, 183
Brown, Peter, 106, 107
Brown, Robert, 101
Brown, Thomas, 101, 102, 182, 183
Bryan, Laurie, 171
Buandig, 78, 175, 176
Buchanan, Alexander, 34, 140, 145
Buffalo, 20, 147
Bull, John Wranthall, 54, 136, 150, 165
Bundaleer, 97
Bungaree, 49, 91
Burtt, Corporal, 105
Buttfield, Sub-Protector John, 118
Buxton, Sir Thomas Fowell Buxton, 1

C

Cameron, J.B., 171
Cape Radstock, 95
Carter, William, 82, 83
Castle, Tim, 3
Centenary of Federation, 179
Central Australia, 95, 123, 140, 143
Charley, 60
Chesterman, John, 144
Chief Secretary, 61, 96, 104, 105, 106, 112, 113, 121
Cleland, John Burton, 151
Clyne, Robert, 27
Cockburn, Rodney, 116, 145, 163
Coffin Bay, 46, 48, 50
Commemoration Day. See Proclamation Day
Commissioner of Crown Lands, 95, 96
Commissioner of Police, 27, 30, 64, 66, 79, 80, 85, 88, 89, 91, 93, 94, 103, 105, 106, 108, 109, 110, 111, 137
Congreve, Henry John, 137
Coniston Massacre, 145, 173
Coolmultie, 137
Cooper, Judge Charles, 26, 29, 56, 60, 74, 75
Cooper, William, 149, 150
Coorong, 28, 56, 57, 150, 161, 162, 164
Coronial inquests, 63, 67, 68, 69, 72
Corporal punishment, 42, 52, 53, 72, 110
Corroboree, 119, 132
Crawford, James, 33
Crawford, Max, 158
Curran, Owen, 81

D

Darke, Charles, 52
Darling River, 33, 34, 38
Darling, Governor Ralph, 18
Dashwood, Police Commissioner George, 96
Davies, Susanne, 4
Day of Mourning, 149, 152
Dean, Henry, 115, 116, 119, 122
Dean, William, 114
Destitute Asylum, 109
Diyari, 117
Donnelly, James, 70, 71, 72
Dowling, Chief Justice James, 75
Driver, Government Resident Charles, 44, 45, 47, 50, 51, 52, 53, 87, 164, 174
Duffield, William, 26
Duguid, Dr Charles, 152
Dunstan, Don, 168, 169, 184
Dutton, Charles, 43, 49, 174
Dwyer, Patrick, 64, 85, 162, 164
Dying Race, 131, 132, 142

E

Ealing Studios, 155
Earl Grey, Secretary of State, 95
Easton, Annie, 84, 85, 137
Eastwood, 70, 162
Elder, Thomas, 115, 116, 122
Elkin, A. P., 149, 150
Ellis, James, 124
Elliston, 86, 137, 171, 172, 173
Elliston massacre, 137, 171
Empire Pageant, 146
Encounter 2002, 172
Encounter Bay, 25, 91, 162
Executions, 3, 4, 30, 31, 32, 51, 52, 62, 70, 71, 72, 121
Eyre Peninsula, 40, 53, 61, 64, 87, 110, 164, 174, 176
Eyre, Edward John, 33, 37, 38, 40, 41, 42, 53, 58, 59, 61, 64, 88, 91, 173, 174

F

Fastings, James, 44
Federal Council for the Advancement of Aborigines and Torres Strait Islanders, 171
Federation, 131, 133, 143, 144, 147, 152, 153
Ferguson, William, 149
Field, George, 69
Field, Henry, 34, 35
Finnane, Mark, 67, 69

Firearms, 27, 33, 36, 50, 101, 106, 108, 112, 114, 118, 119, 120, 125
First Report of the South Australian Colonisation Commission, 20
Fisher, James, 23, 24, 75
Flinders Ranges, 67, 68, 92, 100, 104, 105, 110, 114, 117, 139, 155, 156, 176, 178, 182
Flinders, Matthew, 147, 173
Ford, Norman, 171
Frank and Freddy, 122
Franklin Harbour, 84, 106
Fuller, Hugh, 64

G

Galligan, Brian, 144
Galway, Governor Sir Henry, 134
Gason, Police Trooper Samuel, 114, 116, 119, 120, 121, 124
Gawler, Governor George, 24, 25, 26, 27, 29, 30, 32, 34, 35, 39, 56, 59, 152
Geharty, Sergeant James, 88, 96, 106, 107
Genders, J.C., 149, 152
Gillen, Frank, 132
Gipps, Governor George, 4, 37, 38
Glen Helen, 140
Goessling, Reverend, 119
Gold rush, 76, 97, 101
Goldsmith, Charles, 84
Gouger, Robert, 14
Goyder, Surveyor-General George, 100
Goyder's line, 98, 100, 101
Granite Creek, 124
Great Australian silence, 9, 145, 159, 173, 182
Greenwood, Gordon, 158
Grey, Governor George, 32, 35, 37, 44, 45, 49, 52, 56, 65, 91, 138, 161, 173
Grey, Sir George, 16, 17
Griffiths, Tom, 7, 8, 139
Guichen Bay, 91
Gundagai, 154

H

Haggis, Jane, 175, 176
Hailes, Nathaniel, 49
Hale, Archdeacon Matthew, 88, 96
Hallett, John, 82, 83
Hamilton, Police Commissioner George, 119, 120, 121, 124
Hamp, John, 62, 84, 164, 165
Hamp, John Chipp, 164
Hanson, Advocate-General Richard Davies, 26, 28

Harcus, William, 135
Hardwick Bay, 69
Harris, George, 32
Hassell, Kathleen, 170
Hastings, Gordon, 161
Hawker, George, 64, 65, 82, 150
Hawker, James, 35, 36, 48, 136, 165
Hawker, Ruth, 150
Hawson Jr., Frank, 40, 42, 43, 150, 174
Hawson Memorial, 174
Hawson, Captain Frank, 40
Hayward, Frederick, 110, 139, 145
Hermannsburg mission, 140
Hermannsburg Missionary Society, 118
Hill, Ernestine, 150
Hindmarsh, Governor John, 2, 5, 20, 23, 57, 62, 134, 142, 147, 151, 183
Hirst, J.B., 135
Hobart, 25
Holdfast Bay, 133, 147
Holdfast Bay City Council, 184
Holroyd, Police Inspector Henry, 94, 104, 106, 107
Homann, Reverend Ernst, 120
Horn, Thomas Cooper, 86
Howitt, Alfred, 117
Hughes, J.B., 65, 97
Hughes, Jonathan, 114
Hugonin, Lieutenant, 45, 46, 47, 48, 49
Hunter River, NSW, 18
Hunter, Ann, 76

I

Imperial Waste Lands Act of 1842, 25
Inman, Henry, 34
Inter se cases, 3, 4, 56, 73, 76, 121
Inverary, 79
Investigator, 147

J

Jacob, John, 105, 109, 114, 117
Jeffcott, Chief Judge Sir John, 22, 62
Jerrold, John, 114
John Martin's Department Store, 156
Jones, Henry, 60, 69
Jones, Philip, 117
Jubilee, 132, 135, 152, 155, 158
Justices of the Peace, 63, 64, 68, 82, 83, 87
Justifiable homicide, 65, 66, 68, 69, 110

K

Kangär Wodli, 74

Kangaroo Island, 14
Kappawanta, 86
Karagarni, 156, 157, 158
Katyetye, 124
Kaurna Heritage Committee, 184
Kertameru, 57
Killalpaninna, 118, 119, 120, 124
King George's Sound, WA, 40
King, Governor George,, 17
King, Wally, 157
Kingberrie, 70, 71
Kirton Ward Progress Association, 174
Kleinhert, Sylvia, 152
Kopperamanna, 118, 119, 120
Krichauff, Skye, 61
Krygier, Martin, 58
Kudnutya, 60, 82, 83, 84
Kulgalta, 62

L
Lady Nelson Discovery Centre, 175, 176
Lake Blanche, 117
Lake Bonney, 35, 91
Lake Eyre, 114
Lake Gregory, 117
Lake Hamilton station, 84
Lake Hope, 112, 114, 115, 116, 117, 118, 119, 121, 122
Lake Leake, 79
Lake Torrens, 101
Langhorne, Charles, 35
Larry, 73
Lawson, Dr George, 52, 53
Leake, Edward, 78, 80, 81
Leake, Robert, 78, 79, 80, 81, 145
Letters Patent, 9, 23, 24, 142, 169, 184
Liston, Ellen, 137
Little Jemmy. See Ngarbi
Long Pond station, 44
Lord Bathurst, 18
Lord Hobart, 18
Lord Melbourne, 15
Lord Stanley, 65
Lovelock, 43
Lower South East, 33
Lydon, Jane, 179
Lyndoch Valley, 30

M
MacDonnell, Governor Richard, 183
Magistrates, 37, 38, 42, 58, 63, 64, 65, 67, 68, 92, 97, 109

Malgalta, 62
Mann, Charles, 57, 61
Maraura, 35, 36, 38
Maria, 25, 26, 27, 28, 29, 30, 32, 35, 37, 56, 59, 136, 138, 150, 161, 162
Markus, Andrew, 152
Martial law, 3, 18, 26, 28, 56
Mason, Corporal George, 94
Maude, 153
Mayurra station, 70
McCourt, Tom, 164
McCullock, Sergeant, 69, 70
McEllister, Sergeant, 43, 47, 51, 53
McGrath, George, 57
McIntyre, John, 78, 80
McKay, Captain, 67, 68, 118
McLeod, 34
Melaityappa, 61, 69
Melrose, 100, 104, 176, 179
Melrose Police Station Museum, 178, 179
Melville, Henry, 38
Merltalla, 51
Mid north, 82, 84, 87, 91
Military, 96th Regiment, 38, 45, 47, 48, 50
Miller, Alexander, 110
Milmenrura, 28, 30, 31, 56
Mincham, Hans, 164
Minchin, Henry, 92, 93, 98, 110
Mingulta, 62
Mitchell, James, 104
Model Aboriginal State, 149, 152
Mongarawata, 28
Moorcangua, 28
Moorhouse, Protector Matthew, 23, 24, 33, 36, 38, 57, 58, 60, 61, 62, 81, 82, 83, 90, 91, 92, 93, 96, 162
Moorundie, 37, 38, 40, 58, 91, 94, 97
Moravians, 118, 119, 120
Moreton Bay, 5
Morgan, David, 64
Morldalta, 43
Morris, Thomas, 60, 69
Morton, Corporal, 119
Morton, Nugget, 145
Mount Arden, 57, 101, 182
Mount Brown, 92
Mount Deception, 111, 117
Mount Fytton, 110, 114
Mount Gambier, 78, 91, 147
Mount Remarkable, 67, 91, 97, 100, 101, 104, 108, 109, 179

Index

Mount Serle, 105
Mounted Police, 8, 38, 47, 49, 94, 102, 103, 104, 107, 108, 117, 120, 147, 160, 176, 178, 179
Mudnowadna, 111, 117
Multalta, 74
Multulti, 137
Murray Bridge, 154
Murray River, 16, 35, 94, 154
Murray, Mounted Constable William George, 145
Murrumbidgee River, 153
Myall Creek massacre, 4, 173

N

Naltia, 51
Nantariltarra, 69
Narrandera, 154
National Museum of Australia, 173
Nationalism, 131, 132, 141
Native Location, 90
Native Police, 4, 93, 94, 95, 98, 124, 176, 179
Native School, Adelaide, 90
Nauo, 42, 46
Neumann, Charles, 116, 122
New South Wales, 3, 4, 5, 18, 33, 37, 59, 72, 73, 75, 76, 95, 135, 148, 149, 159, 173
Newland, Simpson, 138, 141, 163, 165
Ngadjuri, 176
Ngarbi, 43, 44, 51, 52
Ngarka, 47, 48
Ngarrindjeri, 161
Ngulga, 47
Ngulta Wikkania, 74
Nicholls, Governor Sir Doug, 184
Ninalta, 62
Norrie, Governor Willoughby, 154
Northern Territory, 6, 121, 124, 125, 143, 144, 145, 173
North-West Bend, 154
Nuccaleena, 115
Nukunu, 176, 179

O

O'Halloran, Police Commissioner Major Thomas, 27, 30, 35, 36, 50, 51
Ochre, 68, 117, 118, 122
Old Gum Tree, 2
Overland Telegraph Line, 6, 124, 147

P

Pageant of Progress, 147, 148
Pannenum, 64

Parachilna, 68, 117, 118
Parnkalla, 46
Parrallana Jacky, 114
Parrallana Tommy, 114
Parramatta, 17
Pastoral leases, 95, 97, 98
Patten, Jack, 149
Penton, George, 69, 165
Perigundi, 119
Perria, 61
Phillips, Police Constable, 101, 102
Pike, Douglas, 9, 159
Pillaworta, 47, 48, 53
Pinkerton, William, 84
Pinya expedition, 120, 121
Pioneer legend, 131, 135, 137, 144, 145, 146, 150, 151, 163, 164, 178, 185
Point McLeay mission, 132, 154
Point Pearce mission, 132
Poisoning, 85, 137, 162, 163, 164
Pompey, 68, 110, 117
Poonindie Mission, 88, 96
Pope, Alan, 62, 76
Port Augusta, 93, 94, 176
Port Ferguson Police station, 110
Port Lincoln, 40, 42, 43, 44, 45, 46, 47, 48, 49, 50, 52, 54, 71, 72, 84, 85, 86, 87, 88, 89, 91, 93, 95, 96, 103, 106, 107, 136, 137, 138, 150, 162, 173, 174, 175
Port Lincoln Caledonian Society, 174
Port Lincoln Pioneers and Descendants' Club, 174
Port Phillip, 4, 5, 23, 33, 70, 72, 90, 93, 95
Poynter, Police Trooper, 114, 116
Price, Henry, 64, 82, 84, 87, 88
Proclamation, 2, 9, 20, 21, 22, 26, 29, 31, 32, 62, 125, 133, 134, 142, 147, 151, 154, 169, 181, 183, 184
Proclamation Day, 2, 133, 134, 147, 183, 184, 185
Protector, 133
Protector of Aborigines, 6, 16, 19, 20, 23, 24, 25, 33, 36, 37, 38, 42, 47, 51, 57, 58, 60, 61, 62, 66, 70, 81, 82, 83, 84, 88, 89, 90, 91, 92, 93, 95, 96, 108, 109, 111, 112, 125, 143, 144, 162, 169
Pullen, Captain, 25
Putaba Bob, 104

Q

Queensland, 4, 5, 59, 67, 69, 94, 124, 143, 155
Queensland Aborigines Protection Act 1897, 143

Quorn, 156

R
R. Vs Murrell, 3, 73
Raglass, Benjamin, 101
Rankine, George, 152
Rations, 26, 42, 58, 88, 91, 92, 93, 94, 98
Raukkan. See Point McLeay
Red Cliffs, 154
Referendum, 167, 169, 170, 171, 172
Reynolds, George, 114, 116
Reynolds, Henry, 7, 170
Richards, Jonathan, 67, 69
Richardson, Robert, 139, 140
Rilka, Joseph, 66
Rivoli Bay, 70, 80
Robe, Governor Frederick, 52, 85, 91
Robins, Corporal, 66
Robinson, George Augustus, 23, 90, 95
Robinson, William, 36, 37
Roe, Police Inspector, 116, 122
Ronkurri, 73
Rose, Deborah Bird, 183
Rowley, C.D., 170
Rufus River, 32, 33, 36, 37, 38, 91, 136, 138, 150, 161
Rule of law, 2, 5, 6, 7, 8, 9, 20, 32, 37, 55, 58, 63, 69, 72, 89, 95, 98, 111, 121, 122, 123, 124, 125, 139, 181

S
SA Aborigines Act, 1911, 144
Salt Creek, 107
Scarce, Governor Rear Admiral Kevin, 184
Schurmann, Reverend Clamor, 43, 44, 45, 46, 47, 48, 50, 51, 53, 85
Scott, Sub-Protector Edward Bates, 97
Sculpture on the Cliffs, 172, 173
Select Committee of the British House of Commons, 1837, 1, 19, 110
Select Committee on Aborigines, 1860, 111
Select Committee on Aborigines, 1899, 132
Self defence, 36, 65, 66, 67, 102, 105
Sergeant Major Alford, 80
Shaw, Sub-Inspector of Police Barnard, 36
Shelton, 64, 65
Simpson, Police Trooper, 105
Smith, Christina, 162, 175, 176
Smith, Stipendiary Magistrate G.B., 68
Solomon, Emmanuel, 125
Souter, Gavin, 149
South Australia Act, 1834, 15, 16, 17

South Australian Colonisation Commission, 15, 16, 17, 20, 23, 27, 159
South Australian Museum, 132
South, William Garnett, 143
Stanner, W.E.H., 7, 9, 145, 168
Stephen, James, 15, 20, 26
Stephen, Milner, 165
Stevenson, George, 23, 31
Stirling, Edward, 132
Stirling, Lieutenant-Governor James, 5
Stoney Point station, 84
Streaky Bay, 95, 100
Strehlow, Ted, 168
Stretton, Mounted Trooper, 124
Stuart, John McDouall, 173
Stuckey, Samuel, 68, 69, 110, 117, 145
Sturt Expedition re-enactment, 153, 154, 155
Sturt, Anthony, 153
Sturt, Charles, 13, 14, 15, 16, 33, 79, 134, 135, 147, 152, 153, 154, 155
Sturt, Evelyn, 79, 81
Sub-Protector of Aborigines, 90, 91, 94, 97, 98, 109
Supreme Court, 5, 22, 51, 57, 60, 62, 63, 69, 70, 73, 74, 76, 109, 162
Sydney, 33, 34, 140, 148, 153

T
Takkarm, 74
The Prohibition of Discrimination Act, 1966, 168
Thomas, Julian, 146
Thomas, Mary, 32
Thomas, Nicholas, 146
Thompson, James, 26, 110
Thompson, Janna, 9, 185
Tindale, Norman, 158
Tolmer, Alexander, 27, 53, 136, 165
Tornto station, 84
Torrens, Robert, 17
Treaty, 15, 184

U
Umberatana, 110, 114
Unaipon, David, 149, 152
Underwood, Edward, 50

V
Van Diemen's Land, 3, 15, 16, 18, 23, 38
Venus Bay, 84, 110
Vogelsang, Reverend Hermann, 119

W

Wadlata Outback Centre, 176, 177, 178
Wakefield, Edward, 14
Walker, Protector James, 92, 112
Warburton, Police Commissioner Major Peter Egerton, 6, 94, 102, 103, 104, 105, 107, 108, 109, 110, 111, 112, 113, 118, 120
Warburton, Robert, 158
Ward, Russel, 159
Waterloo Bay, 86, 171
Wauhop, Corporal James, 111, 117, 118
Wekweki, 57
Wellington, 91, 94
West Coast, 156, 171
Western Australia, 5, 40, 59, 76
White, Mr, 49
Willshire, Mounted Constable William, 124, 176, 179
Wilson, Mark, 152
Windschuttle, Keith, 7, 182
Wira Maldira, 57
Wiradjuri, 3
Woods, Police Trooper, 106, 107
Wurmbrand. Mounted Constable Erwin, 140

Y

Yailgalta, 52
Yorke Peninsula, 74, 87, 160, 164, 165
Young, James, 173
Yultalta, 50, 51

Wakefield Press is an independent publishing and
distribution company based in Adelaide, South Australia.
We love good stories and publish beautiful books.
To see our full range of books, please visit our website at
www.wakefieldpress.com.au
where all titles are available for purchase.
To keep up with our latest releases, news and events,
subscribe to our monthly newsletter.

Find us!

Facebook: www.facebook.com/wakefield.press
Twitter: www.twitter.com/wakefieldpress
Instagram: instagram.com/wakefieldpress

www.ingramcontent.com/pod-product-compliance
Lightning Source LLC
Chambersburg PA
CBHW030824230426
43667CB00008B/1367